*The Elephant Paradigm*

D0123483

ALSO BY GURCHARAN DAS

**Novel**

*A Fine Family* (1990)

**Plays**

*Larins Sahib: A Play in Three Acts* (1970)
*Mira: Rito de Krishna, translated by Enrique Hett* (1971)
*Three English Plays* (2001)

**Non-Fiction**

*India Unbound* (2000)

# The Elephant Paradigm

## India Wrestles with Change

**Gurcharan Das**

PENGUIN BOOKS

PENGUIN BOOKS
Published by the Penguin Group
Penguin Books India Pvt. Ltd, 11 Community Centre, Panchsheel Park, New Delhi
110 017, India
Penguin Group (USA) Inc., 375 Hudson Street, New York, New York 10014, USA
Penguin Group (Canada), 90 Eglinton Avenue East, Suite 700, Toronto, Ontario,
M4P 2Y3, Canada (a division of Pearson Penguin Canada Inc.)
Penguin Books Ltd, 80 Strand, London WC2R 0RL, England
Penguin Ireland, 25 St Stephen's Green, Dublin 2, Ireland (a division of Penguin
Books Ltd)
Penguin Group (Australia), 250 Camberwell Road, Camberwell, Victoria 3124,
Australia (a division of Pearson Australia Group Pty Ltd)
Penguin Group (NZ), cnr Airborne and Rosedale Roads, Albany, Auckland 1310,
New Zealand (a division of Pearson New Zealand Ltd)
Penguin Group (South Africa) (Pty) Ltd, 24 Sturdee Avenue, Rosebank, Johannesburg
2196, South Africa

Penguin Books Ltd, Registered Offices: 80 Strand, London WC2R 0RL, England

First published by Penguin Books India 2002

Copyright © Gurcharan Das 2002

All rights reserved

15  14  13  12  11

For sale in the Indian Subcontinent and Singapore only

Typeset in Adobe Garamond by SÜRYA, New Delhi
Printed at Chaman Offset Printers, New Delhi

This book is sold subject to the condition that it shall not, by way of trade or otherwise,
be lent, resold, hired out, or otherwise circulated without the publisher's prior written
consent in any form of binding or cover other than that in which it is published and
without a similar condition including this condition being imposed on the subsequent
purchaser and without limiting the rights under copyright reserved above, no part of
this publication may be reproduced, stored in or introduced into a retrieval system,
or transmitted in any form or by any means (electronic, mechanical, photocopying,
recording or otherwise), without the prior written permission of both the copyright
owner and the above-mentioned publisher of this book.

*For Manni, Bina, Tutu and Geeta*

# Contents

# Introduction

*. . . there is nothing more difficult to arrange, more doubtful of*
*success, more dangerous to carry through than initiating changes . . .*
*The innovator makes enemies of all those who prosper under the old*
*order, and only lukewarm support is forthcoming from those who*
*would prosper under the new.*

—Nicolas Machiavelli, *The Prince*, 1513

*E*ach age has a unique temper, and it seems to reflect the mood
and the spirit of the people, especially the young. The mood that
is most famous in recent times seems to have belonged to Europe
at the end of the nineteenth century when a spirit of intense
vivacity—an almost desperate joy in being alive—led to some bold
experiments in the arts. That temper came to be called *fin de siècle*
or 'end of the century' and it was a rebellion, in part, against the
Victorian 'middle class morality' that Bernard Shaw made famous
with great wit.

If I had to define the Indian temper at the beginning of the
twenty-first century, and if I went by the newspaper headlines and
reports, I would conclude that we lived in pretty dispirited times—
a sort of post-reforms, post-Nehru, post-Mandal and post-modern
menopause. Its cause seems to be the depressing state of governance
in our country. But if one were to pause and reflect, and widen
one's horizon beyond current events, one would see in the nineties
a revolutionary decade during which we decisively broke with old
dogmas and the *ancien régime* in significant ways. If I had to give
it a name, it would be liberation—the rallying cry of the French
Revolution, as it has, not surprisingly, been of mass movements for

over 200 years. The difference is that ours has been a quiet revolution—so quiet, in fact, that few have noticed it. I admit 'the liberating nineties' does not have the same zing or style as *fin de siècle*, but the reality behind it has solid substance, and it is our best guide to understanding the decade.

When we think of 'revolution' we conjure up images of the events in Paris in 1789 or in Russia in 1917, when revolutionaries seized the state in order to change the social order and destroy the existing one. These revolutions were violent and apocalyptic. In the Indian context, however, I refer to profound economic, political and social transformations 'both within and on the margins of the constitutional framework'.

If one is to believe Eric Hobsbawm, the English historian, then the twenty-first century began in 1991 with the collapse of communism and the Soviet Union. In his book, *The Age of Extremes,* he calls the twentieth century 'short' because it started late in 1914 with the beginning of the First World War and ended in 1991. In contrast to the seventy-seven years long twentieth century, the nineteenth lasted 125 years—from 1798, the year of the French Revolution, to 1914. The year 1991 was also the one that we began our economic reforms in India, and these were part of a liberal revolution that seemed to sweep the world, as country after country began to turn democratic and capitalist. Historian Francis Fukuyama described this movement in grandiose terms as the 'end of history', and by this he meant that the triumph of democratic capitalism had ended the battle for ideology. With only one superpower, he predicted, the world would become less violent, as people gradually became absorbed in the peaceful pursuit of the middle class life.

If one accepts Hobsbawm's formulation, then our decade of the nineties was an especially significant one, and as the first decade of the twenty-first century, it might tell us something about our future. As I have said, what happened in India in the nineties was revolutionary, although it did not make the noise that accompanied the 1919 or the 1789 upheavals. Like our struggle for Independence in the first half of the twentieth century, it was non-violent. In this 'silent revolution' there were deep changes in our society. More important, there were mental changes as the nation's world-view began to change.

Such was our optimism in the early days following the 1991 economic reforms that many thought that our moment in history had finally arrived. We felt that we had the same sense of possibilities as our parents did in the early fifties. We believed that by dismantling the old socialist institutions we would be economically free and eventually overcome our degrading poverty in the same trusted way as the West had over the past hundred years and East Asia in the last quarter of the twentieth century. We began to look forward to the day, sometime in the first half of the twenty-first century, when half our country would turn middle class. Our cheerful confidence during this post-modern decade harked to the hopeful modernist tradition of the eighteenth century Enlightenment in Europe, which had taught us the concept of progress and the possibility of change for the better. We felt our world was turning rational as more and more countries became market-based democracies. We might not approve of globalization on aesthetic grounds, but it was unquestionably a powerful force that could lift our economy and the poorest with it.

Ten years later, at the beginning of the new century, this mood has turned sober, as the reforms are stuck and the economy has slowed. After growing at an average 6.8 per cent a year for four years after the reforms, it had slowed down to 5.4 per cent in the last four years of the decade. But what causes the greatest anxiety is the appalling state of day-to-day governance. Something has clearly gone wrong. Were we over-optimistic? Were the new ideas in themselves wrong? As the decade wore on, more and more people seemed to agree that we needed to enhance the sphere of individual freedom at the state's expense, dismantle the socialist institutions of licence and inspector raj, and re-focus the state on the basic functions of governance and building human capital. We have also realized that our biggest failure over the last fifty years has been of administrative and institutional incompetence and our inability to implement rather than of ideology.

Moreover, the growing consciousness of religious identity and the rise of aggressive nationalism in the nineties adds to our unease. We had been warned of it by Samuel Huntington, who had predicted precisely this coming de-secularization of the world in his provocative book, *The Clash of Civilisations*. But Jawaharlal Nehru had bequeathed us a cosmopolitan attitude—that all human beings were equal and all differences of colour, caste and religion were superficial and had little impact on the human capacity for living the good life. Now Hindu nationalism seemed to challenge these ideals. Nationalism might have had a place in the first half of the twentieth century, when we were fighting for Independence; it might even have made sense when we were building a nation in the fifties. But now, forty years later, when we should have been more confident and secure in our nationhood, its value seemed doubtful. And when that nationalism was linked with religion it seemed to have a sinister quality; when it was linked to swadeshi economics it seemed altogether bizarre and irrational.

This book has grown out of a series of thin, 800-word rectangles that I began to produce regularly in the nineties for the *Times of India* on Sundays (and occasional pieces for the *Wall Street Journal, The Financial Times* and other papers). I quickly realized that one cannot merely paste columns together and produce a book. It isn't fair to the reader, who expects a continuity of ideas, and needs a single argument that runs throughout the book and unfolds chapter by chapter; only then does it become an organic and wholesome experience.

Writing a newspaper column is an eternally ephemeral trade, and although last week's sensation is always forgotten by the following week, it has always looked, or was made to look, as though it was carved in stone. When I laid the raw material—the more than 200 newspaper articles—on the bright, sun-drenched veranda of my home in Delhi, I slowly realized that all of them seemed to describe in one way or another how our country was

changing in the decade of the nineties. So, the idea was born to write a story of India's nineties as a series of essays.

The essay is a wonderful thing. It can refer to practically any piece of non-fiction prose—from a short newspaper column by Tavleen Singh trashing Sonia Gandhi to an 800-page formal academic treatise on local democracy. In recent times, however, young Indians in their quest for careers and obsession with information technology have lost touch with this form, as they have turned increasingly away from a liberal to a technical education. When some of them began applying to American colleges for admission and were asked to submit a personal essay with their application, they began to rediscover this form.

The word essay was introduced by a sixteenth-century French magistrate, Michel de Montaigne, who temporarily retired from official life in the 1570s and set up a room in his chateau where he began writing and publishing a series of short prose works that he called *essais*. He published three volumes in all, the last in 1588, and with these he assumed a place among the world's most respected writers. In Old French *essai* meant an attempt, a test, or a trial. Montaigne often uses the word as a verb—to *essay* something, meaning, 'to attempt' something. In France the verb 'essayer' routinely refers to try out—for example, to test-drive a new car. I, too, regard the essay as a trying out of ideas rather than a fully shaped formulation.

My own hero of the essay is the liberal American writer E.B. White. When I get discouraged or downcast I go to my study and pick out a small anthology of his essays. From E.B.White I have learned to distrust my own ideas and display the trait of modesty. He has taught me to be self-critical and to be keenly aware of one's limitations. I have also learned to use colloquial language, to adopt an informal and flexible approach to subjects, which also tends to reinforce the tone of modesty. Sometimes, claiming a deficient memory helps to warn readers not to expect a systematic treatment of the subject. These are some of the ways one learns to pretend to be more modest and credible than one is.

I learned similar lessons from my other hero of the essay, George Orwell, who teaches how to offset what might seem like irritating egoism and self-absorption when writing in the first person. He opens his famous essay, 'Shooting an Elephant', in a way that both establishes his importance and downplays it in the same sentence: 'In Moulmein, in Lower Burma, I was hated by large numbers of people—the only time in my life that I have been important enough for this to happen to me.' He ends his essay with an unflattering remark that undercuts any heroism the reader might attribute to him. Why did he shoot an elephant? He says he did it 'solely to avoid looking a fool'.

Even though most of the essays here are impersonal, I find that I cannot avoid the 'we' and sometimes the 'I'. I have discovered that the 'we' on the page is not necessarily the same as the 'we' of real life. I employ the first person plural sometimes to embrace 'all reasonable human beings', but more often a subset of that, 'all reasonable Indians'. This pronoun, I have learned, helps to build equity between the reader and the writer. However, there is a temptation lurking to overuse it, and I find that I am often guilty of this fault. When I use the 'I', I find that I inevitably reveal one thing and suppress another; I recount one experience but distort another; I remember one incident while fabricating another. This is inherently a part of this hazardous business of essay writing. Indeed, in no other genre does one need to pay such close attention to personal pronouns as in the essay.

The history of the English essay is intimately connected with changes in publishing technology. With the steady improvement of the printing press in the seventeenth century, the essay in the hands of polemical writers like Jonathan Swift and Daniel Defoe grew into a popular form of pamphlet literature. I like to believe that I am a modest part of this distinguished tradition—for behind my essays of advocacy is a moral vision of a good society. What drove me to write the columns in the first place was polemical—to passionately advocate reforms in our society. But slowly I learned that one had to go beyond the current reform agenda. One needed far-reaching social and political change in order to implement it, and I have realized our great failure in not having paid sufficient attention to the reform of our education, health and administrative institutions.

I am at heart an old-fashioned liberal, more at home with ambiguities and cautious of certainties. If I sound as though I have excessive faith in the market, it is because I have deep suspicion of state power. I also think we have to right the pendulum in India, which has swung too far to the other end. We have to dismantle the phoney institutions of the licence-permit-inspector raj that have taken away our liberty and continue to humiliate us to this day. In the social sphere, I favour aggressive support by the state to build human capabilities. In the economic sphere, I prefer market outcomes to intervention by bureaucrats. If we were to redefine socialism to mean our wish for a rational and compassionate society—rather than state ownership of the means of production—we would all be socialists today, and this vision might describe the society that we would want our grandchildren to live in.

This, then, is a book about the spirit of contemporary India. About a third of the essays are about individual or private concerns and the other two-thirds deal with collective or public matters. I have divided the book into three parts. The first part, 'The Temper of Our Times', sets the stage; the second deals with the private space, and part three focuses on public issues. I begin the first chapter, 'Our Liberating Nineties', with an essay in six parts, which tries to catch some aspects of the changing age. I describe the revolutionary, political, social, economic and mental changes that we have experienced in India in the nineties, and which have had the combined effect of liberating us. 'Understanding Our Times', the second chapter, attempts to draw some lessons from the past, mainly from economic history. For forty years after Independence we seemed to learn the wrong lessons from history and we need to unlearn them now, and this unlearning too is part of our liberation. Yet, despite all the release, I ask in chapter three, why is our temper so low?

The stage having been set, the book now divides itself into the private and the public spaces. The essays in part two focus on our personal concerns, expressed in the next four chapters. These essays have a lighter touch, in contrast to the weightier issues of the public space. The private space begins with the fourth chapter, which looks at our sacred and philosophical concerns, and its second essay, 'Dance of the Debonair God', is my favourite. The following chapter, 'A Sentimental Education', is based on the premise that the business of going through life is, in some ways, similar to that of acquiring an education; it offers humanistic enthusiasms ranging from 'what to read' and 'how to write well', from 'how to live' and 'how to die'—all of them informed by a commitment to liberal values; its second essay, 'Who Will Roll the Chapatis?' is about the changing role of women in contemporary India. 'Playing to Win', the sixth chapter, is about succeeding in the competitive post-reforms market place, and a theme running through it is that attention to execution and detail will bring the real rewards.

Now I move to part three, from the private to the public space. The seventh chapter, 'Learning to Live, Living to Learn', deals with the reform of various aspects of our education system. Chapter eight turns to the Indian village and examines two themes: how local self-government is unfolding in rural India, and the urgent need for agricultural reform. In chapter nine, 'To Reform or Not to Reform', I blame our poor governance on weak institutions and advocate their reform. The following chapter, 'What Slows Us Down', is concerned with the interface of democracy and capitalism, and it attempts to understand why governance is failing us and why the pace of Indian reforms is so slow. Finally, the last chapter, 'Making the Nation Competitive', discusses the issue of competitiveness from the perspective of the government and of policy makers, and is about the reforms we must do to make the nation perform.

Since I give my address at the bottom of my Sunday column, I usually get a fair amount of email and snail mail. And being a diligent sort, I endeavour to read and reply to most letters. One indignant reader wrote to say that I had come between him and his son. 'You see, we always read the Sunday paper together as a family under a banyan tree in our ancestral home. We drink tea leisurely and there is harmony in our home; that is, until we read your column. Then we begin to argue like mad and our peace is shattered. My wife always seems to take my son's side and my brother mine. I fear that my son and I are drifting apart, thanks to you.' If my book succeeds in provoking argument, then I shall feel that my work is done.

# PART ONE

## *The Temper of Our Times*

*The tranquillity or agitation of our temper does not depend so much on the big things which happen to us in life, as on the pleasant or unpleasant arrangements of the little things which happen daily.*

—La Rochefoucauld, *Maxims* (1665)

# 1

## Our Liberating Nineties

*Liberation is not deliverance.*
—Victor Hugo, *Les Miserables*, 1862

*A* decade, it seems to me, is long enough to look right through the arc of time and ask if there are any definitive things that can be said about a changing nation. There are, of course, no permanent conclusions to anything, and when the nation is a 'daily performance', the challenge lies in making sense out of a decade full of daily performances. The Americans, who, more than others, tend to live in the present, have made an industry of characterizing their decades—'the roaring twenties', 'the swinging sixties'. If I had to do the same for the 1990s in India, I would call the decade 'our liberating nineties'.

The decade started nervously. Communism had collapsed around the world, and in India we faced an unprecedented fiscal crisis—we were bankrupt as our foreign exchange reserves plunged. When the decade began, the world was fiddling with the fax machine; when it ended, we were zipping around the world through e-mail, scanning and forwarding photographs, and talking of bandwidth and gigabytes. The meaning of globalization began to sink in when we could search and find almost any piece of information in the world on the Net. Of the two factors that had shaped human history in the twentieth century—technology and ideology—the latter was gone, but the former ruled triumphant, symbolized by the Internet, surely the brightest story of the decade.

The integration of the world economy was another distinctive feature of the decade, and it made spectacular progress through communications, capital and technology flows. There had been a similar age of globalization a hundred years ago, but it seemed primitive compared to the present process. Only in one respect was it more advanced: it encouraged the movement of labour through mass migration; today there are immigration barriers everywhere.

With the collapse of communism, democratic capitalism seemed to be triumphant, and by the end of the decade 119 nations claimed to be liberal democracies, although only eighty-nine genuinely qualified. Even so, this was a huge gain for the world, since there were only thirty-one such nations in 1975 and sixty-one in 1990. The state was in retreat everywhere and more than seventy nations were engaged in some form of economic reform. Clearly, a liberal revolution had taken place around the globe, and the liberal idea had emerged victorious, based on political rights, universal suffrage and free markets. However, although the totalitarian tyrannies of both the right and the left were forgotten, nationalism and religious bigotry—the other bequests of history—were reasserting themselves. By the end of the century, we were again groping for answers to old questions: what ought to be the right relations between human beings, and how should we live our lives? With the discarding of ideology, no one asked any more if there was a supremely good society. The only goal we seemed to agree on was freedom.

In contrast to the general mood of diminished expectations in the West, it was an age of rising expectations in India. Although we did not have a grand vision of the future, as China seemed to, thanks to Deng Xiaoping, we knew that the lives of our children would be better than ours or those of our parents. Our ruling elite did not have a clue about the globalized world of the twenty-first century and continued to be absorbed with the irrelevant.

Nevertheless, there were marvellous intellectual debates during the decade, and even though some ideas did not get translated into policies, they did increase our understanding of the world.

## Our Many Liberations

We were liberated politically, economically and socially in the nineties in India, but the biggest change by far has been in our minds. Politically, we were freed from the rule of a single party—nay, from the dynastic rule of a family—but more significant was that power had increasingly begun to filter downwards to the states. Local self-government in the form of panchayati raj has slowly become a reality, thanks to the Seventy-third Amendment to the Constitution in 1993. Economically, liberalization began to free us day by day from the heavy hand of bureaucrats and politicians. Socially, the lower castes have continued to rise through the ballot box and thanks to growing literacy. In Bihar and Uttar Pradesh, the newfound freedom is palpable in the body language of the other backward castes. Technologically, the Internet is a great liberation, and although its immediate impact is limited in India, it holds the potential of breaking barriers to knowledge and levelling the playing field. Mentally, our minds became decolonized in the nineties.

*Political Liberation* After the enactment of the Seventy-third Amendment, local elections were held for the first time in almost all the villages and municipalities across the country. Over three million legislators were elected—a world record of sorts—of which roughly one million were women. Of these a quarter of a million were chairpersons of local bodies. The initial impact of this revolution has been mixed. Though the Dalits and other backward castes have risen in many villages, power continues to be monopolized by the old feudal forces in the majority. The average panchayat, like the average village, has turned out to be hopelessly factionalized, but the important thing is that a beginning has been made. The old village headman can no longer take power for granted, for there will be a next time. Our Constitution has let loose new forces of liberation and the average Indian villager is slowly getting empowered.

In this devolution of power we seem to be returning, curiously enough, to the India of yore, to Mahatma Gandhi's India of the autonomous village. In the past, no matter who ruled India— whether the centralized empires of the Mauryas, the Guptas, the Mughals or the anarchy of a thousand local rajas and nawabs—the ordinary Indian's life had begun and ended in the village. Now again authority was coming closer to the individual, and he could influence it and take charge of his life. This is liberation.

*Economic liberation* Economically, it was the age of globalization and liberalization. With the collapse of communism, the big debate of the twentieth century was settled—for the time being, at least. The market had decisively won over socialism. The power to take decisions was visibly shifting from bureaucrats to the market. Any young person with ambition and skills could start an enterprise without having to grovel for a licence. Globalization was opening our doors and windows and letting foreign winds blow through our house, and this too seemed right, for the continuity of our civilization rested on our remarkable ability to absorb foreign influences and to transform them into something that belonged to us. True, there were many voices of swadeshi, but they were fighting a losing battle and would eventually get blown away by the voices of openness. One of these new voices is the ubiquitous yellow STD/ISD/PCO sign in our village bazaars, which symbolizes the benign influence of the global communications revolution. Beneath the sign can be found mothers talking to their sons working in distant cities and farmers enquiring about market rates in the mandi towns before they harvest their crops.

Some argued that globalization curtailed individual freedom because it gave effective power to large multinational monopolies that had the resources to exploit global markets. Globalization's defenders countered that it would lower barriers to trade and investment. Indian consumers would then benefit not only through better products at lower prices but also more job opportunities. The test came in the bazaar and here the Indian consumer began to see visible improvements in quality accompanied by declining prices under the pressure of competition. The real problem now was to choose from dozens of offerings of Indian and foreign manufacturers.

*Social liberation* Socially, the mood of the underprivileged became more defiant in the nineties. The Dalits and the backward castes had been rising through the ballot box since the fifties, but this trend accelerated in the nineties, especially in the north, and assumed the proportions of a social revolution. The south, of course, had experienced its revolution many decades before; hence, it is more advanced socially than the north. The leaders of the backward castes like Laloo Prasad Yadav in Bihar and Mayawati in Uttar Pradesh may have followed some bizarre policies, but they had given their people a new self-esteem. There was a visible change in the electoral arithmetic in the large Hindi-speaking Gangetic states and it became difficult to predict political outcomes. Although the better-off Dalits and backward castes were the main beneficiaries of reservations and affirmative action, caste discrimination could no longer be taken for granted.

Census 2000 also brought the news of significant gains in education, as literacy figures for the decade rose from fifty-two to sixty-five per cent. The biggest gains were reported from among the backward social groups and in the most backward states. Although their leaders did not articulate it, the lower castes began to realize that their best ally was education of their children. The backward castes continued to complain throughout the decade, but their temper reflected a more liberated and empowered world-view.

*Mental liberation* The most profound change occurred among the youth. Their minds became decolonized and there was a new feeling of confidence in the air. Gone were many of our inhibitions and hang-ups. Economists and businessmen instinctively understand the value of confidence in entrepreneurial success and in creating a climate for investment. Historians also understand the power of confidence in national success, and they point to examples in Roman history and Japan's success after the 1868 Meiji reforms. We began to observe the same in India during the nineties.

I don't think we know why this happened. Perhaps, it was the impact of television, especially with the advent of competitive cable television. Perhaps, it was due to the reforms. What we did see was lots of young Indians moving about in all manner of new ways, with a 'can-do' attitude that didn't need approval from others, especially from the West. People began to speak on these television channels in a curious mixture of English and Hindi—Hinglish—in a most relaxed manner. Pop stars like Daler Mehndi and A.R. Rahman displayed an exuberant nonchalance, as did the new breed of young Bollywood heroes and heroines. So did new fiction writers in English, fashion designers, beauty queens and cricket stars.

This new mindset was particularly evident among business people and students, but many politicians, bureaucrats, trade unionists and housewives had also been infected. Even in their complaints I noticed a sense of urgency.

Making money became increasingly a legitimate route to success and our earlier hypocrisy towards it began to disappear. It was a positive attitude and all sorts of unlikely people began to take risks with their savings, either by starting new businesses or on the stock market. The discourse in India gradually began to shift from politics to economics. The business pages of newspapers, which had been their dullest section, became much more vibrant, specially whenever the stock market was on one of its periodic—and spectacular—climbs. Chief ministers in the states scrambled for private investment. Judges became more even-handed in industrial disputes; they no longer assumed that capital always exploits labour. Many trade union leaders began to rethink their mission.

## Winds of Change

My young nephew returned home to India in 1998 during the Kargil skirmishes. He came back after six years in the United States, and he was asked if anything had changed. 'I don't see anything different, except for a few new cars on the road,' he said. He is a high-flying bond trader on Wall Street and his pressured world changes daily at the speed of light. He might well have come from another planet. He found that most Indians were living in a strange twilight world, discussing issues that were settled long ago. He thought it strange that Indians still talked as though they had a choice about whether or not to globalize when it was a fait accompli.

For a start, I told him, Kargil had burst into seventy million homes through television and watching our jawans fighting at 16,000 feet night after night has generated new emotions and created a new spirit in our first televised war. Just ten years ago, we would have been grateful for stiff bulletins read by stiff newscasters on Doordarshan. The media revolution has created a whole new industry and Zee Television alone claims to have created more than a quarter of a million jobs by outsourcing content. Doordarshan has also improved, though its in-house programmes are still dismal. This is why we have around thirty-five million cable television homes—more than all of Latin America put together.

Not so long ago, I reminded my nephew, it took years to get a telephone. We had to run about to find someone with influence to get the minister to allot us a connection. Today, we can have a telephone almost on demand. How did this happen? Telecom liberalization sent a shiver of fear through the Department of Telecom (DoT) and it decided to wire up the country and pre-empt competitors. Hence, the number of telephones rose from five million in 1990 to more than thirty million by the end of the decade. Simultaneously, DoT modernized its equipment and laid 76,000 km of fibre optic cable, and this has improved performance exponentially. Of course, if DoT had not deliberately sabotaged the entry of private competitors we might have had fifty million telephones. Fortunately, at the end of the decade, the government finally got its act together. It took away the authority for making policy from DoT and corporatized it. Now our telecom future seems to be more secure.

I told my nephew about other quiet changes in our life. Not long ago, we had to beg a minister's personal assistant to get cooking gas. The Supreme Court had to finally step in and ban ministers from giving out-of-turn connections. Today, we can get a liquefied petroleum gas (LPG) cylinder on demand. Again, this change has happened because of modest liberalization. Nor do we have to bribe anyone for a railway ticket any more because the ticketing system has been computerized. Flying is now as easy as taking a bus to Ghaziabad—probably easier. Earlier, there would be panic if one had to attend a meeting in another city at short notice. There were only three flights between Mumbai and Delhi and they were always late. Now, with the advent of competition, there are twenty-four flights between the two cities and they are almost always on time.

No one seemed to complain about inflation in the nineties. In fact, prices of some consumer durables actually declined. In the past three decades, almost every election had been fought on rising prices, but in the nineties this was not an issue—except for the aberrant 1998 'onion election' in which the Bharatiya Janata Party (BJP) lost in several northern states.

Gone also is our paranoia over foreign exchange. Ever since the fifties, we lived in fear of dwindling foreign reserves. Every time they came down we raised tariffs, tightened import licensing, and destroyed the prospects of our exports, our industry and our prosperity. The fear was so acute that the Finance Ministry introduced the dreaded 'P Form', which gave one permission to travel. As a result, anyone who wanted to travel abroad had to go through the humiliation of justifying his trip to a clerk in the Reserve Bank of India (RBI). Soon everyone sought a connection in the RBI, but still many flights were missed and many hopes were dashed. With a measly foreign exchange allowance, even J.R.D. Tata could not take his business partner out for lunch abroad without violating the Foreign Exchange Regulation Act, 1974 (FERA). All this finally changed in the 1990s as our foreign exchange reserves burgeoned and touched an unbelievable $50 billion by February 2002 (compared to $1 billion in the 1991 crisis). The humiliating way that customs treated our citizens returning from abroad changed as well (although the same attitude and obstacles did not go away for business people and they continue to be harassed by customs inspectors).

Soon after the decade ended, the Aditya Birla group made two bold acquisitions—it acquired the menswear business and brands of Madura Coats (Van Heusen, Louis Philippe, Peter England, etc.) and Reliance Industries's stake in the engineering giant Larsen and Toubro (L&T). These were quiet, uncontroversial events consistent with the Security and Exchange Board's (SEBI) elaborate code for the takeover of companies and, significantly, without any government intervention. They stood out in dramatic contrast with what happened eleven years ago when Reliance Industries first bought its stake in L&T. V.P. Singh's government had the financial institutions veto Reliance's efforts to get on the board and prevented it from taking control of the company.

So, I told my nephew, this is not a complete inventory by any means, but it is a start. And in the end, India is not a tiger, and change will always be slower than in East Asia. India is an elephant which has stirred from its slumber and has finally begun to move ahead with a degree of determination. However, unlike a sprinting tiger that runs out of steam, the elephant has stamina.

## A Happy Consensus

A successful nation has three attributes: politically, it is free and democratic; economically, it is prosperous and equitable; and socially, it is peaceful and cohesive. But it is rare to find a nation which scores on all three counts. Most Western countries have democracy and prosperity, but they suffer from social disintegration.

The nations in the East have prosperity and social cohesion, but they suffer under authoritarian political regimes. For decades India used to score high on the political front, middling on social criteria and low on the economy, but in the 1990s it has reported considerable gains in all three areas.

The world has fought bitterly over how to achieve these three goals. Even in the last fifty years, when there was relative peace in the world, the Cold War ensured that we remained divided. Now, after the collapse of communism and the slow erosion of ideology in the world, a remarkable consensus seems to be emerging, at least on one of these goals—how to make a poor nation prosperous. It is a consensus based on empirical data, painstakingly gathered by researchers covering a half-century, and can be found in Gerald Meirer's and Joseph Stiglitz's *Frontiers of Development Economics: The Future in Perspective*.

Not surprisingly, the starting point in moving from poverty to prosperity is sustained high economic growth. Nothing reduces poverty like growth. Since India and China together account for more than a third of the world's people, and since both have experienced high growth for two decades, the world as a whole has become less poor and more equal. More than half a billion people in the two countries have lifted themselves out of poverty between 1980 and 2000, and per capita income growth in the developing countries has outstripped that in the high-income countries.

What makes for this poverty-reducing growth? Two things— one, a healthy climate for business and investment, and two, the poor empowering themselves to take part in the growth. A healthy climate is not just about attracting multinational companies (although foreign investment is very important in raising the savings rate of a society). It also means keeping inflation low, for example, so that ordinary people can enjoy the rewards of their effort. A healthy climate is also one where small entrepreneurs are not at the mercy of inspectors and petty government officials. Corruption is the shame of India, as the Global Competitiveness Report reminds us year after year, and this partially explains our low levels of foreign investment. The most troublesome officials are in the excise, customs and tax departments. All of them are in the Finance Ministry, yet none of our distinguished finance ministers in the nineties succeeded in cleaning up his own stables.

The widest consensus is on opening the economy to trade and investment. The record shows that open economies have consistently outperformed closed ones, and the link between economic growth and openness is so overwhelming that it should silence swadeshis and protectionists forever. So, if we wish to be a great exporting nation, we must lower our tariffs, which are still amongst the highest in the world.

There is widespread evidence that an attack on poverty does not succeed through state-run schemes, where most of the funds are eaten up by corruption and administrative expenses. It is vastly more successful when the poor take part in these programmes. This happens where they have access to schools and primary health care. Also, where panchayati raj has taken off, communities report lower teacher and student absenteeism and better-run poverty programmes.

The history of poverty is one of inadequate property rights. A fourth consensus is on the crucial importance of enforcing property rights if one is to realize the benefits of the market. In India, we have an independent judiciary, but judicial delays and our inability to dismantle the accumulated legislation of the socialist era nullify our advantage.

Finally, people everywhere are disappointed with massive bureaucratic intervention in the economy. There is consensus on the need to redefine the role of the state so as to give us good governance and to build up human capabilities that are crucial in raising a society's productivity. For the rest, the state should be kept out and we should go by the Chinese proverb: people are happy when the king is far.

## Search for Civic Engagement

With the ascent of democratic capitalism, middle class Indians understood the importance of strengthening market institutions, but they were less clear about the place of a third type of institution, which claimed to mediate between the market and the state. This was involved in civic engagement and was represented by the voluntary, philanthropic and non-government organizations. These had begun to play an increasing role since the 1980s, and had become a conduit for the idealistic energies of the young. In the nineties, literally hundreds of NGOs became embedded in local communities across the country, as they reinforced the message of self-help, cooperation and civic solidarity. They began to leave a modest mark on issues relating to children, women and the environment.

Community action was effective in influencing the way our forests are managed, for example. The movement to preserve forests spread from Gujarat in the mid-eighties, and the voluntary initiatives have led to a new forest policy, which ensures that local people participate in decisions related to managing them. A civic organization in Bangalore, Public Affairs Centre, began to issue 'report cards' on various government agencies which rated the services provided and assessed the quality and cost of citizens' transactions with government departments. The Bangalore Development Authority (BDA), responsible for housing and other civic services, scored the lowest in one of the early report cards, with only one per cent of respondents admitting to being 'satisfied'. This prompted the BDA director to launch a major citizen–government initiative that resulted in some improvements.

As expected, the best contributions of the NGOs came in education and health. Hundreds of voluntary organizations were running schools for decades, but the massive funding of primary education by the World Bank and other international agencies through the District Primary Education Programme in the nineties encouraged new partnerships between government and NGOs. In some states, such as Rajasthan and Madhya Pradesh, non-profit organizations worked together with the state government to make children's learning more relevant and 'joyful'. In Maharashtra, researchers showed that successful schools depended less on the curriculum or even the quality of teachers and more on a broader fabric of supportive parents and community action. Overall, however, state departments of education were too arrogant to take advantage of the opportunities offered by the NGOs. And, as with any activity that becomes a fad, plenty of dubious NGOs also emerged, giving the word itself a bad odour to some.

Following international fashion, our intellectuals became enamoured with the notion of 'social capital'. They explained that if financial capital is found in one's bank account and human capital in one's head, social capital inheres in one's relations with others. A community where citizens have a tendency to engage in civic affairs and form voluntary associations which lead to collective action for the common good is said to have high social capital. Social capital can thus create fertile ground for political and economic development.

Social capital is, of course, not a new idea. Aristotle praised man for being a social animal. Machiavelli applauded citizens in the practice of *virtu civille* (civic virtue). Alexis de Tocqueville, the French aristocrat, was alarmed by a situation similar to ours in post-revolutionary France, which saw the growth of a centralized bureaucratic state side by side with the expansion of democracy. He encouraged his countrymen to form voluntary associations, the sort he had found during his tours of the fledging United States in the 1830s, as these, he felt, would act as a democratic buffer against state power.

Tocqueville wrote, 'Americans of all ages, all stations in life, and all types of dispositions are forever forming associations. There are not only commercial associations in which all take part, but others of a thousand different types—religious, moral, serious, futile . . . Nothing, in my view, deserves more attention than the intellectual and moral associations in America.' Such associations, he argued, have 'an effect on the inner moral life of those who participate, enhancing their sympathies and understanding for fellow humans . . .'

Then as now, 175 years later, Americans still seem to have the most intense civic life in the world. They join everything—Boy Scouts, Red Cross, Lions and Rotary Clubs, book clubs, Parent–Teacher Associations, Little League baseball, bowling leagues and you name it. But Americans today are concerned that their social capital may be eroding. Memberships in all voluntary clubs have declined significantly since the sixties, primarily because of the intrusion of television. In 1958, Edward Banfield published a classic, *The Moral Basis of a Backward Society*, which was a study of underdevelopment in a village at the southern tip of Italy. 'The extreme poverty and backwardness of which,' he wrote, 'is to be explained largely by the inability of villagers to act together for their common good.' Thirty-five years later, in 1993, Harvard professor Robert Putnam returned to the same theme in *Making Democracy Work: Civic Traditions in Modern Italy*. He concluded that local government works in north Italy but fails in the south because northern Italians are more likely to get involved in neighbourhood activities—singing groups, football clubs, cooperatives and networks of small entrepreneurs, while the southern Italians remain aloof and backward.

Putnam's book influenced Indian intellectuals, who began to avidly seek examples of community life in India. I suggested in an article that the neighbourhood cricket clubs, which had experienced explosive growth in the past two decades, might be fertile ground for seeking out social capital. The popularity of cricket clubs often cut across socio-economic groups. Since twenty-two people are needed to play, I had seen that often players from different strata of society were coopted, and this lent a nice, democratic air to the proceedings. While the younger people played, the older ones watched and gossiped about neighbourhood concerns—the condition of the schools, roads, garbage, water supply, etc.

Social capital seemed especially relevant to an India invigorated by economic reforms. We desperately sought transparency from the government and were trying to shake off the dead weight of bureaucracy; we were eager to embrace the fruits of local self-government. Tocqueville's vision was in keeping with our ethos today—we wanted to decentralize decision-making, devolve power to the states, municipalities and panchayats and have people rely on themselves. This stood in contrast to Nehru's socialist vision that had prevailed during the past fifty years, with its emphasis on centralization, command and control bureaucracy and mammoth public sector monopolies. Socialism tended to destroy social capital because it made us depend on the government for everything (a dependence that also suited our politicians). People forgot that they could rely on themselves. And the best work of some of the NGOs has been to remind people on the virtues of self-reliance.

Intellectuals searched for social capital in the villages where two-thirds of Indians lived. Village studies by sociologists had shown that Indians were warm, gregarious and seldom alone. They interacted incessantly, usually in their extended family, but also with caste brethren. They showed concern. If someone fell sick, the entire village showed up at the hospital (and practically willed the patient to get well!). In short, we seemed to be intensely connected. Interactions outside one's caste were, however, limited and formal. As a consequence, the Indian village was heavily factionalized.

American scholar Suzanne Rudolph, writing in the *Economic and Political Weekly* in May 2000, gave examples of how democratic processes could actually deplete social capital. She quoted a study of four north Indian villages by Sudha Pai, a scholar at Jawaharlal Nehru University, and of two Himalayan villages by Niraja Jayal. Both these studies showed that civic engagement during the panchayat elections united caste brethren, but divided them from other caste groups; in other words, it did not meet Tocqueville's second test. Jayal's story is of how the panchayati raj processes and the government undermined a vibrant case of self-help activity of the Chipko movement that had existed before the elections and that had been nurtured delicately by the whole community. Elections came and divided the community. Participative volunteerism in this case made the members more divisive, selfish and parochial.

Thus, social capital has an ambivalent nature. While it might help NGOs to get collective action from within a caste or community, and it might empower villagers to solve their own problems, it can be divisive when it comes to the whole village. Nevertheless, the movement for participation is a huge step forward in the India of the nineties, as communities and local and state governments have seen the value of people's involvement in development.

The best example of collective action that I came across in the nineties was of Civic Exnora in Tamil Nadu. A resident of Vadapalani Road in Chennai wrote to say: 'Our street used to be one big garbage dump; the bin outside our home was always overflowing because the corporation van did not often show up. My neighbours in frustration would set the garbage on fire, but the smoke irritated my asthma and I would douse it with water. So, we fought all the time.

'One morning the dustbin disappeared and a brightly painted cart stood at my door with a boy in uniform and gloves. Called the "street beautifier", he taught us to separate our garbage at home. Each morning he empties the organic waste into the green section of his cart and the recyclable waste into the red section. When he has covered the street, he takes the cart to our Zero Waste Centre, where he empties the organic waste into a storage tank that has holes at the bottom and where it is converted to compost. He sells the recyclables and the compost to augument his income. I pay Rs 20 a month and our street is now spotlessly clean. Where there was garbage outside each home, we have now planted trees.'

All this happened because of an Exnora Club. Started by M.B. Nirmal, a bank manager, this civic movement rapidly spread across the south, and by mid-2002 it covered 40 per cent of Madras city, 75 per cent of its suburbs and had clubs across Tamil Nadu and the three southern states. Its 17,000 street chapters provide clean, scientific garbage collection to approximately 17 lakh homes. Having realized their collective negotiating power, many clubs are solving other civic problems (sewage, street lighting, water supply) through their municipality. Exnora was recognized by the United

Nations Conference on Human Settlements in 1996 as among the 100 Best Urban Practices. If you too want to transform your community, write to: Exnora, 20 Giriappa Road, Chennai 600 017 (exnora@vsnl.com) or call 044-8153377.

## English Becomes an Indian Language

Ever since the British left we heard constant carping against the English language. And then one day in the 1990s, it suddenly seemed to die. Quietly and without ceremony, English became one of the Indian languages. English lost its colonial stigma, oddly enough, around the same time that the Hindu nationalists came to power. The Hindi protagonists lost steam because they lost their convictions—their own children wanted to learn English and get ahead in the world and their wives reminded them that English was their child's passport to the future.

Based on present trends, India will, predicts English linguist David Dalby, become the largest English-speaking nation in the world by 2010, overtaking the United States. Dalby, the author of *Linguasphere Register of the World's Languages and Speech-Communities*, says India will then become 'the centre of gravity of the English language'. Thus, it would seem just as intrusive to want to remove English from India today, as it was to introduce it during the time of Ram Mohan Roy and Lord Macaulay in the nineteenth century.

We are more comfortable and accepting of English today, I think, partly because we are more relaxed and confident as a people. Our minds have become decolonized and 'Hinglish' increasingly pervades our lives. For a hundred years the upper middle classes had mixed English words in their everyday talk, but the present media argot is a creature of the new satellite channels. Zee, Sony and Star, supported by their advertisers, have created this uninhibited hybrid of Hindi and English. Avidly embraced by the newly emerging middle classes, this new popular idiom of the bazaar is rushing down the socio-economic ladder. The purists naturally disapprove, but most of us are resigned to it—we know this is how languages have usually evolved. Over the decades we have learned painfully that it is often better to go with the tide than to impose one's will. All those damaging experiments in West Bengal, Gujarat and other states, which deleted English from the school syllabus, are being quietly rolled back.

That English is one of our Indian languages should neither be cause for mourning nor of rejoicing. It is the way in which the world is going. English has become the global language at a time when technological breakthroughs have shrunk the globe. Yet, one wonders why Hindi nationalists did not invest more energy and creativity into making Hindi richer and a more attractive alternative. Why did they not translate all the world's great literary and scientific works into Hindi? Why have we not had an efflorescence of regional writing in the past half-century? Certainly a few fine writers have emerged, but not the renaissance that everyone hoped for. The deck has been stacked against our vernaculars for 150 years, I realize, but our language intellectuals could have done more.

It is sad that our languages are not held in esteem by their speakers. Parents prefer to send their children to English-medium schools because they have higher standards than vernacular schools. Knowing English also means getting a better job. Whatever the reason, more and more Indians are growing up today feeling more comfortable in English than their mother tongue. They are still a minority, but if this trend continues for a couple of generations, then one day that minority will become a majority. What could stop this is a sudden resurgence in the quality of vernacular schools, and a renaissance in the regional literatures. But this appears unlikely, given the mesmerizing hold of English, along with its global ascent.

Indians have made a pact with the devil. Fluency in English gives them a competitive advantage in the global society, but losing their mother tongue runs the risk of impoverishing their personality. For, language is not only a means of communication, it is a source of new ideas and emotions. Some of us are aware that we cannot think without language, but we do not realize that we cannot feel without it either. I am able to feel certain emotions when I speak Punjabi that I do not when I use English. I have always wished that I could write in Punjabi, for then I could express a whole range of new feelings.

It is unclear where we are headed. What is clearer is that more and more Indians are speaking and writing English and finding a market for their work both in India and abroad. Since the publication of Salman Rushdie's *Midnight's Children* in 1981, Indian writing in English has become not only more visible but also respectable. Earlier, Indians were suspicious of their countrymen writing in English; they argued that one could only write creatively in one's own mother tongue. But they forgot to notice that English was becoming a mother tongue to more and more Indians.

The English that we speak and write originated with the professional middle class that emerged in the nineteenth century under British rule, and the introduction of Western education. This class not only produced clerks for the East India Company but also lawyers, teachers, engineers, doctors, bureaucrats—all the new professions that were required to run a country. Since passing an examination was the only barrier to entering this class, its members came from various castes and backgrounds, although the upper castes were the first to seize the opportunities. These professionals became the new elite, and like every elite, it closed ranks. However, the English that Indians tried to speak and write naturally mimicked that of the masters, and this continued well into the post-colonial years.

If it is any consolation, the Americans faced a similar dilemma. Until the mid-nineteenth century, the Americans were ashamed of their accents and suffered from an inferiority complex. They too were imitators. You only need to read the novels of James Fenimore Cooper to see that. But then Mark Twain came along, and he made the Americans feel that English was their language. Rushdie did the same for us in the 1980s.

The problem, however, is that less than five per cent of Indians are comfortable in English, another ten per cent negotiate it in varying degrees of discomfort, and the remaining eighty-five per cent don't know it at all. I am reminded of Ursula Mistry, a deaf woman in Mumbai, who wrote to say that she feels 'shut out because she cannot communicate'. She likened her situation to that of Indians who did not know English and were excluded from serious economic, social and political discourse. 'Not to know English in India,' she said, 'is worse than being deaf.' The middle ten per cent also have their sorrows. Not being comfortable in English, they make a heroic effort to understand and to speak correctly. Their intellectual energy is wasted in copying others. In the end, they have no confidence left and all their originality and creativity is lost. They are fettered in an imitative world, their education wasted, their culture replaced by an English whitewash. This means that the five per cent sit prettily on top of the heap, receiving all the rewards and favours of our society. They are the real brahmins of India and have been for more than a hundred years.

What is the answer to this great problem? The development of regional languages has been uneven across the country, but nowhere have they been able to supplant the rewards that come from knowing English. Also, stopping English is clearly not feasible, nor a good idea. It is our window to the world and a source of great competitive advantage in the global economy. The young regard English as a skill, like working with the computer, and it helps them to negotiate the modern world. Nor is English any longer a carrier of the English or American flag, for every mother in every country knows that it is a ticket to her child's future. The only workable solution is to face the unpalatable truth, which every Indian knows in his heart—accept English as our own language. Everyone must learn it along with his mother tongue. Let us shed our hypocrisy and eliminate the distinction between English and vernacular-medium schools.

## Heroes for Our Times

Every nation must have its heroes. Having lost its stars of the Independence era, Indians were desperately seeking new ones who might inspire them in this unheroic decade. P.V. Narasimha Rao, like Deng Xiaoping in China, could have been a hero. Deng had created an economic revolution in China and he had supplanted Mao in many Chinese hearts. Rao too created an economic revolution in India between 1991 and '93, but, unlike Deng, he turned out to lack vision and conviction. He was a reluctant reformer, and by the end of the decade, he was mired in corruption cases and no longer respected.

V.P. Singh could also have been a hero. He had released a social revolution as he attempted to 'mandalize' our society and raise the status of backward castes. He proposed quota-based affirmative action on behalf of the backward classes, as suggested by a commission headed by R.P. Mandal. But the middle class and even the backwards saw through his electoral ambitions, and his efforts only ended up in dividing society and seriously compromising standards. If he had genuinely cared for the backward classes, he would have attempted to deliver education and health to them, and that would done more for them over the long term. The actions of several backward class leaders later proved how undeserving he was.

Manmohan Singh and P. Chidambaram, former finance ministers, were candidates. Indeed, with a solid record of achievement in reform, they did become heroes to many young people in the business world. But, in the end, politics was not kind to them and they were languishing by the end of the decade. The nineties were not kind to politicians as a class, and they fell even lower in public esteem than before. It can be argued that democracy is best run by modest men and we should not look to democratic leaders to become our heroes. We should look elsewhere to persons with tangible achievements. To V. Kurien, for example, for making India the largest milk producer. To Sam Pitroda, for initiating the STD booths and letting loose a telecom revolution in the bazaar.

To C. Subramaniam for ushering in the green revolution. To Amartya Sen, the Nobel laureate, for reminding us constantly about the importance of investing in primary education and health. To Mother Teresa and others in our civil society who were making a difference. To Sachin Tendulkar for becoming the best batsman in the world and inspiring a million youngsters every time he comes to bat. There are other such examples and they are better qualified to be our heroes in these non-ideological times.

The ones who truly captured the nation's imagination were the warriors of the information technology revolution, both in Silicon Valley in the United States and in Bangalore. Their rags-to-riches stories resonated with our times. They single-handedly changed India's image in the world from a failed economic state to a potential economic power, and they inspired a whole generation of young Indians to believe in themselves. There were so many heroes to choose from, but N.R. Narayana Murthy, the smallish, bespectacled and soft-featured chief of Infosys Technologies, won the nation's heart. He had created not only the best performing company, but also the one most respected for its integrity and its values.

In 1962, Murthy got admission to the Indian Institute of Technology (IIT), Kharagpur, but he could not go because his father could not afford the monthly fee of Rs 150 for the hostel. Narayana Murthy then had to settle for the local engineering college in Mysore. But that did not discourage him. From there, he went to the Indian Institute of Management (IIM), Ahmedabad, where he got his Master of Business Administration (MBA) degree. After hopping through several early jobs, he landed at Patni Computer Systems in Mumbai, where he and his friends struck upon the idea of starting their own software company in which all employees could have a stake. That dream came true.

Started by six computer engineers with a capital of Rs 10,000 at the beginning of the nineties, Infosys was worth Rs 16,000 crore in February 2000. It developed software for the best global companies, and its sales had grown at a steady pace of 40 per cent a year for a decade. With the gradual appreciation of its stock, more than a hundred of its managers had become millionaires in dollar terms and more than 400 managers had become crorepatis as the company spread its wealth through stock options. Narayana Murthy was the glue that kept this enterprise of 10,000 professionals together, inspiring and motivating them.

Towards the end of the decade, I came across Ashish Nandy's fascinating book, *An Ambiguous Journey to the City*. In it he wrote about Karna, the mythic hero of the Mahabharata. Karna, as every schoolchild knows, was born of the princess Kunti, who had a boon that allowed her to have a child by any god that she wished. Whilst still young and unmarried she invoked through her prayers the sun god, and as a result, she conceived and gave birth to Karna. Fearing a scandal, she stealthily placed the child in an ornate casket and left it to float on the Ashva River, where a humble charioteer, Adhiratha, and his wife, Radha found him, and brought him up to be their son. Kunti, meanwhile, married the sickly Pandu, the prince of Hastinapur, who was cursed to die if sexually aroused. So Kunti exercised her boon and had children by the gods. These were the famous Pandavas who went on to fight the Kauravas in what became the Mahabharata.

Karna grew up into a brave and gifted warrior. But he was constantly subjected to jibes about his humble birth and his princely ambitions. He challenged his half-brothers to an open competition in the field, but they refused on the ground that competing with princes was a royal privilege reserved for their peers. He was again humiliated when princess Draupadi refused to marry the charioteer's son, even though he had won her in fair competition.

Embittered, Karna turned to the Kauravas for friendship. This worried the god Krishna, who revealed to Karna the secret of his birth on the eve of the great battle and pleaded with him to join the Pandavas. In return, Krishna offered him Hastinapur's kingdom and Draupadi's hand in marriage. Kunti and Surya, his natural parents, begged him as well, but Karna was loyal to his word and refused to betray the Kauravas, who had elevated him to a Kshatriya and a prince. In the end, like a good hero, Karna knew when to die, and he went down unvanquished, killed by Krishna's trickery.

Although he walks out of the pages of the Mahabharata, this Karna, I believe, seeks power and legitimacy for a new ethic and a new mindset that resonates with our age. He defies his low caste, he celebrates achievement in a competitive society, he stands for individualism and a confident attitude of achievement. He seeks legitimacy for the rustic and low-born in a secular city. Like Narayana Murthy he has come up through self-help and self-reliance. He could well be another hero for our times.

# 2

## Understanding Our Times

*To be ignorant of what occurred before you were born is to remain always a child. For what is the worth of human life, unless it is woven into the life of our ancestors by the records of history?*

—Cicero, *Orator* (46 BC)

The decade of the nineties brought to a close the most violent century in world history. An unbelievable 187 million people were killed in two world wars, in Hitler's holocaust, Stalin's gulags, and Mao's genocides. This is equal to killing one in every ten persons alive in 1900. More people were decimated in the twentieth century than in all the centuries put together.

For us in India, however, it was a different story and a good century. We won our freedom peacefully in 1947, with practically no English or Indian casualties—and this happened in the shadows of Hitler, Stalin and Mao. It is true that unspeakable violence accompanied the Partition, but we escaped the century's ideological devastation, and we set about building a proud nation based on the idealistic institutions of democracy, secularism and socialism. In the past five decades, democracy has been our biggest prize, although statism prevented us from creating an industrial revolution and realizing our economic potential. Nevertheless, compared to fifty years ago, the average Indian lives twice as long in 2000—sixty-three years compared to thirty-one—and two-thirds of the people are literate versus only seventeen per cent at Independence.

The twentieth century brought unparalleled prosperity almost everywhere. Across the globe, people now live longer, they are taller, better fed and better educated. The earth supports three times more people than it did a hundred years ago, and they are all better off than their grandparents. In a sense, we have fulfilled the nineteenth century's faith in progress. There are, admittedly, vast inequalities, but even in the poor countries the average person is better off today than a hundred years ago. This material progress will continue in the twenty-first century, and it is likely that mankind's age-old economic problem of want and hunger will be a thing of the past by 2050. This will happen because of two of the most powerful forces of the twentieth century—technology and globalization. It is these forces that have brought a degree of convergence in the standards of living among the Western countries (and more recently in East Asia), and they will do the same broadly across the world in the twenty-first century.

The twentieth century also brought more freedom. There were only thirteen democracies in 1900, covering less than fifteen per cent of the world's people. In 2000, more than seventy per cent of the people on the earth lived in eighty-seven democracies. This trend is also likely to continue. The essays in this chapter will describe the mood and spirit of our times against an historic backdrop of a world that is increasingly turning liberal and is wary of ideological conflict.

## Coping with Democratic Capitalism

True to the temper of our times, there are no heroes, no big-chested ideologies, no utopias that will provide complete solutions to our problems. We are witnessing the quiet triumph of democratic capitalism, and it is in the nature of its institutions that they are best run by modest men. In India, too, the rapidly growing middle class is absorbed in the pursuit of prosperity, gradually becoming consumers and busy acquiring material possessions. Instead of resting content with the knowledge that people have eschewed wars for the peaceful arts, our intellectuals are, however, discontented by the loss of ideology.

In our parents' time in the 1950s, many reasonable people looked forward to a bright socialist future in which private property and capital would be abolished. By contrast, we have trouble imagining an order today that is not essentially democratic and capitalist. Many improvements could, of course, be made to this new order—a stronger safety net for the poor, better quality of health and education, less unemployment, more care for the environment. But it is, to our minds, a better order than any other we can realistically imagine.

It is reassuring that democratic capitalism seems aware of its limitations. It does not pretend to offer a utopia but accepts a plural society such as ours with diverse castes and creeds and interest groups, and it modestly offers a civil society with 'private space' for each person to pursue his or her passion. It does not prescribe what a person should do in his private space. Unlike feudal societies, capitalism does not celebrate war and heroes; unlike religious societies, it does not venerate saints or spiritual feats. Instead, it values the boring, domestic virtues of thrift, restraint, prudence, trustworthiness and hard work. It begins and ends with the ordinary person's desire to 'better his condition', in the words of Adam Smith. As to happiness, enlightenment and heroism, it leaves those for the individual to find on his own.

We are told that capitalism, with all its faults, works better than any other economic system. That evidence, its supporters point out, is no longer in dispute. A series of controlled experiments were conducted in the last fifty years on a scale that is the envy of every social scientist. After the Second World War, Germany, Korea, Vietnam and China had been cut into two and capitalism was installed in one part and socialism in the other. In every case, the capitalist part outperformed the non-capitalist one by a vast margin. Over the past 200 years, in country after country, capitalism has delivered unparalleled prosperity after the Industrial Revolution.

It started with England in the eighteenth century, spread to the European continent and North America in the nineteenth century, and moved to East Asia in the last quarter of the twentieth century. Although this prosperity has been unequally shared, over time, the whole society has benefited visibly and significantly, including the poor.

The private space that a democratic capitalist order offers is the personal liberty of the individual. However, personal liberty is not synonymous with capitalism, as some defenders of free enterprise seem to suggest. In recent times, a number of countries in East Asia have permitted a good deal of economic freedom but have placed heavy curbs on political and social freedom. But, yes, capitalism is a necessary condition for individual liberty, even if it is not a sufficient condition. There seems to be no example in history of any nation that has delivered true liberty without it having a market economy. Although the market has an inherent tendency to diffuse wealth, this will happen more easily if the system is open— where there is equality of opportunity, where talented youngsters from poor families can get an education, where there is social mobility and the benefits of liberty are widely shared. Over the past fifty years in India, we have made some progress in opening our system to the lower castes, but true equality of opportunity is very far away.

However, the West's experience has taught us that democratic capitalism creates its own problems. With rising affluence, as more and more people are liberated from basic wants, the majority seems unable to cope with the demands of autonomy. Since people do not know how to sensibly fill their private space, they appear to get bored and suffer from a spiritual malaise. They either pursue insatiably the acquisition of material goods or they rebel against this spiritless life and seek refuge in adversarial cultures, as the young people in the West did in the sixties and seventies. However, where there are strong religious and family traditions, people appear to cope better with these problems. Ordinary people seem to need a moral authority to order their lives, which is, of course, beyond the agenda of the democratic capitalist society.

These problems might appear distant to many, but they are relevant to the question of what sort of society do we want to build in India? Our economy has grown at an average of six per cent annually between 1980 and 2000 and if it keeps growing that way in the future, then these problems will be upon us in the first half of the twenty-first century. Fortunately, religious and family traditions remain strong in India, and this gives many Indians the confidence that we may be able to absorb some of the shocks and cope with many of the difficulties. The history of the twentieth century has taught us that it is dangerous to be too enthusiastic about any ideology or system. Communism, fascism, socialism have all inflicted incalculable harm; so has nationalism of various enthusiastic varieties. Too much passion about one's ideals is not a good thing.

## The Difficulty of Becoming Rich

Contrary to what many believe, the economic lives of our ancestors is a story of almost unrelieved wretchedness. Everywhere, a small number lived well while the great majority lived in abysmal squalor. We forget their misery, in part, by the grace of literature, poetry and legend, which celebrate those who lived well and forget those who lived in the silence of poverty. The eras of misery have been mythologized and are remembered as golden ages of pastoral simplicity. They were not. In truth, survival was the only order of business.

The move from poverty to wealth began in England in the mid-eighteenth century and it was based on harnessing technology and organization to the satisfaction of human wants, while keeping the economy free from political control and ensuring that private individuals, rather than bureaucrats, made decisions. For the first time, prosperity touched the lives of more than a tenth of the population and offered the common person the possibilities of education, privacy and a variety of experience. The striking character of the West's miracle was its gradualism. There was no sudden change—just year-to-year growth at a rate that somewhat exceeded population growth. The gains, at first, were not noticeable and it was widely believed that only the rich experienced them. As economic growth compounded through the twentieth century, it became obvious that the working classes were increasingly turning into middle classes. Poverty also declined in the West from ninety per cent of the population to twenty per cent, or less, depending on the country and its definition of poverty. In contrast, most of the people in the rest of the world still lived in poverty.

As economies expanded, so did their stocks of capital, their expenditures on education and public health, and the accumulation of skills by their workforces. Innovations needed to be tested in the market place and this required money and competence in engineering, manufacturing and marketing, especially if the innovator was to capture the rewards of the innovation. These resources came to exist in the ordinary firm. Comparatively free of political and religious controls, markets determined who won the rewards of innovation. The response of the market was the test of success or failure. Competition was, of course, central to innovation. The market rewarded innovators with a high price for a unique product or service until such time as it was imitated or superseded by others.

Economic historians sometimes take a longer view and see different phases in the West's economic expansion. Beginning in the fifteenth century, there was an expansion of trade and commerce and this is sometimes called a mercantile revolution. Three centuries later, in the eighteenth century, there began the first industrial revolution, about which I have already spoken. At the end of the nineteenth century and the beginning of the twentieth, the introduction of electric power and the internal combustion engine amounted to a second industrial revolution. In our own day, developments in electronic storage and switching networks, embodied in communications systems and computers, have led to an information revolution.

In the seventeenth century, the West developed a scientific procedure, based upon observation, reason and experiment. Although artisan-inventors developed their own technology in the beginning, over time the contributions of science became increasingly numerous. Late in the nineteenth century, the paths of pure science and industrial technology converged in the fields of chemistry, electricity and biology. The introduction of the industrial research laboratory at the beginning of the twentieth century systematized the links between science and industry.

Did the West grow rich through colonialism? Karl Marx certainly thought so. He attributed some of the new wealth of the West to its imperialist conquests and its commercial acquisitions of raw materials from overseas, beginning in the sixteenth century. The striking accomplishment of British colonialism was the fact that it seeded several advanced Western economies, to the substantial benefit of the colonies—the United States, Canada, Australia, New Zealand, Hong Kong and Singapore. The economic accomplishments of these colonies also benefited Britain, for trade with an advanced country is far more beneficial than it is with an economically backward colony.

The claim that Western economic advances arose from imperialism is based on the claim that the poor colonies provided markets for the manufactured goods of the advanced countries. This line of thought cannot be pressed beyond a point for poor, undeveloped countries do not, as a rule, provide large markets. So the possibilities of exploitation are also relatively small. Markets large enough to encourage a major expansion of production in the advanced countries are, almost by definition, in countries that are themselves economically advanced (though not necessarily industrialized). Another reason for doubting this hypothesis is the absence of correlation between the timing of a Western country's economic growth and imperialism. Imperialist Spain and Portugal did not achieve long-term growth. Switzerland and the Scandinavian countries, which did grow, were not imperialist countries. Germany and the United States, which achieved long-term growth, were latecomers to imperialism. Imperialist Britain and Holland grew, but they were already strong before they became imperial powers and they continued to grow after they gave up their empires.

～

We have grown up in a world divided between rich and poor nations. We also take for granted that the rich will keep getting richer and the poor poorer. When I was young, we learned that countries became rich through creating an industrial revolution. But we were resigned to the idea that this would take a lot of time. We believed that technical progress was the result of centuries of scientific learning and attitude building. Catching up with the industrialized countries was a pipe dream. Then the Asian miracle happened and today we no longer take national inequalities for granted. In the second half of the twentieth century, the history of East Asia demonstrates that a poor nation can become rich, and very quickly at that. If China maintains its dynamic growth, its standard of living will catch up with that of the rich countries in the second quarter of the twenty-first century. Indeed, this optimistic outcome is also the fate of India. It may not happen as quickly as in China, but it will happen faster than we think.

The convergence between rich and poor nations was always expected. Adam Smith suggested 200 years ago that when rich and poor nations were linked through trade, their standard of living would eventually converge. It makes intuitive sense because the standard of living depends on productivity, and productivity, in turn, depends on technology. When a poor nation is connected, it merely adopts the technological innovations of the rich one without having to reinvent the wheel. Hence, it grows faster and eventually catches up. In the forties, Paul Samuelson, the American Nobel laureate, demonstrated the same outcome in the 'factory price equalization theorem'. He asked that if there are only minor wage differences within a country, why should these differences be so large *between* countries? Thus, remove barriers between countries and wages will eventually equalize. But the nagging question is, why did convergence not happen? Why have the poor countries not caught up in the last fifty years?

The simple answer is that poor countries were not linked to the rich in the past fifty years. After the Second World War, almost the entire Third World, except for some East Asian countries, closed its economies to international trade. The East Asian nations, led by Japan, traded vigorously. They imported technology and, gradually, real wages rose and soon they became prosperous. Between 1970 and 1990, the per capita income of the seventy-one closed, developing countries grew 0.7 per cent a year, while the income of the thirteen open, developing countries (most of them in East Asia) rose 4.6 per cent. Similarly, after the Second World War, the incomes of the poorer, southern European countries—Spain, Portugal, Italy—converged with the richer northern European countries primarily as a result of trade and their joining the European Economic Community. So, convergence does take place.

How to make a poor nation prosperous is not an easy question. The answer seems to lie in technology and institutions. Since Britain's Industrial Revolution, there came about, for the first time in recorded history, a continuous flow of inventions, and they were absorbed commercially as profitable innovations. History teaches us that a nation's ability to absorb these innovations and create an industrial revolution depends on having the right institutions in place—for example, property rights, schools and stable governance.

Although we have not so far experienced this miraculous transformation in India, it is only a matter of time before we do, thanks to economic reforms, and as long as we keep our economy open and keep vigorously reforming our damaging socialist institutions. We will thus expand the autonomy of the economic sphere and protect it from the mischief of political interference. However, it will take more than deregulation to succeed. Widespread prosperity needs the reform of our education and health institutions as well. Even after we replace inefficient bureaucracies with competitive markets, we will still need honest constables and efficient judges to dispense speedy justice. Hence, we need to strengthen our institutions of governance.

## Another Age of Liberalism

The world at the beginning of the twenty-first century bears a striking resemblance to the world at the beginning of the twentieth century. What we are witnessing today is the second emergence of globalization. The chip and cyberspace are to our age what the telegraph, the railway and the large steamship were to the twentieth century, bridging distances.

That era of free trade began when Britain scrapped export duties and lowered import duties in 1842. The unification of Germany also gave a major push to trade in the early 1870s. Russia joined in with the foreign financing of its railway. Japan dramatically opened to the world economy based on low tariffs imposed by Western powers. Latin America experienced enormous growth from the 1870s based on raw material exports and capital imports, mainly for railroad construction. India too enjoyed rapid export growth between 1870 and 1914. A network of bilateral agreements kept protectionism in check and trade barriers low.

Marx made some disastrous predictions, but he also got a few things absolutely right. One of these was to foresee the globalization of the world economy. He correctly prophesied that technology and communications, combined with the productivity of the market economy, would lead to a global capitalist world. In the biting language of *Communist Manifesto*, he and Friedrich Engels wrote: 'The bourgeoisie, by the rapid improvement of all instruments of production, by the immensely facilitated means of communication, draws all, even the most barbarian nations, into civilization. The cheap prices of its commodities are the heavy artillery with which it batters down all Chinese walls, with which it forces the barbarians' intensely obstinate hatred of foreigners to capitulate . . . In a word, it creates a world after its own image.'

I try sometimes to imagine the days when George V was

emperor of India and when Mahatma Gandhi had yet to enter politics. The Japanese controlled most of eastern Russia and the Germans were preparing for the First World War. It was also the time when a tiny middle class, which had spread a thin covering over the whole of India, was rapidly and insistently becoming confident goaded on by Bal Gangadhar Tilak and Gopal Krishna Gokhale (who provided it with differing visions of a future India). Despite colonial rule, a law-abiding Indian before 1914 could pass through life hardly noticing the existence of the state beyond the policeman and the postman. He could produce and sell what he pleased without a licence or a permit, and without an inspector who insisted on a cut. He could leave the country without a passport, and exchange his money freely without any restriction.

The world before August 1914 was an age of liberalism. Between 1870 and 1914, the world had experienced true globalization, and had enjoyed more than forty years of continued export-led growth. What was the result of this globalization? An exhaustive study of forty-one countries by economic historian Lloyd Reynolds, *Economic Growth in the Third World 1850–1980*, shows that the open global economy significantly promoted rapid economic growth in much of the developing world. Another scholar, Dean Williamson, shows that the gap in real wages between the rich and the poor countries narrowed during this global export boom.

The spirit of this age was captured by John Maynard Keynes in a famous passage:

What an extraordinary episode in the economic progress of man that age was which came to an end in August 1914! . . . The inhabitant of London could order by telephone, sipping his morning tea in bed, the various products of the whole earth, in such quantity as he might see fit, and reasonably expect their early delivery upon his doorsteps; he could, at the same moment and by the same means, adventure his wealth in the natural resources and new enterprises of any quarter of the world, and share, without exertion or even trouble, in their prospective fruits and advantages; . . . most of all, he regarded this state of affairs as normal, certain, and permanent . . .

This age ended when the world trading system collapsed with the First World War and Britain's leadership of financial markets ceased. The gold standard failed in the twenties and financial instability contributed to the Great Depression in the thirties. Commodity prices slumped, ending the export-led growth of the poor countries. Protectionism in Europe and the United States stopped capital flows. Russia's Bolshevik Revolution and the rise of fascism in Italy and Germany undermined liberal trade regimes. Faith in markets, free trade and international institutions died along with all this. It was Keynes once again who caught this new spirit in a surprising turnabout:

> I sympathise, therefore, with those who would minimise, rather than with those who would maximise, economic entanglements between nations, ideas, knowledge, art, hospitality, travel—these are things which should of their nature be international. But let goods be homespun whenever it is reasonably and conveniently possible and above all, let finance be primarily national!

The international economic system was in ruins at the end of the Second World War. In the fifties, only five countries had convertible currencies and more than eighty per cent of the world's population lived in closed, non-market economies. The Europeans established currency convertibility in 1958, but it wasn't till 1993 that fifty per cent of the world's people began to live in open economies. In 1994, India crossed Jeffrey Sachs's and Andrew Warner's threshold of openness (that the authors describe in 'Economic Reform and Global Integration' in the *Brookings Papers on Economic Activity*, 1:1995). When Russia and China also implemented their trade reforms in 1995, eighty-seven per cent of the world began to live in open economies. And another age of free trade, global markets and liberalism had begun.

What are the lessons that we can draw from this story? One certainly is that globalization and free trade are fragile and we should not take them for granted. The world trading system, which collapsed in 1914, took eighty years to rebuild. In our euphoria over global integration we should not assume that we are at the 'end of history'. Certainly, the World Trade Organization (WTO) and the International Monetary Fund (IMF) will inhibit unilateral adventurism today, but the lesson of history is that we should guard this unique and rational state of economic affairs.

Another lesson is that free trade contributes to growth and raises standards of living. Reynolds' and Williamson's data confirm that the poor countries also benefited from the export boom in the nineteenth century. Sachs and Warner argue that in the second half of the twentieth century, poor nations did not close the income gap with the rich nations because their markets were closed.

A third lesson for a newcomer to world trade like India is that we must jealously protect our newly-won 'openness'. This commitment must not diminish despite protectionism among our trading partners, despite short-term imbalances between export and imports, and despite panic raised by Indian business in the face of global competition. Let us remember that of all our achievements since 1991, the most important one has been to open our economy.

## Socialism Doesn't Live Here Any More

I have no illusions that the market economy is perfect. It is like democracy: with all its flaws it is still better than any other system. As I think of the market's lack of perfection, I am reminded of the distinguished physicist Freeman Dyson at Princeton. His five-year-old stepdaughter accidentally walked into the room when he was naked and about to get dressed. 'Did God really make you like that?' she asked with some astonishment. 'Couldn't he have made you better?'

'The only honest answer is, of course, yes,' admitted Dyson wryly.

It's the same answer for the free market. It creates inequalities, it makes the workplace insecure and it commercializes life. But it is better than any other system we have found.

Will our government not lose control over resources if we open up, privatize or become dependent on market forces? People have insistently asked these questions since 1991. I believe liberalization will lead to higher growth in India, as it has everywhere else. Higher growth will bring more resources for the state through taxes and duties. If the government spends its funds wisely it can dramatically improve the quality of life of the common people. Primary education and eradication of illiteracy is clearly the highest priority, followed by public health. Next in priority is our creaking physical infrastructure—roads, ports, railways, power, etc. Once the government gets out of the negative job of running and controlling economic activity and puts its best people (and there are many of them) in implementing social action and infrastructure, then it will enhance the quality of life of the worst-off members in our society.

Although socialism died around the world circa 1991, in India it continues to exercise a mesmerizing influence in many influential pockets. The Communist Party of India (Marxist) unveiled a new manifesto in 2000, and although it recognized that much had changed, it still hankered after state control of economic activity. The Congress Party, too, often harbours dreams of a return to Nehruvian socialism. The rest of the Opposition regularly invokes socialism to block economic reforms, but what it really wants is a return to cheap populism. The question is: why does a bankrupt system, which brought untold misery to millions around the world, refuse to die in India?

Socialism is attractive because it appeals to our idealistic wish for a rational and compassionate society. Robert Heilbroner, the eminent American thinker, suggests that socialism can still serve as the vision of a society we would like our grandchildren to live in.

Such a society might have, for example, the level of social welfare of Sweden, civil liberties of Holland, income distribution of Norway, health care of Germany, the public culture of France and, till recently, the security of employment of Japan. In other words, the collapse of socialism should not put an end to our social imagination. If we think of socialism as the improvements we would like to make in our society, it is clear that we must make economic peace with the demands of our environment. Making that peace means that we do not contaminate 'the green-blue film on which life itself depends'.

But Heilbroner confuses the issue, for he makes socialism synonymous with idealism. Socialism, strictly defined, means the ownership of the means of production by the state. In this sense, socialism has failed everywhere, and it is misleading to confuse the two words. The ideas of the Russian Revolution were seductive—the equality of men, women and nations, the right of everyone to work and to have a fair share in the distribution of the wealth they produce, the undesirability of an idle leisure class. But these ideas were lost in Soviet practice. Yet, as ideals, they retain their validity. They will be remembered long after the lies and perversions of Stalinism are forgotten.

The worst indictment of the Indian brand of socialism is that, in the end, it did very little for the poor. It is ironic that men and women of goodwill created this order and they were widely admired. The second irony is that they pig-headedly refused to change course, even when there was clear evidence that this path was doomed. They feel no humiliation that India has lagged behind in the Third World, while its neighbours in East and Southeast Asia have gone ahead, and done so much for the poor.

In all likelihood, we are now moving in the direction of some sort of capitalism in India. Capitalism's strength is that entrepreneurs and companies innovate, expand, contract and change in the market place daily. In the process they create jobs and wealth for society. But all this energy of a market-driven society also needs governance and public goods (education, roads, public health) and it needs to avoid deleterious outcomes (damage to the environment). We need the state to create public policy and public goods, which is very different from central planning or the licence raj.

The commercialization of life is not a pleasant prospect, but it is the price we have to pay for prosperity and efficiency. We have to put up with it as we have to put up with politicians in a democracy. In the short term, capitalism increases inequality; but in the long term, it leads to a much more democratic society. It is merciless to the weak producer and uncompassionate to the worker who loses his job, but it rewards the economy as a whole by creating more jobs, lowering costs and prices, improving the quality of the products and raising the standards of living.

The free market leads to inequality because of the unequal ability of people to work and make money. Some people are just more productive than others, whether they are labourers or farmers or managers. Capitalism rewards them unevenly, according to their productivity. But the market also breaks down conventional barriers to equality because of the continually changing demands of labour. Indian cities today are far more socially egalitarian than the village society that they are replacing. What is emerging from this equalizing process is the Indian middle class.

Middle class society does not achieve Marx's 'classless society', but a high degree of social mobility within it permits more and more people to identify with its aspirations. Social inequality is not eliminated, but the source of inequality is now due to natural differences in talents, productivity and the division of labour rather than the old, arbitrary, man-made hierarchy of the village. In successful economies the vast majority of the population becomes the middle class. In India, our biggest failure is not that we did not eliminate poverty, but that we failed to create a middle class. Our middle class was only eight per cent of the population in 1980 and even in 2000 it was only eighteen per cent.

There are other flaws in capitalism. It tends to concentrate economic power in a few firms, and it needs a policeman to ensure free and fair competition. Capitalism needs a strong judicial structure to enforce contracts and to catch crooks who fix prices or engage in insider trading. Capitalism also leads to a greedy consumer society, where people only care about their own interest and have lost faith in religion or idealistic ideologies; they are left with little to do except to go shopping. The answer to capitalism's flaws is not to hanker after socialism, but to insist on good governance, transparent regulation and vigorous institutions that protect the consumer, the producer and society.

## The Future Belongs to the East

The nineteenth century belonged to Europe, the twentieth went to America, and many believe that the twenty-first century is likely to be Asia's. Whether it belongs to China (and greater China) or China *and* India depends largely on our ability to sustain rapid economic growth in the coming decades. Japan's situation is problematic because it has lost confidence after suffering more than ten years of continuous deflation since the beginning of the nineties. What is more serious is that it has an ageing population, and its demographics are wrong.

East Asia has begun to influence the course of world history because of its sheer economic weight. In 1960 East and Southeast Asia had only four per cent of the world's wealth (gross national product or GNP), while North America had thirty-seven per cent. In 1990, both had become equal with twenty-four per cent of the world's GNP. Since more than half the world's economic growth in the 1990s has taken place in East and Southeast Asia, it has become progressively larger relative to the world.

In the 1960s Japan emerged to become a significant force in the global economy, followed soon by the four Asian dragons in the seventies. Southeast Asia joined up in the eighties and China and India in the nineties. Simultaneously, the world also became a global economy, abetted by the incredible expansion in world trade, communications and cross-border capital flows.

By the end of the century, the picture changed somewhat. After becoming one of the richest societies in the world—periodically lecturing the United States on successful business practices during the eighties—Japan's economy suffered ten years of agonizing contraction in the nineties. The other East and Southeast Asian countries (except China) also suffered a terrible economic blow in the summer of 1997. Although many recovered, they went into a shell once again when the American recession hit the world soon after the new century began. But China and India, both continental economies and less susceptible to the shocks of global trade, continued to grow. Although the GDP growth rate of both slowed down by one to two percentage points, China continued to outpace India. Despite the setbacks, there is growing realization among Asians that their moment in history has arrived. Their minds, which were shackled by colonialism, are becoming liberated. With economic success, there is greater confidence. China exemplifies this more than any other society as its income per head has doubled in ten years.

East Asia's experience spells good news for India as well, because our economy has been growing six per cent a year on the average for twenty years since 1980. Although this is a percentage point slower than the Asian tigers, India nevertheless faces the happy prospect of dramatically reducing poverty in the early twenty-first century if it keeps growing as it has in the past two decades. As long as it continues on the virtuous path of opening up its economy, dismantling controls, raising literacy, the momentum of the global economy—with its relentless spread of technology, capital and ideas—will carry it on its shoulders. By 2025, according to World Bank projections, India could see its share of world output rise from six to thirteen per cent, making it the third largest economy in the world. By then China will be number one with twenty-six per cent, and India and China will account for thirty-nine per cent share of global output, which is about equal to the present share of United States and Europe combined. Add to this Japan and the rest of East and Southeast Asia and you are well above fifty per cent. Hence, there is good reason to believe that the twenty-first century might belong to Asia.

~

The greatest burst of sustained economic growth that the world had ever seen came to an end in 1997 when the East Asian miracle slowed. The economic success of the region had thrilled the world for twenty years. The East Asian nations exported, created jobs and prospered. As their economies grew, inequality declined dramatically and they virtually eradicated poverty. Japan created this model of success when it began to export simple, but quality, products like toys and textiles in the fifties. Gradually it moved up the value chain to export more sophisticated products, such as steel and electronics. Eventually, it became a producer of high-technology products and financial services. Taiwan, South Korea, Hong Kong and Singapore followed Japan in the late sixties and seventies. Malaysia, Thailand, Indonesia, China and the Philippines came thereafter in the eighties. Apart from a strong commitment to export, the other features of the East Asian strategy were to build on a successful agricultural base, give high priority to education, and create an effective partnership between government and industry.

By 1997, however, most of these economies were in trouble, and precisely at a time when they had budget surpluses, high foreign exchange reserves and among the highest savings rate in the world. So, what went wrong? The economist Ashok Desai made a lucid analysis of this crisis and I have drawn upon it with much gratitude. The Asian crisis of 1997 began in Thailand, precisely at the moment when it was healthiest and strongest. According to Ashok Desai, its economy was 'picture perfect': it had been the world's fastest growing country, with GDP having grown 9.8 per cent a year for a decade between 1985 and 1995. Contrary to what many thought, this growth had not been fuelled by foreign capital inflows—they were less than fifteen per cent of investment. Thailand was fiscally prudent—its fiscal deficit of 3.7 per cent of GDP in

1985 had become a surplus of 7.8 per cent by 1995. Exports had been growing 16.8 per cent a year for a decade, its exchange rate had remained stable and its investment rate had risen to a spectacular 41.5 per cent of GDP, while inflation remained below five per cent between 1985 and 1995.

Thailand's human and social performance was also extraordinary. In 1995, its population was growing only one per cent (versus India's 1.9); life expectancy was sixty-nine years (versus sixty-two for India); infant mortality was thirty-five per thousand (versus sixty-eight for India), proportion of poor ten per cent (versus India's thirty-five per cent), adult illiteracy six per cent (forty-nine per cent in India), and eighty-seven per cent of the population had access to sanitation against twenty-nine per cent in India's case.

Thailand's soft underbelly was its high current account deficit—7.8 per cent of GDP in 1994—but it did not squander the capital inflows in consumption; nor did it use the investment inefficiently. Its domestic savings ratio rose much more than its capital imports; domestic savings financed most of its capital formation, and its incremental capital–output ratio in 1990–94 was only 4.8.

So, what failed? First, Thailand's export growth came down suddenly from twenty-five per cent in 1995 to 0.1 per cent in 1996, primarily due to the slower growth in world demand. Thailand's exports had consisted mainly of low technology and labour-intensive goods like garments, electronic goods and leather goods. As its unemployment rate came down to three per cent, wages rose three to five times compared to China, Indonesia and Vietnam. The stable dollar exchange rate, combined with appreciation of the dollar against other major currencies, contributed to the growing uncompetitiveness of Thai exports.

Second, its property market collapsed. Loans to the private sector went up from thirty-nine per cent of GDP in 1992 to 123 per cent in 1996. A high proportion of it went into real estate, whose prices collapsed at the end of 1996. To finance the real estate development, Thai companies had borrowed abroad. Owing to the stability of the exchange rate, they failed to hedge against exchange risk. Two-thirds of the foreign debt of $90 billion in 1997 was in short-term loans. As a result, Thai banks ended up with high bad debts and their impending insolvency set off panic among foreign investors.

Could the crisis have been avoided? It is difficult to say. A fixed exchange rate led Thailand towards mis-investment. Since there was no exchange risk, both the properties market and the stock market seemed to offer wonderful returns to potential investors. Had the government let the exchange rate find its own level, it might have received quicker signals about impending troubles.

Of course, every government wants to eliminate exchange risks. Sometimes it does so by fixing the exchange rate; at other times by deliberately undervaluing its currency to encourage exports. The Thai government should have allowed the baht to appreciate when foreign investment was pouring in. It might have then given the right signals to investors. If the Thai baht had been allowed to appreciate when the world wanted to invest, it would have been obvious that the property and stocks in Thailand were overpriced. The terrible mis-investment would not have been made and Thailand might still have avoided this bizarre crisis.

Why the Indonesian and Malaysian capital markets went into a panic following the floating of the baht is also difficult to understand. Indonesia had been borrowing heavily abroad to fill the gap between domestic savings and investments. Though it had a floating exchange rate, it did not allow it to vary beyond a narrow band. Indonesians also did not cover their foreign exchange risks involved in foreign borrowing. Indonesia had the same unreformed banking system as Thailand, which slumped after big lending to the property market. Although Malaysia was in far better shape than Indonesia, its use of foreign capital for grandiose projects left it vulnerable to currency shocks, particularly when the current account of its balance of payments was in substantial deficit.

The case of Hong Kong is even stranger. It has one of the soundest banking systems and a currency board that fully guarantees repayment of all foreign exchange liabilities in the event of an emergency. Hong Kong does not rely on manufacturing exports, which might have felt the impact of exchange decline in neighbouring countries. Yet, Hong Kong became the victim of foreign investors who started withdrawing money from its capital market and its banking system. The fixed exchange parity of the Hong Kong dollar with the US dollar could be blamed, but the behaviour of investors was bizarre considering that Hong Kong had foreign currency reserves of $85 billion of its own and another $125 billion of China's.

Equally difficult to explain is the case of South Korea. Its balance of payments crisis was precipitated when international banks refused to roll over its short-term debt, and this led the government to approach the IMF for a bailout. The bulk of the debt consisted of borrowings of private sector companies from international commercial banks. While the external debt was not really excessive, its short-term component was high. The South Korean government could not wash its hands of the problem because much of the debt was owed by corporate groups who employed too many people and were too important to the economy. Allowing the chaebols or the big commercial banks to default would have created a bigger problem.

The Asian crisis caught everyone by surprise because the economies of East Asian countries were in sound health. Hence, the risk premia on loans to Asia were low. Credit-risk agency ratings remained favourable and International Monetary Fund (IMF) reviews of the region continued to paint a rosy picture. The common features between the countries were high capital inflows, pegged exchange rates, low interest rates and expansionary overseas credit. The large capital inflows had predictable consequences: currencies appreciated, current account deficits widened, credit expanded in the banking system and bank financing shifted towards real estate. The capital inflows were used mainly for investment, rather than consumption.

The financial crisis, as many have pointed out, was not on

account of weak fundamentals. The Asian economies had strong fiscal policies, market orientation, strong export sector, low tax rates and rapid economic growth. The panic was caused by the herd instinct of capitalists: the sudden withdrawal of foreign credits was caused by each creditor wanting to flee because other creditors were also fleeing. Since financial markets in these capital-importing Asian countries were poorly regulated, the lack of prudential regulations added to the panic. The pegged exchange rates contributed to the crisis.

What are the lessons for India? One, we must have commitment to flexible exchange rates; two, retain capital adequacy standards, though implement them gradually in order to avoid a sharp credit squeeze; three, prudential controls and limits on short-term capital inflows from abroad, especially into the domestic banking sector and other leveraged financial institutions; four, avoid excessive reliance on short-term foreign capital. This means we should reduce reliance on the deposits of non-resident Indians (NRIs), who nearly caused the balance of payments crisis in 1991. Finally, we must urgently reform our creaking banking system. India's financial sector is far weaker in some respects than those of the Asian countries that suffered in the 1997 crisis.

The debacle raised non-performing assets (NPAs) or bad loans of the banking sector in Indonesia from eight per cent to sixteen per cent of total assets. But in India, NPAs were almost seventeen per cent in 1997. The committee on capital account convertibility had suggested that NPAs should come down to five per cent before India thinks of total convertibility. That may never happen, or at least not in the foreseeable future. As long as directed lending continues and government banks have to keep looking over their shoulders at their political masters, our NPAs will not fall to anywhere near five per cent. Privatization of public sector banks may happen if a bill to reduce government holding to thirty-three per cent is passed. The bill has been pending since 2000. In sum, our financial sector looks much too weak to deal with large capital inflows and outflows. So, no matter how desirable convertibility may theoretically be, the preconditions for its success do not exist.

Our anti-globalizers had a field day when the Asian crisis happened. They had found yet another reason to promote the bad old ways. Not long ago some of them had been pointing to South Korea as the proper way of 'governing the market' and the way India should globalize. There were others who extolled the Japanese interventionist model over the Anglo-Saxon model. These alternatives have proved to be fragile. By having a close and non-transparent nexus between banks, industrial companies and the government, they enhance fragility and corrupt lending/borrowing practices and expose the system to meltdown. The Anglo-Saxon reliance on the stock market, with all its short-term traits, is more transparent, less corrupt and more robust.

Many have pointed out that the East Asian economies (with the exception of Hong Kong) were, in large measure, 'planned', with the government exercising significant control over investment and industrial policy. They are partially correct. However, the irony is that these very planners were the root cause of the problems in 1997. They continued to push exports of cars and electronics when world demand had slowed. They forced over-savings at the expense of domestic consumption; they protected financial markets and kept capital cost artificially low. To some extent, the Asian bureaucrats did learn from the crisis—they cut down tampering with the market and instituted liberal reforms. As a result, many countries recovered fairly quickly.

For a long time, we did not understand the dynamics of the East Asian success model. Leftists claimed that their markets were closed to multinational companies and free imports and had strong government controls. Rightists praised the capitalist and free trade approach of the exporting economies. Both the leftists and the rightists, it seems, were wrong. The East Asian economies were certainly more open, more market-based and they did not distort prices. But their spectacular success was also due to the guidance provided by policy makers in channelling credit and investment into the export-oriented sectors where they had competitive advantage. Whereas the interference of bureaucrats in the closed, import substitution economies like India had evil consequences, government intervention in the exporting nations was benign. But both had government intervention.

It is precisely this intervention that must now stop if the East Asians are to sustain growth in the next phase of their development. The reason is that the global market is becoming crowded with suppliers as more and more nations have adopted the same export strategies. There is fearful competition for markets in the West and Japan and these developed markets are not growing.

It was easier for the early exporters, and it will be more difficult for the followers. The East Asian countries must now pay equal attention to expanding their domestic markets in order to drive growth. This requires a change in mindset among the Asian policy makers. They need to learn to depend on the market, allow more domestic consumption, and reduce the excessive level of savings. They have to stop trying to create strategic competitive advantage in their favourite industries. The East Asian nations must also focus on institution building. Japanese politics demonstrates the failure of weak political institutions.

There is a growing lobby in India led by leftists and bureaucrats that wants to emulate East Asian interventionism. The lessons from East Asia suggest that this would be a mistake. But we can certainly learn many other sensible lessons from the miracle there: how to educate our people, how to build exports, and how to have equity with growth. Finally, Indians should remember that the East Asian crisis was more like a tyre puncture rather than an engine failure (in the analogy of eminent Pakistani economist Mahbub ul Haq) and the reason for that is the sustained attention to human capital.

## Europe in the 'Age of Fear'

The death of communism and the triumph of global capitalism and free trade did not usher in a golden age of prosperity in

Europe. Instead, economic insecurity spread. Some of the emerging economies in Asia, Latin America and eastern Europe, meanwhile, did far better. And the great American economy came into its own and experienced amazing growth in the last five years of the nineties.

In 1994, I spent a great deal of time on both sides of the Atlantic. In this 'dual-located' life, I was struck by the gloomy employment picture in Europe while relative optimism prevailed in the United States. There was a 'jobs crisis' in Europe and unemployment was at a record level of eighteen million rising to twenty million the next year, which meant that about a quarter of those aged between eighteen and twenty-five were without a job. And while the picture improved a bit later, high rates of joblessness continued to plague Europe for the rest of the decade. In contrast, the flexible American economy not only created thirty-eight million jobs between 1970 and 1990 (versus ten million in Europe), it also went on to its lowest levels of unemployment in the nineties.

Indians will find the explanation for this contrast between Europe and the United States fascinating but hard to swallow. The phenomenal American success in creating jobs in the eighties was largely due to President Ronald Reagan's market-oriented economic policies, whereas Europe's failure stemmed from its inability to shed rigid socialist policies, especially those related to employment. Jean-Claude Paye of the Organization of Economic Cooperation and Development (OECD) said that for twenty years Europeans 'had gone on adding to the social safety net without taking into consideration fundamental changes in the world economy'. As a result, European industry had become a high cost one and, therefore, less competitive. As it lost market share, factories had to close down and jobs were lost.

Europe's inability to transform costly social habits in order to allow its private sector to compete globally is similar to India's lack of political will when it comes to eliminating subsidies and introducing an exit policy for labour. Both Europeans and Indians are agreed on the desirability of slashing regulatory red tape and bringing about flexible American-style labour policies, but both have been unable to do so. And because they did not 'bite the bullet', their economies remained less competitive.

But there is another philosophical difference between the Europeans and the Americans and it might mean something for India. Americans have opted for hard work and the Europeans have opted for leisure. Americans are working harder than they have ever worked, often holding two jobs. Europeans—and especially the French—are responding to the problem of high unemployment by cutting the number of working hours or reducing the work week. This path, of course, runs the grave risk of making European products uncompetitive. The Chinese, too, have opted for an ethic of hard work. What will India, with its spiritual heritage, choose, I wonder.

The Europeans argue that they are more mechanized and hence their productivity is higher. They also argue that the jobs created in America are low-skilled (short-order cooks at McDonald's restaurants, for instance). But the United States Bureau of Labour Statistics shows that the majority of the new American jobs were in the new economy, or at least in areas related to it. The Europeans argue that the Reagan years widened income inequalities. But the widening had actually begun in the seventies and started to slow down after growth resumed in 1983, and dramatically reduced in the second half of the nineties. Income inequality has turned out primarily to reflect education differentials in an increasingly knowledge-based economy, and has little to do with 'the decade of greed'.

Europe's dilemma is that corporate restructuring increases joblessness in the short term, as companies reduce workers and automate their plants and offices. Europe continues to lag behind the United States in bringing efficiency to the workplace. Eventually, it will catch up and restore its competitiveness, but, in the meantime, the drive to restore industrial competitiveness will be hostile to employment. The question troubling many European minds is whether people in the West are likely to become poorer while the Third World gets richer? They ask this question more insistently when the recession is deep and unemployment is high, and young people face the grim possibility of not being able to get a job for years together.

All through the nineties, people in the West continued to blame cheap labour in China and India for taking away their jobs. Industrialist Ross Perot led this attack in the United States and Sir James Goldsmith in France. They argued that with the advent of the global economy, workers in the newly liberalizing countries of the Third World would create an unprecedented glut of cheap labour, which would put severe downward pressure on the wages of the richer Western workers. And this would inevitably lead to a downward levelling of standards of living worldwide.

Daily reminders promoted this fear. People in the West could not go shopping without being hit by products from China, Malaysia, South Korea, Mexico and any number of Third World countries. These were not merely cheap readymade garments but also sophisticated electronics, computers and upmarket accessories. It had got to the point where merchants like Marks and Spencer began to appeal to the nationalist sentiment of their customers with such advertising slogans as 'Our products are made in the UK'.

Peter Jay, the economics editor at the British Broadcasting Corporation (BBC), talked about the nineties as the 'Age of Fear'. He referred to the widespread anxiety among young people of all classes in the West that they might never find a job, and even if they did it would be a low-paid one. The young feared, he said, that with the integration of the world economy, and impediments to market forces being removed by liberal reforms, a single world market for labour was emerging. The market, in turn, must equalize prices, including salaries and wages for the same job or for persons with equal skills. Because of the huge increase in the effective supply of labour from China and India, the equalization of wages would be downward. So, while the rest of the world became richer, people in the West would become poorer.

To an extent, these European fears are legitimate. It is also true that the multinational companies will seek the lowest cost solution to making a product. Hence, more and more work will be transferred to India and China, and the same activity will be valued at lower real wages in Europe. However, the American experience after the coming of the North American Free Trade Area (NAFTA) suggests that while many low wage jobs were transferred to Mexico, these were more than compensated by higher value jobs that were created in the United States, especially in the second half of the nineties.

*The Times* in London rightly took exception to Jay's thesis. In an editorial entitled 'Level Up: the economic rise of the Third World is opportunity, not threat', it said 'the case for a worldwide levelling of living standards downwards will almost certainly turn out to be wrong'. Karl Marx made the same mistake in believing that competitive capitalism would inevitably lead to the pauperization of the proletariat. He, too, was wrong. Living standards of the 'proletariat' in the West, Japan and, more recently, East Asia have risen dramatically. *The Times* concluded that the levelling 'will be up, not down' and 'the poor countries of the world may converge with the rich faster than the rich and the poor converged in Europe'.

I agree with the *Times*, but what does this mean for India? So far, the benefits of global trade have eluded India or touched us only marginally. Despite the improvements after a decade of reforms, India is far behind in its share of exports and in the race to attract foreign investment. If India wants to take advantage of this opportunity for labour arbitrage, it must become a better place to do business. Most multinational companies still find the ground realities of doing business in China and Southeast Asia far better. India will have to take its reforms much deeper—to the level of the excise inspector—in order to be on par with its competitors. It will have to remove red tape in all transactions; it will have to implement an 'exit policy' and make its labour market more flexible. It will have to implement value-added tax (VAT), scrap octroi and local levies and remove other barriers to the free movement of goods within India. It will have to privatize its public sector and rapidly modernize infrastructure. It will have to reform and invest in primary education so that our workers can acquire the skills needed by the global economy. Only then will Indian products find a place on the High Streets of the First World and Indian workers enjoy the fruits of global trade and prosperity.

## At the Millennium

The essays in this chapter have described an India and a world that has grown more practical and less ideological at the beginning of a new century. Entering a new millennium is a daunting enterprise, especially when the past one has been so unkind to us in India. Historian Felipe Fernandez-Armesto, in his brilliant book *Millennium*, explains why: 'India has been the Cinderella civilization of our millennium: beautiful, gifted, destined for greatness, but relegated to the backstairs by those domineering sisters from Islam and Christendom'. This, however, was not true of the previous millennium. He adds that the 'history of the first millennium of our era would have [had] to give India enormous weight: the subcontinent housed a single civilization, characterized by elements of a common culture, conterminous with the geographical limits; the achievements it produced in art, science, literature and philosophy were exported, with a moulding impact, to China and Islam; and it was a civilization in expansion, creating its own colonial New World in Southeast Asia'. Yet somehow, Fernandez-Armesto says, 'with bewildering suddenness, the inspiration seemed to dry up, the vision to turn inward, and the coherence to dissolve.'

If the past millennium has been painful, the future one holds promise. Our situation in India is dramatically changed. At the beginning of the last millennium, in contrast, it was an untidy mess. Then, a large number of tired states filled the subcontinent in uneasy equilibrium. They were quarrelsome, fractious and inefficient, and they collapsed under the strain of mutual emulation and Muslim adventurers of the smash-and-grab variety. The invaders ground down the Hindu–Buddhist culture, our intellectuals were decimated and creativity was destroyed. Today, India has rediscovered its common culture. This rediscovery project has taken over a 150 years to mature, beginning with Raja Ram Mohan Roy, and it has helped to create a confident, modern consciousness that now reaches beyond our borders to embrace the twenty million members of the Indian diaspora spread across the globe. In the decentralized information economy of the twenty-first century this is a huge advantage. Today, India is a strongly unified state that is a beacon of democracy, and it has had consistent high economic growth for two decades.

Many people in India follow the Vikram samvat calendar that began in 58 BC, and according to it we are already in 2059. Only for Christians, who calculate their calendar from the birth of Christ, are we in 2002 AD. Clearly, the last millennium belonged to the West. This was not true of the previous one, nor will it necessarily be true of the next one. Christianity, the faith synonymous with the West, has been decaying in its homelands, while Islam is in a state of revival. China, and, to a lesser extent, India, are nations on the move.

The greatest achievement of the past millennium, according to the *Economist* of London, is the 'astonishing multiplication of human wealth, of the human race, and of the knowledge' that supports it. I agree. For the first time in history, it is possible for more than a tiny minority of the people to be comfortable and to live beyond the meanest level of subsistence.

Since this has been the Western millennium, naturally a great deal of hype has surrounded it and everyone has been busy making lists. Not to be left out, I too have made mine. My top team for the millennium, not surprisingly, is heavily filled with Westerners, and consists of the fifteen who have most influenced our way of looking at the world.

My team begins with three German Jews—Einstein, Marx and Freud. Einstein changed the way we think about space, time and the universe. Our view of society and the relations between human beings will never be the same after Marx. No longer do we think of man as a 'rational animal' since Freud's discovery of the unconscious. Similarly, Darwin, the English naturalist, took humans off their pedestal with his theory of evolution, which proved that we are not unique but are descended from the apes. What Einstein did for us, Newton and Galileo did for pre-modern man—they decimated the dogmatic Christian view. Martin Luther saved Christianity by founding Protestantism—he did to the Catholic priests what Buddha had done to the Brahmins 2,000 years before. Adam Smith discovered the 'invisible hand' and laid the foundations of capitalism (just as Marx would do for communism).

The artists who changed our conception of the world were easy choices. What Shakespeare was to drama, Rembrandt was to painting. What Beethoven was to music, Dante was to poetry and Michelangelo to the human form. These artists of the last millennium created our world of beauty and emotion and taught us that truth, beauty and love are one. (I must confess that I found it painful to exclude Picasso and Cezanne who created our 'modern' world of art; the same for Baudelaire and T.S. Eliot in literature). Apart from Luther, two men of action qualified for my team—a Russian and an Indian. Lenin made the Bolshevik Revolution and 'created' the political history of the twentieth century. Mohandas Karamchand Gandhi was arguably the greatest of human beings. For, amidst the disastrous killing in the past century, he exemplified the value of humanity and justice. Some will complain that my list is heavily Western. But as I have said, the West wrote the history of this millennium. The West influenced us; we did not influence it. If I had to do an Indian list of the millennium, I would have included Guru Nanak, Kabir, Tulsidas, Chisti, Khusrau (among others) for it is these persons who truly determined our Indian world-view. I would not forget the architect of the Taj Mahal either.

# 3

## *What is Wrong with Our Temper?*

*Out of timber so crooked as that from which man is made nothing entirely straight can be built.*

—Immanuel Kant (1724–1804)

*I* began by suggesting that there is a unique temper that seems to attach to each age and it reflects the mood and the spirit of the people. I also said that Indians seem to think that they live in pretty dispirited times. The question naturally is, why? What accounts for our low temper? Why is there a general feeling of malaise, and that too at the beginning of a new century? It is a puzzle all right, particularly as we have experienced a veritable revolution in the nineties.

I also alluded to how our day-to-day lives have changed. No one talks about rising prices these days, and the ugly shortages and long lines for our daily needs are part of history. Services have gradually improved and we don't need to pay a bribe to get a railway berth or cooking gas. Gone is our constant insecurity over foreign exchange and food grains. Neither are we hostage to the monopolies of Doordarshan and Indian Airlines. We have quietly accepted these changes and they have unthinkingly become a part of our lives. We have also had world-class performers to root for— Booker Prize winner Arundhati Roy, chess grandmaster Vishwanathan Anand, Nobel laureate Amartya Sen, cricketer Sachin

Tendulkar, not to mention our beauty queens.

And yet, despite all this, our national mood is down and out. Is it because we are in the midst of an economic slowdown, and this affects our mood? After the sensational years, 1993 to 1997—when economic growth averaged 6.8 per cent a year—growth has slowed down in the last five years to an average of 5.4 per cent a year. But in the middle of the global recession of 2001-02, we remained one of the fastest growing economies in the world. There is some sort of irony in the fact that even as our people's material condition continues to improve in every way, they continue to sit around complaining that things are getting worse.

The real culprit behind our malaise, I think, is the depressing state of day-to-day governance in the country. What blackens our day is the state electricity board (SEB) employees who steal thirty per cent of the nation's power. They do not steal power in Mumbai because distribution is in private hands. Yet, knowing this, we have not been able to privatize power distribution elsewhere. The first attempt has been made in Delhi in 2002. If only half this theft stopped there would be enough money to build new power plants. It costs more to ship goods from Delhi to Mumbai than from Mumbai to London because the railways have failed to carry freight economically and honestly even as truckers continue to be victims of poor roads and incessant delays and bribes at octroi and police posts. In Uttar Pradesh and Bihar, one-third of the teachers do not show up in village schools, and sixty per cent of the contraceptives supplied by the health ministry are stolen or misused. No one has calculated the loss of trust and the enormous cost to the nation that a simple bounced cheque causes and our inability to quickly repair the damage because of judicial delay. In Rajasthan, primary health centres perform at forty per cent of the efficiency of Andhra Pradesh, and, despite knowing this, they are unable to reform.

Contributing to our unhappy mood is the loss of idealism and ideological certainties. We feel betrayed that Nehru's socialism has led us into a ditch, and that his secularism has turned out to be hollow—out of tune with the people's ethos and unable to stop the rise of Hindu nationalism. It is difficult, meanwhile, to feel enthusiastic about the market because the 'invisible hand' is, in fact, invisible. The loss in today's jobs is more striking than tomorrow's rewards that will trickle down subtly. What we can see instead is the failure of our politicians to invest in education and health in order to build the capabilities of our young. Finally, the great gap between thought and action in our public life is the real reason for the lack of success of our institutions rather than bad policies or ideology.

So, maybe there is a reason for our low spirits. The essays in this chapter examine some of our disappointments. I begin with our crumbling institutions. I take a look at our bureaucracy, the railways, the SEBs and the judiciary. I follow up with a short piece on corruption. After that, I briefly flag the end of the Nehruvian age as another source of anxiety, and end the chapter with a longish essay on the rise of Hindu nationalism, which has added to our low temper.

## Our Crumbling Institutions

We are used to thinking of India in terms of dualisms: the rich versus the poor, upper versus lower castes, illiterate villagers versus sophisticated city dwellers. But the dualism that causes the greatest anxiety is the contrast between the vibrant private space of India and the impoverished and callous public space. And no single institution has contributed more to our disenchantment with the public space as our bureaucracy. No single institution has disappointed us more. When we were young, we bought the cruel myth of the 'steel frame'. We were told that Britain was not as well governed because it did not have the Indian Civil Service. Today, our bureaucracy has fallen dreadfully in public esteem and has become the single biggest obstacle to development. Indians think of their bureaucrats as self-servers, rent seekers, obstructive and corrupt. Instead of shepherding economic reforms, they are responsible for blocking them.

Experts widely believe that East Asian bureaucrats helped in engineering their economic miracle. Why did they succeed and Indian bureaucrats fail? In my thirty years in active business, I did not meet a single bureaucrat who really understood my business, yet he had the power to ruin it. Even under a socialist democracy our institutions could have done well with better public management. A South Korean businessman told me that man for man our bureaucrats are smarter. 'But, whereas your bureaucrat is a know-it-all, ours listens to us and collaborates with the citizen,' he added. Secondly, East Asian bureaucrats are specialists; as they are not shifted from job to job, they acquire expertise and commitment. Third, their bureaucracies are smaller, with shorter lines of authority, and this makes for quicker decisions. Fourth, when you bribe, your work gets done in East Asia. In India, even after paying a bribe, you are never sure!

What is the answer? Clearly, it is not to abolish the bureaucracy. Every country needs governance. But we must cut down our government and make it result oriented. It can be done as Britain has shown—it had forty per cent less people in government in 1999 than in 1979, saving £1 billion a year. Twenty out of our eighty secretaries to the government ought to come from the outside, suggests a senior IAS official. Certainly, experts should run our economic ministries and our regulatory agencies. Another variant to this proposal is to make every job beyond the level of joint secretary contractual, open to both insiders and outsiders. In the end, however, outsiders will also fail unless we reform the work processes in the government.

The real solution is to change systems and procedures and reward bureaucrats for results and not for adherence to process. To achieve result orientation, we must decentralize decision-making, give more autonomy to officers, and delegate authority to those lower down in the hierarchy. Secondly, we should relentlessly invest in training civil servants. We should empower them with managerial skills, such as 'management by objective' and 'total quality'. We should educate them in the economics and the values of a market economy. Now, how do we get this reform on the agenda of the political parties?

⁓

A similar lack of performance and managerial skill pervades the railways. I was stupefied to read in March 2002 that the railways plan to bottle water. In that case, I thought, why don't they also grow tea (and wheat and rice) for their catering department? And cotton for their conductor's uniforms, and make shoes for the drivers while they are at it? Perhaps then we can get someone to run the trains safely. The issue is not bottled water but the astounding mindset of the Railway Board that is ignorant of the basic managerial concept of core competence and thinks that the railways, with its inefficient, high cost labour, can do it cheaper.

The purpose of Indian Railways is not to serve India's citizens but to tend to the comforts of its fifteen lakh employees. This is seven times more manpower per km than in the developed countries. The railways admit that five lakh employees are surplus; that is, one out of three persons should not be there. Railway families occupy, on the average, forty out of a hundred berths in the two-tier (AC) sleeper class, and they (and their relatives and friends and friends of friends) get priority in bookings because of 'connections'. Staff accounts for fifty per cent of total railway costs with productivity that is amongst the lowest in the world.

Because of rising payroll costs, expenses on repairs and maintenance have been steadily declining, while employee negligence (called 'human error') is the main cause of accidents. When a serious accident occurs, the site managers are typically found tending to the visiting ministers and board members, while accident victims are left to fend for themselves. When the Rajdhani Express derailed on the Tundla–Kanpur section in January 1992, the chief area manager of Kanpur was transferred because he was aiding the injured passengers and not looking after the chairman of the Railway Board!

There was a time when railway journeys were filled with pleasure. Now, filth on the tracks at the premier New Delhi railway station puts off every decent person, and the first twenty kilometres of the journey are a sanitation disgrace. It is easy to blame the habits of our people, but couldn't some of the five lakh surplus employees be deployed to clean it up? When questioned, railway authorities frankly admit that the *safaiwallas* mark attendance in the morning and for the rest of the day pursue their real profession, which is to play in marriage bands.

These examples are symptoms of a bigger disease that has infected the railways management and it is destroying a great institution that will soon be 150 years old. The railwaymen blame the politicians and to some extent they are right. Among its chief destroyers have been three ministers in the past twenty years whose names are well known. But we now have a good minister, Nitish Kumar, whose budget has finally reversed a pernicious ten-year trend (wherein freight subsidized passengers), but does he have the will to do the surgery?

The real problem lies in the managerial culture and systems of the railways. It begins with a Railway Board that centralizes decisions, some of which should be taken at the operating level. Board members are mediocrities who have come up through a perverse seniority system. When they reach the board level, they have only a few months of service left. They see it as a reward, enjoy a few foreign trips, and retire happily without upsetting the status quo.

Yet, the situation is not hopeless, for the railways can be turned around. This happened between 1980 and 1982, when a good Railway Board chairman, M.S. Gujral, came in and stemmed the rot. He transformed the institution so dramatically that India enjoyed the fruits of his labours through the eighties. Fortunately, we now have an excellent blueprint for reviving this great institution in the Rakesh Mohan Committee's report. It raises many issues, and in the chapter 'To Reform or Not to Reform' I write about how to reinvent the railways and create a vibrant, outward looking commercial institution with a customer focus.

$\approx$

The same managerial failures of the bureaucracy and the railways beset our SEBs and have made India 'a nation of thieves'. The winter of 1999 had been one of the coldest in years. We were shivering at the home of some friends at Delhi University. Their bright young son was busy completing a project report for an overseas customer who was in town. Their daughter was preparing for an exam the next day. And the lights went out. We sat in darkness, trying to make small talk. But the children screamed. They had not yet learned to hide their feelings in polite conversation. The son moaned that he would lose the most important customer of his company and it might cost him his job. The daughter wailed that she would fail her exam. The power did not return, and our anger slowly gave way to a profound feeling of helplessness.

This unhappy scene is played out in millions of homes in India every day. We have put up with this indignity for decades. We are also aware that our neighbours in Southeast and East Asia do not suffer this daily humiliation. In the rest of the world, people turn to the power company when this happens, but in India we turn to our SEB, and that is part of the problem. The SEB tells us that our blackouts are caused by a shortage of power. This is a lie.

Out of hundred units of electricity that we generate in the country, we lose, on the average, ten units in transmission, thirty units are stolen, and farmers get twenty units either free or at a hugely subsidized price. Honest citizens pay for only forty units. Thus, less than half our power is properly paid for. In Delhi, people steal a staggering fifty-eight per cent of the electricity, according to the estimates of the Delhi government. Nationally, our power shortage is less than the theft of power.

Contrary to what most people think, it is not the poor who steal. They do not run air-conditioners. Surveys show that small businesses and the well off (you and I) steal most of the power. A colony of IAS officers in Lucknow has allegedly not paid for electricity in twenty years. Recently, a friend of ours reported receiving a bill for Rs 12,000 when it normally never exceeded Rs 5,000. She complained to the linesman, thinking it was a faulty meter. The linesman suggested, with a straight face, that they split the difference. He would 'fix' the meter so that her bill would be around Rs 1,000, provided she paid him Rs 3,000 regularly. This is how theft typically takes place.

It is no use blaming our character. We have to reform our institutions. The same Indians who steal power in India pay for it abroad. The answer is to create accountability and split the SEBs into three companies for distributing, transmitting and generating power and privatize them. Orissa has already made a start. The Bombay Suburban Electric Supply (BSES), a private company, distributes power there, and the assumption is that a private company will not allow its power to be stolen. There are huge problems in Orissa, however, because it is not easy to make honest people out of dishonest ones in a short period. Uttar Pradesh is trying to do the same, and that is what the strike of the U.P. engineers was all about in the late nineties. The strike failed because people had no sympathy for the dishonest employees. In 2002 Delhi finally privatized its power distribution, but it is still beset with many problems.

The assumption that a private distributing company will not allow its power to be stolen is fundamentally correct. BSES doesn't allow its power to be stolen in Mumbai, just as Bajaj Auto does not allow its scooters to be stolen from its showrooms. The distributor will also have to pay the generating company promptly, otherwise its source of power supply will be cut off. Once this virtuous circle gets going, the generating companies will have the money to invest in new power plants to meet the needs of a growing nation. Some countries have multiple distributors and the consumer decides from whom to buy power, in the same way as she decides whether she wants a BPL or a Samsung TV. Everywhere, with the coming of competition, service has improved and, in some cases, the price of power has come down. There have been problems in California to be sure, but these are a result of a faulty regulatory model, and not because of a flaw with competitive markets in power.

If we persist in reforming our SEBs with sufficient will, thieves will be the only losers. We must not surrender to the threats of the electricity employees. Hence, every state government's courage is on test. We must stand firm to electricity thieves better than we did to the hijackers at Kandahar and redeem the rule of law, decency and a future for our children without blackouts.

The inability of our judiciary to hand out speedy justice is another manifestation of managerial failure. We have long despaired over judicial delays, but we did not know how bad things were until economist Bibek Debroy collected the data. Soon after the 1991 reforms, we began to realize that a market economy could not succeed unless contracts between buyers and sellers in a free market could be speedily enforced in the courts. Debroy headed a project in the Ministry of Finance in the early nineties and discovered that our legal system had a backlog of more than twenty-five million cases. It can take up to twenty years to settle a dispute, and, at the current disposal rate, it would need 324 years to dispose of the backlog. He also found that some 1,500 out of 3,500 Central laws were obsolete and could be scrapped, as could half the 30,000 state laws.

Digging deeper, Debroy found that things were not quite as alarming as they seemed at first. He found that the average civil case is, in fact, settled in two years once you exclude tax disputes, land and tenancy quarrels and government-to-government litigation. When VAT comes into force, the tax area will see some improvement. With computerization of land records, land disputes too will get sorted out eventually.

What has shocked the nation's conscience is that the main culprit behind judicial delay is the government, which appeals automatically all adverse judgements, only to lose them again. Thus, it crowds out the private individual in the judicial system. This happens because the decision to litigate is made at the lowest level in the bureaucracy but the decision *not* to litigate is made at the highest level. If this process were simply reversed, government litigation would come down. Pressure has been building to punish bureaucrats who launch frivolous litigation, but nothing is likely to come of it because of poor accountability of bureaucrats. Another practical solution is to remove the disputes between government departments and settle them outside the court system. This was agreed, in fact, in a 1994 conference of state law ministers.

Lawyers are the other reason for judicial delay. For years they fought all attempts to amend the Civil Procedure Code, which was finally done in 2002. The amendment is not ideal, but it will speed up the legal system. It permits summons to be sent by registered post (rather than a corrupt bailiff); it introduces pre-trial hearings, which disciplines both lawyers and judges; it shortens verbal arguments in favour of written submissions; it reduces adjournments and speeds up post-trial decree.

I have always believed that individuals make history rather than the other way around. Our green revolution would not have happened without C. Subramaniam's wilfulness. England would not have possessed Bengal without Clive's stubborn wish to teach Siraj ud Daula a lesson. In the same way, two achievements on the judicial front would not have happened in the nineties: the lok adalat in Chandigarh would not have cleared 20,000 court cases in seventeen months without S.K. Sardana. And the Supreme Court would not have disposed of 76,000 cases in twelve months were it not for two chief justices—Justices M.N. Venkatachelliah and A.M. Ahmadi.

How did these individuals achieve their miracles? First, they computerized the cases. The computer found that most pending cases were related. The Chief Justice then made the judges specialize.

All environmental cases, for example, went to Justice Kuldip Singh. Computerization also ensured that all related cases were scheduled on the same day. If the Supreme Court can do it, so can the high courts. Wilful subdivisional magistrates (SDMs) can also achieve the same miracles in the lower courts. Why don't they just do it?

Sardana also discovered that the computer was his best friend. He found that most of the 100,000 cases pending in the Union Territory of Chandigarh related to landlord–tenant disputes, motor traffic violations and divorces. He brought together retired judges and social workers, gave them desks, called in the feuding parties and made the lok adalats mediate. He forbade lawyers and court processes, and pressured the parties to reach a voluntary agreement which was final and could not be appealed. In the same way, mediation has dramatically reduced the backlog of cases in Andhra Pradesh, indirect tax cases in Tamil Nadu and land cases in Gujarat. We have lok adalats in most states, and if Sardana can do it in Chandigarh, why can't they?

I have learned from long years in business that it is not intelligence but will that moves the world. The more you believe in a thing, the more it exists. Just as Don Quixote thought that the barber's basin was a knight's helmet, so the world is what it seems and wisdom consists in making it in the image of our will. You have to learn to insist loudly and clearly and courageously defend your claim. It is martyrs who make a faith and not the other way around, and if we want justice to prevail we need wilful men like Sardana, Venkatachelliah and Ahmadi. Better still, hundreds of SDMs across India should say, 'We too can do it.' Remember, the feeling of injustice born of delay is insupportable to the human spirit, and when justice does not prevail, the judge is condemned.

## Oh, Corrupt India!

Every discussion of public affairs in an Indian middle class home sooner or later goes off the rails. Someone moans, 'Oh, but we are a corrupt people!' Another says, 'The problem is our character.' That effectively stops the show. The fact is that the Indian middle class is simply wrong. Corruption has nothing to do with national character and everything to do with institutions. People are, by and large, the same everywhere. They tend to respond to incentives in the same way. They are more corrupt in some societies because their institutions send them the wrong signals. If we want to end corruption, we have to reform our institutions.

When I was young, I used to wonder why banks closed in the middle of the day. My mother explained that banks were different. Bankers had to reconcile their accounts and balance their books every day before going home. So they needed the afternoon to consolidate the morning's transactions. Now I am older, and I discover that our public sector banks haven't reconciled their accounts for months, and in some cases, for years. Even the Reserve Bank of India (RBI) is laggging in this respect. As a result, we have paid heavily for their indiscipline. The now deceased stockbroker Harshad Mehta was one of those who, in the early nineties, took advantage of this information gap. Had the public debt office of the RBI been computerized, his scam would have been immediately detected. Had the banks been up to date in their reconciliation, the scam might not have happened. Later in the decade, banks did computerize under pressure, but it was a bit like locking the stable after the horse had bolted.

Before the 1991 reforms, there were three great sources of corruption: licensing, public sector monopolies and high taxes. Contrary to what many think, corruption did decline enormously in the nineties. Since there is no need for a licence, industrialists no longer bring suitcases to politicians and officials. Since Indian Airlines has lost its monopoly, there are plenty of seats available and passengers do not have to bribe airline officials for a ticket. Tax officials admit that the number of taxpayers and tax revenues have risen dramatically as tax rates have come down to a reasonable thirty per cent. There are no statistics on black money, but it too must have waned. Certainly, the cash component in land transactions has diminished. People will pay taxes when tax rates are reasonable and not when they are extortionate. Traders and doctors still shy away from complying, but that is because they do not want to deal with our corrupt and venal tax department. There have been a few improvements in tax administration, but these are not enough to make a difference.

Despite all the improvements, corruption remains because economic reforms are only half complete. We may have got rid of the licence raj but we have not, as I have already pointed out, touched the inspector raj. Our entrepreneurs still have to bribe dozens of officials in the states. Our exporters are still at the mercy of huge amounts of red tape of the commerce ministry, and customs officials continue to take advantage of ambiguities in the rules. If we liberalize the unreformed sectors—for example, mines, pharmaceuticals, petroleum and agriculture—businessmen and farmers will not have to bribe officials. Corruption persists because our judicial system has also failed us. It is so slow that there is no effective punishment. If a few crooks were to go to jail every month, it would deter others.

We have realized that corruption hurts the poor even harder. For example, street hawkers and rickshaw pullers pay an estimated Rs 550 crore a year to the police and the local inspectors as bribes in Delhi alone. This corruption would diminish if we reformed our policies on urban land use, recognized the legitimate place of these economic activities, and regulated them in the common interest.

Despite the feeling of despair over widespread corruption, more and more Indians have begun to understand the connection between corruption and reforms. We seem to be talking less about character and more about making rules simple and transparent, about breaking public monopolies and about speeding up justice.

## The End of Nehru's India

Despite our many liberations, we seem to live in anxious times. Compounding the failures of governance and our eroding institutions is the loss of the certainties of the Nehruvian consensus which had helped to guide our parents. That consensus had been based on the values of modernism—a rule of law founded on the pillars of democracy, socialism and secularism. The idealistic nationalism of our grandparents' freedom-fighting age has receded even further, replaced by an odd sort of illiberal, exclusionary nationalism. We are being asked to make sense of this world amidst the ruins of communism, the triumph of democratic capitalism in a world that is increasingly suspicious of national borders and ideology.

We can no longer accept Nehruvian socialism because it has done too much damage, and its variants have failed everywhere. We are suspicious of Nehru's secularism because it does not value the ordinary Indian's faith in transcendence—the possibility of human liberation from our fragmented, finite and suffering existence. It is unable to resonate with the average Indian because it lacks a reverence for the old Indian idea of undivided wholeness—that our world of distinct objects must be a manifestation of a more fundamental unity. Nehru's secularism failed because it was too intellectual and empty of content. Nor was it robust enough to stop the rise of Hindu nationalism.

Democracy is the only value that remains from the old consensus, and Indians have embraced it avidly. Indians are moderately nationalistic, like most persons, but they cannot accept the BJP's exclusionary and militant brand of Hindu nationalism. They remain wedded to the decent idea that religion of any kind ought not to intrude into our public life. This also explains why the BJP has not been able to expand its popularity at the polls beyond a point. It became big enough, however, to allow it to form a coalition government with a large number of regional partners, headed by the moderate Atal Bihari Vajpayee.

It is a symbol of our mental liberation that we are now able to criticize the legacy of Jawaharlal Nehru. Young people today cannot begin to imagine Nehru's hold over earlier generations. The criticism of Nehru's economic policies, which was muted in the

1980s, became general in 1990s. That it was the Congress Party that finally began to dismantle the institutions of Nehruvian socialism means something, even though it did so by stealth. But the party was not strong or courageous enough to make a break with its unsavoury, sycophantic culture that had developed during Indira Gandhi's time. As the nineties progressed, the rhetoric of succeeding governments turned to efficiency over equality, of individual over state enterprise, of building human capability over subsidies and affirmative action, of people's participation over bureaucracy. The actions of the governments, however, did not keep up with the intentions—hence our huge disappointment with the pace of our reforms and the general feeling of unfulfilled promises that pervades the country. Having lost Nehru's age of innocence, we are now resigned to a world without ideology and continue to grope for a new set of beliefs that will help us cope with our frustratingly pluralistic society.

I happen to think, like Isaiah Berlin, that this search for a new ideology for our age is a misguided quest. The idea of a perfectible world, in which all good things exist, is not only unattainable but also dangerous. Those who allow themselves to come under the spell of dogma of any kind, religious or secular, become victims of myopia and, in the end, become less human. Spontaneity is the fundamental human quality, and it is not compatible with 'total solutions' or organized planning. The history of the twentieth century is littered with the graves of ideologies, all of which had some great benign aim and were meant to be for the greater good of mankind. This was the faith of Lenin, of Mao, even of Hitler and, who knows, maybe even Pol Pot. In India, we escaped these tragedies, but our modest experiments with Fabian socialism led to statism, and we are still trying to shake off that yoke.

It is true that some problems can be solved and should be. We should do everything we can to reduce hunger; we should fight against injustice and social oppression; we should resist state-induced suffering such as torture and wars; we should help the homeless and the sick. I think the most important obligation of a decent society is to avoid the extremes of suffering. This may sound like a boring answer to idealistic young Indians of today who seek to build a noble society based on great truths. The fact is that there are no great truths, and we should be wary of anyone who thinks that he might have found one.

With the rise of nationalism in recent years, we are being exhorted to look nostalgically at 'our glorious past'. The truth is that ancient Indians were cruel, barbarous, mean and oppressive to the weak; but they also created the wonderful Mahabharata and Ramayana. It is something that we cannot even imagine doing today in our more 'enlightened' age. But these great epic masterpieces belong to the ancients and that world is long gone; there is no point in trying to slavishly recreate it, even if we could. Our world has science, democracy, the Internet and the prosperity engendered by rapid economic growth. The best we can do with our past is first to read about it with a critical eye as the source of historical materials and myths; then, learn from it, with a legitimate expectation that it might help us to understand ourselves better.

If we read the Mahabharata and Ramayana and other ancient classics thus, we would find in them a deeply moral quest. They are concerned with the same things as we are—what is responsible for injustice, oppression and falsity in human relations. They care profoundly for the human condition and for human weaknesses— ego, anger, attachment, greed, cruelty and envy. They were searching, just as we are, for the roads to peace, justice, love, human dignity and spiritual fulfilment.

## The Rise of Hindu Nationalism

On 6 December 1992, a screaming mob tore down an unused mosque. The Babri Masjid in Ayodhya, Hindu fanatics claimed, had been built on the birthplace of the god Rama. Ordinary, peace-loving Indians of all persuasions were aghast. It was such an un-Indian thing to do. Our ethos is pluralistic—we worship all the gods—and this exclusionary extremism was alien to our character. In the following months, it was strange to read of the rise of Hindu fundamentalism because Hinduism is a religion without fundamentals. It does not have one sacred book, one organized church or one prophet. This is why we had rejected the two-nation theory earlier in the century, along with the idea that religion should determine nationhood. Instead, we had firmly separated religion and the state in our Constitution in 1950, and had begun to pursue secularism as a cherished principle after Independence. But something had clearly gone wrong. Did our secularism fail us?

There was also an odd nationalistic component in what happened at Ayodhya, and its timing was strange because it had happened when the world was turning global. The assertion of nationalism might have made sense if we had been fighting for our freedom from a colonial power, or if we had been building a nation from scratch, as in the fifties, or if we had been threatened by disintegration. If anything, the problem of Sikh separatism in Punjab had been resolved; and though the Kashmir issue was smouldering, it had been around for fifty years. Thus, the demolition of the mosque looked suspiciously like political posturing—a grab for power.

In the late nineties, when the nation voted a Bharatiya Janata Party (BJP)-led nationalist government to power, albeit in a coalition, it thought that the party would bring about some change. Many voters who did not belong to the party or were not persuaded by its ideology believed that it was a party with a difference. They were willing to overlook the party's inclination towards militant communalism, as long as it might change the way India was governed. But after trying out this government, many people felt disillusioned. It was not so much that the moderate Atal Behari Vajpayee had been a bad Prime Minister; but he seemed to be merely perpetuating a Congress-type rule. He inherited a corrupt and inefficient system of governance, and he seemed to have done too little to change it.

In 2001, General Pervez Musharraf, the chief executive of Pakistan, made an entertaining but largely ineffectual visit to India. He did achieve one thing, though. He made us look within ourselves and ask, once again, who we are as Indians, and how we are different from our neighbour. For the past fifty years, we have grown up with the belief that Pakistan is a monolithic, theocratic state with one religion, one language and one mind. India is the opposite, with many religions, many languages, many communities and many minds.

With the ascent of the BJP, a second conception of India has become popular with, perhaps, a quarter of our voters. Instead of the plural India of the first conception, it views the nation as singular and essentialist, which will be energized by Hindu nationalism. In its view, India has been victim of a thousand years of foreign invasions, and it is now threatened by multinational corporations and, particularly, American culture. It wishes to restore it subliminally to a pure, pre-invasions and eternal Hindu past and advance rapidly toward superpower status in the future.

The first concept of India, by contrast, is more relaxed, liberal and self-confident. It celebrates the opening up of India to foreign trade, investment and, most important, to ideas. It thinks of India as a mixture of different peoples and cultures that settled here. In this view, India never had an authentic past; it was always a moveable feast and the moments of mixture were, in fact, the most creative. Historic migrations and the wanderings of many peoples and tribes over thousands of years created this India. The subcontinent, in this view, is a deep net into which various races and peoples of Asia drifted over time and were caught. Hence, diversity is India's most vital metaphor—it is a 'multinational' nation. It is what plural Europe would like to be—a united economic and political entity in which different nationalities and minorities continue to flourish.

In recent years, a new generation of historians has enriched this plural conception of India. Their innovative studies have illuminated our regional identities, showing how our national identity is superimposed from above and created usually by the grab for power, with little to do with how ordinary people see themselves. Moreover, our recent politics is further reinforcing our regional identities. This liberal view, however, does not deny a shared sense of India. It merely warns us to be careful in positing a unifying conception of India based on nationalism. That our minds have finally got decolonized gives this liberal view of India a quiet reassurance and self-confidence.

Sam Huntington proposed the thesis in his *Clash of Civilisations* that an 'indestructible fault line' exists along Islamic borders and clashes with neighbours are inevitable. Hence, the professor wrote, there will be trouble with the Serbs in Bosnia, the Jews in Israel, Hindus in India, Buddhists in Myanmar, Chinese in Malaysia and Catholics in the Philippines. Those who hold the second, singular concept of India fully accept Huntington's premise; they believe that permanent peace between India and Pakistan is impossible. Vajpayee is obviously not one of them. Otherwise, he would not have invited General Musharraf to India and taken a number of initiatives to improve relations between the two neighbours.

Vajpayee understands better than his colleagues in the Sangh Parivar that India and Pakistan's future will be determined far more by the relentless push of the global economy and communications, supported avidly by our rapidly growing middle classes. The future preoccupations of both peoples will be with rising living standards, social mobility and the peaceful pursuit of consumer goods. As a result, obsessions with religious identity and fundamentalist attitudes will slowly fade. The issue is not whether Vajpayee holds the singular or the plural conception of India, but which of the two is likely to prevail. Or will India evolve uneasily from the constant clash of these two competing conceptions?

Having put a nationalist government in power, it is important to remind ourselves that nationalism is generally not a pleasant virtue and the world has grown rightly suspicious of it after all the damage it has inflicted in recent times. Nationalism drove the European nations to colonize the world. It made Germany and Japan militaristic and this caused two world wars. It led to the murder of six million Jews in the Holocaust. These were terrible tragedies of nationalism. However, nationalism can have its uses when a nation is young. It can help a country modernize and develop with a sense of urgency, as Japan did after the Meiji Restoration in 1867–68. It can help a people to unite to throw out foreign rule as India did. Nationalism can also help a nation become cohesive, which is a useful thing for a diverse and plural country like ours. We have suffered heavily in the past because we were disunited and did not act as a team. India was lost, first to Babur and then to the British because of parochial quarrels and intrigues among our divisive rulers. Independence too might have come a dozen years earlier had Gandhi, Nehru and Jinnah been able to work together as a team.

Bernard Lewis, the columnist, once observed, 'When people realize that things are going wrong, there are two questions they can ask. One is, "What did we do wrong?" and the other is "Who did this to us?" The latter leads to conspiracy theory and paranoia. The first question leads to another line of thinking: "How do we put it right?" ' In the second half of the nineteenth century, Japan asked itself: 'How do we put it right?'

Contrary to what many believe, Japan was not always unified. Before the Meiji Restoration, the feudal Shogunate was divisive. There was dissension and dissent, often violent. The lords of the great fiefs of the far south and the west, once enemies, finally united against the Shogunate. After the emperor replaced the Shogun, the Japanese decided to become one, under the slogan. 'Honour the emperor!' The second thing they decided to do was to catch up with the West. So, they hired technicians from there and sent Japanese agents abroad to learn Western technology. They did not complain.

Japan began to modernize by sending a high-level delegation to Europe and the United States, visiting factories and schools to learn how they had modernized. The delegation returned to Japan after two years 'on fire with enthusiasm' to reform. One of the reforms that it implemented with characteristic intensity was to give universal schooling to boys and girls. The schooling imparted knowledge, but it also instilled the virtues of punctuality, discipline and a sense of national unity that helped create the modern Japanese personality.

Our nationalists, both within and outside the government, should reflect deeply on Japan's experience with modernity. They will realize that the first thing they must do is to redefine their nationalism and make it inclusionary; they must shed their antipathy towards the minorities. The idea is that as citizens we should not be Hindu but be Indian. Only then will India realize the power of national unity. Meiji Japan did the job so well that Japanese teamwork has become the envy of the world. Next, our nationalists must also be 'on fire with enthusiasm' to reform the economy. Third, they should, with equal intensity, overhaul our education system and not only ensure education to all boys and girls but improve its quality.

Finally, they should remember that all nationalisms run the risk of becoming militaristic, as Japan's did. They should create powerful safeguards against that eventuality, including giving up the nuclear bomb in a negotiated settlement with Pakistan and China. Only thus will India realize the positive benefits of nationalism. If it were my world, I would not have nationalists in it, but since it isn't, the second best thing is to make the best use of what we have.

Like any great tragedy, the communal violence in Gujarat in early 2002 was full of other sadnesses. One of these is that we have begun to lose faith in our ideals. We had already lost faith in socialism, but now we have begun to question the efficacy of secularism as well. Part of the reason is that it was unable to prevent or stop this murderous carnage in Gujarat.

A major failure of contemporary Indian public life is that we do not have voices of moderate Hindus or Muslims. We only hear the shrill voices of extremists at both ends. It was not always so. Earlier, we had sensible public figures who were also steeped in religion. Mahatma Gandhi, Maulana Azad, Vivekananda used to speak with credibility on behalf of the vast majority of religiously minded Indians. Today, there is an unfortunate polarization between an influential and articulate minority of secularists and the vast majority of silent, religiously minded Indians. Neither takes the trouble to understand the other, and what we have as a result is a dialogue of the deaf.

The problem with many secularists is that they are or were once socialists. Not only do they not believe in God, but they actually hate God. They only see the dark side of religion—intolerance, murderous wars and nationalism. They forget that religion has given meaning to humanity since civilization's dawn. Because secularists speak a language alien to the vast majority of Indians, they are only able to condemn communal violence but not stop it, as Gandhi could in East Bengal in 1947. Gandhi trudged through the Bengali countryside like a one-man peacekeeping force and kept Bengal quiet during the Partition. Unfortunately, there was only one Gandhi—had there been a second one, Punjab might have also escaped much of the Partition tragedy.

Our secularists have been influenced by a number of nineteenth century European thinkers, starting with Nietzsche, who declared famously that God is dead. Ludwig Feuerbach argued that God was a projection of the human imagination and thus an illusion. Marx said this illusion originated in the alienation of the capitalist worker to whom religion was like opium, a drug that soothed his pain. Once capitalism was destroyed the drug would not be needed. Marx understood religion's power and he saw it as socialism's main competitor. 'Criticism of religion,' he said, 'is the prelude to all criticism,' as he attempted man's most ambitious attempt to supplant religion with a doctrine about how life ought to be lived.

But Emile Durkheim, a Frenchman, regarded religion as a projection of society; its shared rituals and sentiments bound people together, and thus it wouldn't easily go away. Sigmund Freud, the founder of psychoanalysis, wrote in the 'The Future of an Illusion' that religion, despite its many negative qualities, helped make civilization possible. Without it life in society would be impossible unless everyone could be educated to behave morally. The media has rightly focused on Narendra Modi's failures of governance in Gujarat. His hands are covered in blood and he should be sacked. But once he is gone, what happens next? Whom will we blame for the next communal riot? Communalism is surely more than a governance issue. We need to ask once again, why did a million people die in the 1947 riots? Why couldn't we prevent that tragedy? Fifty-five years have gone by and we still do not have an answer to that question. And, as a nation, until we do, we shall not be able to sleep in peace. That answer too will not come from analysis, I expect, but from literature.

But while we wait for our *War and Peace* to emerge, we have begun to realize that communal harmony in India will not come from converting India into an image of a secular, non-religious West by weaning people away from religion, as the secularists had hoped. It will come when moderate religious leaders come forth in public life and begin to lead ordinary, decent people in the direction of a secular polity, and snuff out the evil voices of fundamentalism. Until these moderate voices emerge triumphant, we have to live with the sad truth that we have all manner of extremists amidst us who feel a passionate ethno-nationalist claim to a vision of a homeland, and a willingness to condone violence, plus a story line that many Indians will buy, in part because it plays into existing prejudices. With that they have probably got a winning hand, whether or not the interests they advance are noble.

# PART TWO

## Private Space

*The saint and the poet seek privacy to ends the most public and universal.*

—Emerson, *The Conduct of Life* (1860)

# 4

## Laptops and Meditation

*To the poet, to the philosopher, to the saint, all things are friendly and sacred, all events profitable, all days holy, all men divine.*

—Emerson, *Essays* (1841)

The antiquity of Indian tradition is, I think, less impressive than its extraordinary continuity, and this is because it has been able to adapt to alien virtues. It has shown an enormous capacity to absorb other traditions and synthesize them and make them into its own face. It survived the Mughals, it survived the British, and it might even be able to survive Coca-Cola, although the latter's challenge is, I am sure, far stronger.

What is the Indian way? An American scholar, John Koller, writes that its central idea is the possibility of human liberation from our fragmented, finite and suffering existence. It is based on the insight that the basic energizing power of the cosmos and of human beings is the same. Because we have an impressive capacity for thinking, imagining and acting to shape our world, the writers of the *Upanishads* believed that there must be a link between the dynamic energy of human beings and of the universe. Our world of distinct and separate objects must be the manifestation of a more fundamental unity. Initially developed in the Vedas and *Upanishads*, this idea of undivided wholeness went on to inspire various Indian ways of the Buddha, the Jains, the Yoga systems, and even the Sufi and Bhakti saints.

Indians have always known that their gods and goddesses are symbols of reality rather than reality itself. As symbols they point beyond themselves to the ultimate. That is why a Hindu can say in the same breath that there are millions of gods, but only one God. Within a family, the father may be attached to Ganapati, an uncle may worship Vishnu, the mother Krishna and the son could be an atheist. In this syncretic attitude originates the spirit of tolerance of the Indian way.

Although Indians are fond of rational argument, they all seem to agree that reason is limited when it comes to comprehending the deepest reality. Reason differentiates and compares and is, thus, a good faculty for exploring the empirical world. It fails when it comes to comprehending undivided and undifferentiated reality. Hence, Indians of various persuasions look to meditation and direct insight.

We regard our day-to-day life as superficial and in bondage to the law of karma, which determines mundane happiness, suffering and repeated births and deaths. We can free ourselves from karma in various ways—by knowledge according to the Jain philosophy, by selfless action according to the Gita, and by devotion according to the bhakti saints and Sufis. Whatever way one chooses, the Indian way is a way to freedom from human bondage based on the wonderful potential for perfection among ordinary human beings. It is also our strongest defence against 'McWorld'.

During the nineties, Indians seem to grow more religious, despite rising prosperity. The growing middle classes seemed avidly preoccupied with a rising standard of living, social mobility and the pursuit of material goods, pushed relentlessly by the global economy and communications. At the same time, they continued to vigorously pursue their age-old spiritual paths towards living the meaningful life. I happened to meet a large number of young entrepreneurs during the nineties, and I discovered, to my surprise, that almost all had a serious religious side to them. It is a mistake to think that people must necessarily grow less religious with prosperity. There was a huge revival of religious movements in nineteenth century England and America experienced the same in the twentieth century.

The essays in this chapter are based on several encounters that I had with 'the holy' in the nineties. The first recounts a quiet weekend at the Radhasoami ashram by the Beas river in the Punjab, where I was impressed with the way they have been able to synthesize tradition and modernity. The second was in the Madras Museum and it contrasts the anxiety in the life of a rational, liberal, museum-going Indian versus the lack of it in a traditional, barefoot Tamil lady's world.

As the Frontier Mail pulled away from the Old Delhi railway station on its nightly run to Amritsar, a young man pulled out his laptop computer. While the others got ready for bed, he prepared for work. After an hour's toil, he seemed to relax, and looked out of the window. He saw me staring at him and asked in a friendly voice, 'I am not disturbing you, am I?' We discovered that we were both going to the same place: Dera Baba Jaimal Singh, the Radhasoami ashram on the banks of the Beas. Whereas I was visiting my parents for the weekend, he was going for the guru's darshan and *satsang*. He was a software engineer and while there, he would also do *seva*, helping the ashram to computerize its records and systems. He explained, 'We have a modern guru and he runs the place like a high-performance manager.'

'I have heard of your guru,' perked up a third passenger in our compartment. 'What does he teach?' he asked.

'To seek the truth,' replied the young man.

'And how do you find the truth?' the man asked.

'Through meditation,' said the young man.

'How do you know when you have found it?'

'Oh, you know when you have found it,' the young man

smiled and returned to his computer.

The Frontier Mail arrived at dawn. In the half-light, I saw my father standing on the platform. He threw up an arm in an awkward gesture of pleasure as he saw me. I stepped out of the train and we embraced with bashful shyness. An old man scrambled to lift my baggage. I hesitated, but my father gestured that it was all right. I stared at the familiar yellow sign on the platform, which proudly proclaimed the existence of our village in three languages. As the old man got ready to load my bag into a waiting van, I suggested we take a tonga instead. I took out a note, but the old man refused, saying that this was his *seva*.

We rode for three miles along the Beas and soon came across a line of buffaloes moving down towards the river, flicking flies with their tails from their gleaming skins. 'Radhasoami!' shouted the milkman. 'God be with you!' replied the tonga driver. I smiled at these old courtesies of the road. It was a fine morning and people were already busy in the rich wheat fields. The sounds of tractors, tube wells and the green revolution filled the air. We passed a tiny hamlet where TV aerials atop brick and cement houses had replaced the old jumble of mud homes of my childhood. Soon we were at the bougainvillaea-covered gate of the ashram, where we got down for a 'security check'. My father explained that this was a legacy of the terrorist days when the ravines along the river had been a hideout of the Babbar Khalsa, the dreaded terrorist gang.

The tonga started and soon the ashram came in full view. We rode past an imposing structure in the Indo-Muslim style with domes and minarets built by the *seva* of thousands in the thirties. We went through immaculate by-lanes, past the water tank, the dispensary, the library, and the red brick houses of the devotees. We stopped beside one of them, distinguished by the ivy on its front wall, and this is where my parents lived. Inside the house it was cool and tranquill. I touched my mother's feet and she offered me tea. After a shower I went to hear the guru's discourse. He was a handsome, bearded man in his forties, and he sat cross-legged on a high platform from where he could be seen by more than

500,000 devotees, whose eyes were adoringly fixed on him and who listened to him in astonished attention.

In a low clear voice he explained the purpose of life: 'It is quite simply to "know yourself" as Socrates had wanted us to do,' he said.

'Who am I? Am I my body? Am I my mind? No, clearly, I am neither my body nor my mind, for I can distinguish myself from them and observe them. Nor is there anything permanent in my perceptions, thoughts, emotions, drives and memories. When everything is stripped away from me there remains consciousness itself. Saints call it the soul. The soul is an expression of the unity of life. All religions have discovered the same divine unity, and they call it God by different names.

'Our purpose in life,' he continued, 'is to connect our soul with God through the practice of meditation. Fortunately, God is within each of us, and a living teacher can teach us to make this connection by helping us conduct a series of experiments with our consciousness. I don't ask you to believe me. I ask you to merely experiment and find out for yourself. This is not a faith; it is a science—a science of the soul, focused on the contents of consciousness, which can yield predictable, replicable results through the discipline of meditation.'

I was impressed with this logic, and moved by the possibilities of meditation. Sceptical by nature and shy of religion, I was surprised to find myself attracted to the scientific temper of the guru and this path of practice, not of words or rituals. 'The chief obstacle in making the connection between the soul and God is our own mind,' he added. He quoted Guru Nanak, who says, 'He who conquers the mind, conquers the world.' He said that renouncing the world or running away into forests doesn't help. 'Detachment is only achieved by attaching the mind to something else. That something else is *shabad* or *naam*. Muslim saints call it *kalma*; the Rig Veda calls it *vak*; the Bible refers to it as the Word. The practise of meditation helps to link us with *naam*. By withdrawing our consciousness behind the eyes, we learn to listen to the *shabad* and link our souls with God. This is what Christ meant when he said, "Seek and ye shall find; knock and it shall be opened unto you." '

The guru spoke thus for forty-five minutes, quoting liberally from the Bible, the Koran, the Guru Granth Sahib, the sufi and bhakti saints—Kabir, Surdas, Bulleh Shah—suggesting that religion is an uncertain, searching path and not an exclusive institution. There was a quiet confidence in his voice, without a trace of world-weariness or denial. With his emphasis on experience and realization, this guru pointed to a way that must be walked. It contrasted with the information overload in my life, which was assaulted by well-packaged and noisily advertised ideologies. I found his unbounded openness and tentativeness attractive. There were no readymade solutions, only hints and suggestions. I must seek out the answer for myself.

Later that afternoon, I met the guru privately in his garden. He looked fresh in a loose-fitting kurta and churidar and, unlike in the morning, he now spoke in English. He had a no-nonsense public school manner ('What the hell, *yaar*'), which was not surprising, as he had gone to the Lawrence School, Sanawar. But I was troubled by what he said in reply to my question, 'How should one live in this world?'

'Like a passenger on a train,' he said without hesitation. 'You mustn't get too attached to the world. A passenger makes the acquaintance of many travellers. Some get off at the next stop, others at later stops. He is civil to them, but doesn't form deep friendships, because he knows that he is unlikely to see them again. This is how you must live. Don't imagine for a moment that your children, your parents have the same stop. We are all passengers. This train is not your true home.' I was disturbed by this analogy. It would be a bleak world if all our relationships were as casual as those of passengers.

'Surely this world,' I said, 'with all its failures and sorrows, is better for the emotion that we invest in it, especially in human relationships. I like the train journey.'

'Yes, but once you reach your destination then you are on your own. So, why don't you try my way? Once you taste the real thing, you will become the train.'

I was puzzled. 'What does it mean, "to become the train"?' I asked.

'Once you have experienced reality,' he said, 'then you are no longer a faded, purposeless passenger who is afraid of death. You are in charge of your rich, full-bloodied life.' He spoke a great deal about the bhakti saints that afternoon.

⟍⟋

The bhakti movement swept across India after the fifteenth century and touched the lives of ordinary people as nothing had since Gautama Buddha. The central idea of bhakti is the passionate belief that one can be united with God through unconditional love and devotion. Love has long been a metaphor for religious experience in India. An ancient passage in the *Brihadaranyaka Upanishad* compares the attainment of freedom and enlightenment to the experience of a man in his wife's embrace. A person, it says, 'in the embrace of the intelligent Soul [knows] nothing within or without . . . [His] desire is satisfied, in which the soul is his desire, in which he is without desire and without sorrow'. Tamil saints first popularized this idea of bhakti, and later it spread across India, thanks to a galaxy of medieval bhakti saints—Kabir, Mirabai, Guru Nanak, Tulsidas, Lalla, Chaitanya, Sant Tukaram, Guru Ravidas and many others.

The chief mood of bhakti poetry is erotic (*sringara*), and it is usually seen from a woman's point of view, whether in its phase of separation or of union. When Mira addresses love poems to Krishna, she adopts the feminine personae of a wife, illicit lover, and a woman with a tryst, even Radha herself. Krishna is her god, but he is also her lover. The most common sentiment is the pain of separation from the lover and the constant theme is self-surrender of the beloved.

In classical times, Indians sensibly pursued multiple ends in life. These were virtue or righteousness (*dharma*), wealth and power (*artha*), pleasure and sex (*kama*), and release or enlightenment (*moksha*). During the prime of life, a worldly householder (*grihasta*) pursued wealth, power and pleasure. Only later in life did he turn to *moksha*. Thus, in ancient times, there was a nice balance in the aims of life and Indian civilization was not as 'other-worldly' as it became later in medieval times when a fifth objective (*pancham purushartha*) swept the minds and hearts of men and women. This was love and it supplanted the other goals, becoming the highest, higher even than *moksha*.

By reaching out to the masses in their everyday languages, the bhakti saints created a veritable social revolution. By offering entry to the lower castes, they forced reform on Hinduism and prevented mass conversion to Islam. Since boundless love of God was the only requirement, all were rendered equal. By promoting a direct relationship between the soul and God, the bhakti saints eliminated the priests (as Martin Luther did in the Reformation and Buddha had done 2,000 years earlier). They offered confidence to the poor masses and helped bind together the diverse elements of the subcontinent into a single functioning society. A new form of musical composition also took shape in their songs, and they continue to be performed today in concerts and on the radio and television.

Although a saint like Mira subverted the traditional ideals of Indian womanhood and challenged the social order, her mystical love for Krishna did not lead to her being burnt, the way Joan of Arc was for her visions. The conservative Rajputs thought she was mad, or a liar or a sorceress, but they did not burn her at the stake.

Some historians contend that bhakti flowered because Muslim rule prevented most Hindu men from pursuing worldly power. They argue that society had become rigid, the caste system more entrenched, and all this checked the ambitions and the mobility of men. Turning inwards was a natural response, allowing people to accept their unhappy material condition. They conclude that bhakti permanently damaged the Indian psyche by making us ambivalent about the value of human action in this world, and this places us at a competitive disadvantage today. Personally, I would be extremely shy to leap to such generalizations based on history and explanations based on culture. I do believe, however, that whether one is a believer or an agnostic, these desperate medieval lovers made a great contribution to world civilization, and traditions like bhakti provide us today with one additional safeguard against the onslaught of the mindless global culture.

~

When I returned home that afternoon, my father handed me a remarkable book, *The Gospel of Jesus*, by John Davidson, a scientist at Cambridge University's Department of Applied Mathematics and Theoretical Physics who had written a number of books on science and mysticism. Davidson wrote that 'modern scientists, delving into the heart of matter, have determined that not only are the forces, molecules, atoms and subatomic particles comprising matter constantly in a state of highly energetic agitation, but that their motion contributes to their existence. If the motion stopped, then the universe would simply disappear . . . Yet, no scientist can say where the primal energy comes from which keeps the universe in existence.' Davidson, the mystic, suggests that this primal energy is the 'word' of the Bible, which is the creative power of God.

Davidson seemed to throw new light on the well-known passage in John's gospel which has mystified people for centuries: 'In the beginning was the Word/and the Word was with God, and the Word was God.' What is this 'Word' that the Bible speaks of? The term comes from the Greek, *Logos*, he explains, and it is clearly not the spoken or written word of our daily life. In the metaphorical language of the Middle East it has been variously called 'the breath of life', 'the tree of life', 'the *nous*', 'the holy spirit'. Plato was familiar with it 400 years before Jesus. In *Phaedrus*, Socrates asked, 'Now tell me, is there another sort of word (*Logos*), that is brother to the written word (*Logos*), but genuine?'

Davidson had exhaustively researched *The Gospel of Jesus* from the Old and New Testament writings, the Dead Sea Scrolls, the Greek mystics, the Manicheans, the Gnostics and other mystics of Jesus's era. In his search for the origins of Christianity, Davidson had uncovered a mystical interpretation of Jesus's teachings, which will resonate with the millions of Indians who are familiar with the teachings of the bhakti and sufi saints. His interpretation is in the tradition of what Aldous Huxley calls the 'perennial philosophy', with its focus on transcendental experience—something that a person lives and experiences, and not merely a doctrine which he reads or studies.

The culmination of the spiritual experience is union with God, and there is a respectable line of Christian mystics—St Teresa, Marina de Escobar, Meister Eckart—which supports this interpretation. The attractive thing about mystics is that they are never lukewarm or detached about anything. They speak from the centre of their being, inebriated with passion, as they suffer the agony and ecstasy of life.

Jesus the mystic is a curious image, but this interpretation may well be closer to life as it was lived in first century Palestine than the hygienic, packaged variety taught in churches today. This image of Jesus is fascinating in another sense, because it closely links up with the universal spirituality common to all the major world religions. It is precisely for this reason that this book seemed to appeal to my mystical father, who was predisposed to believing that 'the roads that lead to a true understanding of God may not be dissimilar after all'.

Davidson's remarkable encounter with the world of Christ, I felt, is a testimony to the change that our world has experienced. For one thing, Christianity has become globalized. Second, scholars have increasingly subjected the origins of Christianity and the gospels to unprecedented scrutiny and analysis. Third, with the spread of democracy and freedom of speech, the world is much more open to new interpretations of Christian teachings. Not so

long ago, unorthodox interpreters like Davidson would have been
burned at the stake.

～

That evening I ran into my 'computer friend' and we went for a
walk along the river. The sun was descending and the air had
turned cool. On the way we saw an endless procession of devotees
with baskets of mud on their heads. '*Mitti di seva*', he called it.
'They are helping to reclaim the land beside the river, which has
changed course in recent years. On the alluvial soil they grow
vegetables in vast quantities. On some weekends this place provides
free food for up to 500,000 people—mostly villagers from the
surrounding districts—and the logistics surrounding this operation
are managed with a great efficiency,' he said. I now realized why
they needed computers in this spiritual abode.

We walked around the river in silence. Along the banks grew
giant reeds and bulrushes, their stems bleached by the sun. We
breathed pure draughts of the river air and gazed at the evening sky
filled with silence and majesty. I looked down the river into the
horizon and I thought of our ancestors who had occupied these
lands and recorded their primordial experience in man's first book,
the Rig Veda. From these river banks, Vedic civilization had flowed
into the valleys of the Ganges, the Narmada, and spread over the
rest of India, evolving into beliefs that touched every inhabitant of
this subcontinent. The guru's words today were inspired by the
same kernel of truth that had been discovered on these banks 3,000
years ago. 'Truth is one,' the Rig Veda had said, 'the wise call it by
different names.'

Occasionally, we might feel the pull of the old culture, I
thought, but we were unable to resist the seductive charms of the
other, more virile one of the West, which had become the dominant
culture of the world. One could not but marvel at the amazing
phenomenon of the surging Western adventure in science and
liberty, which had spread the mellow glow of the European

enlightenment over the world. Yet, it was wise men such as this guru who were able to synthesize tradition and modernity, and make meaningful to our lives a perennial philosophy with its promise of plenitude.

My computer companion spoke of Einstein, who, too, had searched for the fullness of life. In consoling a stranger on the death of his son, Einstein had said, 'A human being is part of the whole, called by us "universe", a part limited in time and space. He experiences himself, his thoughts and feelings, and he regards them as something separate from the rest—a kind of optical delusion of his consciousness. This delusion is a prison for us, restricting us to our personal desire and to affection for a few persons nearest to us. Our task must be to free ourselves from this prison by widening our circle of compassion to embrace all living creatures and the whole of nature in its beauty.'

At the end of our walk, we came to a fork and he suggested we take the low road so that we might have the guru's darshan. 'They say that the guru's darshan is a powerful thing,' he said.

The next evening we found ourselves on the familiar Frontier Mail, this time going back home. My companion looked pensive, and I was inclined to leave him alone. I thought again about living life as a passenger and when it would be time for me to get off. Or would I one day taste the real thing and become the train?

## Dance of the Debonair God

The Infinite is never far in India. A few years ago, I visited the Madras Museum in Egmore. While I was admiring a Chola bronze, a middle-aged south Indian woman came behind me, and without self-consciousness, placed a vermilion mark on the Shiva Nataraja. At first, I was appalled, but then I realized that we lived in two different worlds. Mine was secular; hers was sacred. Both of us stood before the bronze statue with very different expectations. For me, it was a 900-year-old object of beauty; for her, it was God. Mine was an aesthetic pleasure; hers was a divine darshan.

She did not see what I saw, a brilliant work in bronze by an early Chola artist. I admired the weightless joy of the dancer, so skilfully captured by the sculptor. I moved along, passing by other bronzes, and I got irritated that the bronzes were dusty, ill-lit, poorly spaced and badly presented. Suddenly, I felt embarrassed by my petty concerns and my niggling mind. I turned around to look for the lady. She was still there, absorbed by her light-footed, tireless dancing god, whose dance actually brings the universe into being, and without missing a beat, and in the fullness of time, dances it out of existence. I was struck by the contrast of our lives—the fecund richness of her sacred world versus the poverty of my weary, sceptical and secular existence.

I felt drawn to her and to her god. She sees the drum in Shiva's right hand and the drumbeat announces to her that the universe is about to be created. The flame in his left hand tells her that this is how the world was created. The gesture of the lower right hand bestows upon her freedom from fear. And the raised left arm, pointing towards the raised left foot, is a symbol of her release.

For someone who is carrying out such a momentous mission in this universe, I find that her god looks cool, athletic and even debonair. I move on to Shiva's extended family. Nandi, the infant bull that Shiva sometimes likes to ride, has a round, portly persuasiveness. Ganesh, his elephant-headed and flipper-footed son, is loveable and has dignity despite his misshapen figure. The sculptures of the Chola dynasty have breathed life into them and filled them with celestial finesse. They were made primarily between the tenth and the twelfth centuries in the once-great city of Tanjore (now Thanjavur) under the patronage of Rajaraja and Rajendra Chola, the father and son of the great southern dynasty.

This is where our empty secularism has gone awry. Modern, liberal, English-educated Indians are fast losing the holy dimension in their lives. They will never know the depth and opulence of the south Indian lady's life. They are quick to brand her superstitious, illiterate and casteist. She is, in fact, far more tolerant and accepting of diversity because she is capable of seeing God everywhere. I remember a Sikh taxi driver in Bombay who had displayed the pictures of Guru Nanak, Krishna and Jesus on the dashboard of his Fiat. He said, 'I am still looking for Mohammad.' I asked him, 'You have taken out a lot of insurance, haven't you?' He replied, 'No, sir. This is to remind me that there is only one God.' It is from the wonderful worlds of the Tamil lady and the Sikh taxi driver that the BJP and our Hindu nationalists ought to learn the true significance of Hindutva, and the Congress Party and our secularists ought to learn the real meaning of secularism.

A young friend of mine learned to play the sarod from a great teacher, who insisted that he come to him before dawn. For the first few months, the guru insisted that he play a single note; then he was allowed to play a second note; then a third. It was months before he was allowed to play the full scale. Imagine the discipline when you have to play a single note for hours together. 'In those hours of hearing that one note you will begin to hear the sound of the Infinite,' explained the guru, who was teaching the student not only to play but to meditate, to still the mind and listen to the birth of the universe.

Immanuel Kant wrote some remarkable notes in his old age. 'God,' wrote the great German philosopher in one of these, 'is not an external substance, but rather a moral condition within us.' In trying to understand the world of the believer, he rightly pointed to the human desire and potential for transcendence. When Nietzsche said, 'God is dead,' he meant that the modern, secular human being had lost this possibility of faith and this had plunged him into despair over his absurd situation. The courage to face the meaninglessness of life continues to be a challenge for the non-believing secularist. Sartre tries to console him, saying, 'Man creates his own reality, his own meaning.' But that is easier said than done.

In my world of museums, concert halls and bookstores, there is plenty of search for beauty, but there is no place for the holy. We are lost in a de-sacralized world of petty, middle class concerns. Our secularism has robbed us of Kant's 'moral condition'. Partly, it is the fault of traditional religion, which has overlaid and trivialized the original inspiration. The fundamentalists of the Vishwa Hindu Parishad (VHP) and Islam have alienated us further. The answer for an authentic life, I think, lies with the woman in Chennai in whose attitude lies the possibility of a fullness and wholeness of being. Thanks to millions like her, India can never become a sanitized American suburb. Not at least for a very long time.

I return to the main Shiva Nataraja statue at the entrance. He still looks unperturbed and absorbed in the serious task of creating and destroying the universe. But there is something new I notice. Under his raised left leg, there is a marigold flower! So, the next time the world gets too much for you, do what I do—go visit a museum and experience eternity.

## The Will to Live

During the summer of 2000, I read in the papers that a celebrated English couple had killed themselves in Bristol. It was a death that they had planned for forty years. It was a tragic and haunting love story: the wife had terminal cancer, and instead of being divided by disease, the couple chose to be united in death, taking a lethal overdose of drugs and breathing their last in each other's arms. The news item caught my eye because the husband, Stephen Korner, was the author of a book on Kant which I had read as an undergraduate in college. The book had made me reflect on my own beliefs about right and wrong and had taken away some of the pain of reading the almost unreadable Kant in the original. Ironically, though, Kant had argued that it was wrong to take one's own life.

I discovered from Anjana Ahuja's moving account in the London *Times* that this was not an ordinary couple. They were both handsome and brilliant, and had fled to Britain from Czechoslovakia during the Second World War. They met in London, married during the war, and then rose to distinguished positions in British public and academic life. She went on to become a pioneer in the National Health Service and an eminent magistrate, and he became a famous professor of philosophy. When their daughter was twelve, they told her about their suicide pact. It was an unusual conversation to have with a child, but the Korners had always treated their children as adults.

Their daughter, Ann, grew up to become a molecular biologist and married the Noble laureate Sidney Altman at Yale University. When the suicide finally happened, Ann was devastated. I met her first through the Internet, when someone sent her my essay, and she wrote to admonish me for romanticizing her parents' suicide, an event that in the end ravaged her and her family. She exclaimed that no one should ever emulate her parents. Her parents had left a note for the police, and as they had wished, Schubert's *Trout Quintet*, their favourite music, was played at the funeral.

Suicide is an old subject and people have debated it over centuries. In recent years, however, it has acquired significance because modern medicine has made it possible to live far beyond one's useful life. This has raised the question of social cost. Experts calculate that sixty per cent of Western society's health care costs occur in the last nine months of a person's life. Is it fair, people ask, to prolong someone's life at the expense of the rest? Activists of the 'right to die' movement strongly advocate that a person has the right to end his life rather than face the indignity of surviving on life support systems at a hospital. This issue has also got connected in the United States with the debate on abortion, where 'pro-choice' liberals support the individual's right to choose to have an abortion while 'pro-life' conservatives counter that the foetus is a living being and they would jail the mother for terminating a pregnancy.

As a liberal, I certainly think that a person ought to have the choice to end his life. It is his or her life after all. The stigma that attaches to suicide in most societies is unfortunate, but, perhaps, it would go away if the legal framework were changed. Even our Supreme Court had, in 1994, had called for a more sympathetic view of persons who attempt suicide. The view of the Supreme Court had triggered off a national debate, and this suggested that the old mindset was changing.

In the abortion debate also, I am strongly pro-choice. I think it is disgraceful that the extreme right in the United States has forced this on to the Republican agenda. Partly because of this I would never vote Republican if I were American. Neither do I have a desire to live an artificially long life—and certainly not in the humiliating surroundings of a hospital. I have always desired a short and intense life. Like most people, I would prefer to die a natural death, but if it meant prolonging life unnecessarily I would not hesitate to pull the plug.

Yet, I am a conservative when it comes to re-engineering human beings. I like people as they are—with all their foibles and their flaws. Like the distinguished American diplomat George Kennan, I do not wish human beings to be perfected or tampered with. Who knows what we might unleash if we started on that genetic route? I would prefer human beings to remain, in Kennan's words, 'cracked vessels', or 'crooked timber', in Kant's famous description.

Many of my friends and relatives do not agree with my views on suicide and mercy killing. My mother admonishes me, saying that no one has the right to take his life—it is God's gift. Another friend reminds me that one's life is not one's own alone, it also belongs to one's family and to society. By committing suicide, one not only places one's parents' old age in jeopardy, but also infringes on the rights of children and grandchildren to share one's lifetime of experience, thereby ensuring that culture is passed on.

A reader of my columns wrote a most moving letter from Gujarat, and it reminded me of King Lear. After leading an honest life and discharging his obligations, my middle class correspondent retired to live with his children. But soon he found that he was unwanted by his offspring, for whom, he said, he had sacrificed everything when they were growing up. He now felt constantly humiliated, and he wondered if it might not be better to opt for mercy killing.

There is but one truly serious problem in life, wrote novelist Albert Camus, and that is suicide. Judging whether or not life is worth living amounts to answering the fundamental problem of our existence. People have always debated whether it is natural or perverse to escape from life's difficulties. As for me, I have come to believe, like French essayist Montaigne, that to die well requires greater moral stamina than to live well. Heroism consists in facing death with equanimity, and this reflects the highest qualities of a well-resolved life.

I wanted to comfort my letter-writer and tell him that human life is the mystery of undeserved suffering. The innocent always suffer. This is not only the central problem of the human condition, but it also gave birth to tragedy. I commended to him Nietzsche's famous definition of tragedy: 'a reaffirmation of the will to live in the face of death and the joy of life's inexhaustibility when so reaffirmed'. Nietzsche had Greek tragedy in mind, especially that of Aeschylus, the first writer of tragedy, who revealed to the world the strange power that tragedy has to present suffering and death in such a way as to exalt and not to depress. The ancient Greeks had a wonderful ability to see the world clearly and think it beautiful at the same time. They thought freely and deeply about human life, without the burden of religion and priests, and were willing to confront the giant agony of the world.

In India, the Buddha also saw that the world is made up of individuals, each with a terrible power to suffer, and that there is this awful sum of pain in the world. His solution to sorrow was to turn inwards and deny our everyday world of experience. The Greeks were aware that injustice was built into the nature of the world, but they dealt with it in the spirit of enquiry and poetry. And when enquiry met poetry, tragedy was born.

We tend to misuse 'tragic' in everyday discourse. We confuse the word with disaster. Tragic pleasure, as the Greeks knew it and as Aristotle defined it, is the emotion of pity and awe, which purges and purifies us in the end. The result is the feeling of exaltation that Nietzsche spoke about. Aeschylus's Prometheus is an innocent sufferer who stole fire from the gods in order to benefit human beings. He passionately rebels and defies the gods and the powers of the universe. To the messenger of the gods who bids him to yield, he replies that he cannot, just as the wave in the sea cannot fail to break on the sand. With these last words and as the universe comes crashing upon him, he proclaims, 'Behold me, I am wronged!' Thus, the tragic poet shows us that mankind can meet disaster grandly, forever undefeated.

The same is the case with Sophocles's Antigone, the high-souled princess who goes to her death with open eyes rather than leave her brother's body unburied. Instead of giving in to her uncle's unjust law, she cries out, 'Courage! The power will be mine and the means to act.' In another play, Euripides's *Trojan Women*, Troy has lost the war to Greece and a handful of women are waiting for the victors to carry them away to slavery. The Greek messenger comes to tell the Trojan queen, Andromache, that her son is to be thrown from the wall of Troy. She says to the child: 'Go die, my best beloved . . .' When we see Prometheus, Antigone and Andromache on stage, we feel pity and awe. As we identify with their defiance and affirmation of life, we feel purified and freed and better able to face life and death.

## *Life's Secret*—Nishkama Karma

Most Indians have not heard of Donald Hall, the American poet, but I was fortunate to meet him when he visited India in the early nineties and we had an absorbing evening's conversation. He wrote about his Indian visit in an unusual book called *Life Work*, in which he also described an encounter with Henry Moore, the British sculptor. 'Now that you are eighty,' he asked Moore, 'you must know the secret of life? What is it?'

Anyone else would have answered with an ironic laugh, but Moore spoke in a straightforward manner, and without impatience. 'The secret of life,' he said, 'is to have a task, something you devote your entire life to, something you bring everything to, every minute of the day for your whole life. And the most important thing is—it must be something you cannot possibly do!' Moore's work was the high road of art, and doing what he could not possibly do made him, perhaps, the greatest sculptor who ever lived.

I have only met one such person who seemed to know this secret of life—a Sikh carpenter who came to build us a teak cabinet in Mumbai in the early seventies. He used to get so absorbed in his work that he would forget to eat lunch, sometimes even dinner, and my wife would have to go upstairs and remind him at ten o'clock at night to go home. 'Sardarji,' she would say, 'your wife and children are waiting for you.' Not only did he make beautiful furniture, he also forgot to collect his bills. For him, only the cabinet mattered.

Most people, I have discovered, do not like their work. They get easily distracted and find it difficult to get absorbed. They brood, and mostly about themselves. If they work in a company, they worry about how they are doing, their place in the pecking order, where their name appears on the distribution list of a memo, the size of their office, and the next promotion. I have worked in five countries and find this to be true in all cultures. What a waste, I sometimes think.

If most people like to avoid work, there are always a few in every organization who actually like it. They tend to transform their work into a game that requires skill and challenge. Because they are absorbed, they also tend to lose track of the time. We have all experienced this feeling. When a book or an activity engages us, we forget the time. What seemed like an hour turns out to be three. Thus, absorbedness is the quality that matters and you can tell because time gets distorted. At that moment, the difference between subject and object also disappears for we forget our egos. We emerge from what we have been doing feeling strong and self-confident, and our moods do not depend on whether others respect or praise us.

Moore's and my carpenter's secret lies in the ancient Indian concept of *nishkama karma*. If dharma defines the ideal life, karma tells us how to reach it, and the best way to get to it is through detached or desireless action, which is the literal translation of *nishkama karma*. The Gita teaches us that *nishkama karma* means to act for the sake of the act and not for its reward. I, too, have discovered that in a curious sort of way (in the way that Moore might have thought of it), this may well be the secret of happiness. I am not sure if the author of the Gita had this in mind, but the reality of our lives is that we devote more than a third of our existence to our work, and it is tragic if we do not get some sort of joy out of it. Freud was probably right when he told a young man that happiness consisted in loving the work that you do and the woman you live with. This concept teaches us how to get absorbed by our work and to enjoy what we do, but how does one apply it to the sterile market place?

Unions have done much good in the twentieth century, but they have also done great harm. They have turned the worker away from pride in his work, and away from customers and the purpose of the organization. It is especially tragic in our public sector where unions have completely destroyed the work ethic. They, in particular, but most of us as well, need to listen to what Swami Vivekananda had to say about the day's work: 'Do you not see how everybody works? Ninety-nine per cent work like slaves, and the result is misery; it is all selfish work. Work like a master, not like a slave.' This, I am beginning to believe, is also the secret of living.

I felt enthused by this thought and I wrote about it, albeit in a tentative fashion, in an essay called 'Local Memoirs of a Global Manager' in the *Harvard Business Review* of March 1993. At the time, I was based at Procter and Gamble's headquarters in the United States, and I got a telephone call at 11 o'clock one April night. The lady on the phone said that she had just read my piece, and had been especially drawn to the part where I had talked about *nishkama karma*.

She quoted from the article: 'It seems to come down to commitment. The meaning in our lives comes from . . . absorbing ourselves so deeply in the microcosm of our work that we forget ourselves, especially our egos. The difference between subject and object disappears. The Sanskrit phrase *nishkama karma* describes this state of utter absorption, in which people act without ego for the sake of the action, not for the sake of reward from the action. This is also the meaning of happiness.'

'Wow! Mr Das,' she said. 'I have experienced that feeling!'

She went on to say that she was a businesswoman and she ran a human relations consultancy. She had worked with hundreds of managers in the northeastern part of the United States, and had found that most of them were unhappy; as a result, they were not very effective.

'The problem is that most people dislike their work,' I said. 'They get easily distracted, and they can't get fully absorbed in their work . . . Only when you get deeply absorbed in an activity do you do it well or enjoy it.'

She said that she could understand about artists and scientists getting absorbed, but what about ordinary people in ordinary jobs, like a clerk, for example? I responded that there were extraordinary challenges even in the most ordinary jobs, even in that of a clerk and certainly in that of a manager. She agreed with me, but something else had been bothering her. 'We Americans are an individualistic people. We affirm our egos and fight for our self-interest. Don't you think a certain amount of ego is healthy and necessary to get going? Isn't it a necessary condition for getting absorbed in a project?'

'At this point, your mood doesn't depend on the respect and praise you receive from others. Your sense of worth comes from within and is independent of the opinion of others. This is what you mean by a healthy ego, I suppose,' I said.

'Yes. But then how do you resolve the contradiction between having a healthy ego and the need to submerge the "unhealthy" ego?' she asked.

I was not sure about the two egos and felt that they might be two aspects of the same ego. She raised another point: 'We Americans conceive of work as a curse to be avoided at all costs. Hence, our national productivity has not been growing. We have the idea that work must always be less enjoyable than leisure.'

'It is the same in India,' I said. 'I think most cultures regard work as something to be avoided. But there are always individuals in every culture and in every organization who are able to transform their work into a sort of game which requires skill, challenge, clear objectives and immediate feedback. Since they are absorbed, they have no time to worry about themselves, their promotion, or feel envy towards the person sitting next door. They literally transform their work, and their work becomes enjoyable. They feel as if they had freely chosen their work.'

'Meanwhile, the majority feel apathetic and bored with their work, seeing it as mere routine,' she added. 'It seems to me that we are talking about two types of people. The first kind are the few that enjoy work—they seem to have an autonomous personality to begin with. They seem to be able to control their inner selves and gain mastery over their lives. But such people are rare, aren't they? I am interested in the ordinary person in a company who is bored and cannot take charge. How do I get him to commit to his work?'

That was a tough problem, I thought. And it was a problem of an affluent society. In poor countries, I felt that the masses were so occupied with the day-to-day struggle for survival that they did not have the luxury to think about such things. Yet, even in India, she reminded me, there was a growing middle class that was faced with the same issue. She was, of course, right. And it was a more poignant problem, for, unlike in the United States, capitalism did not have the same legitimacy in India. Whereas a worker in the government might feel that he was working for the greater good and did not need to justify his existence, a clerk, for example, in a private company may actually do more good because at least he worked hard. However, a clerk in the public sector didn't even do his job, forget about doing it with commitment.

She wondered if the answer to commitment might lie in the notion of customer focus that I had written about in my article. 'Do you mean that if I, as an employee, identified with the customer, and understood how my product or service affected the lives of ordinary people, then . . .'

'Yes, I think. Knowing all the time how my product or service affects the life of my customer would give me a reason to do my job well, and I would come out feeling more effective and even happy.'

'I would certainly value my work more if I understood its purpose,' she said. 'That's certainly a possibility.'

Both of us were pleased by our little discovery. We felt that we might have stumbled onto a new management philosophy based on *nishkama karma*, which was focused on the customer. This philosophy might give me, a manager, a goal which flowed naturally from the purpose of my business, and achieve a concentration which was so intense that there was no attention left over to think about the petty problems of my ego. At the end of the day, I would come out feeling confident, empowered and happy.

# 5

## A Sentimental Education

*Man is but a reed, the most feeble thing in nature; but he is a thinking reed. The entire universe need not arm itself to crush him. A vapour, a drop of water could kill him. But man knows that he will die, and he knows the advantage that the universe has over him; the universe, however, knows nothing of his.*

—Blaise Pascal (1623–62)

$\mathcal{B}$laise Pascal, the French mathematician and philosopher, pays the greatest compliment to humanity when he characterizes man as a feeble, thinking reed. The prescription for a distinguished human life, Pascal felt, was to know the advantage that the universe holds over us, and to turn it around to our advantage. A liberal education is one way to do it—to defy the universe in this Pascalian manner—because it places the human being at the centre of the quest for knowledge. This seems to have been forgotten with the triumph of the technology and management culture. It is important, I think, to go back and remind ourselves about the place of the liberal arts in building future leaders and citizens. Leaders of tomorrow will need vision; hence, they will need to be familiar with the humanistic ideas of the great books. I find too many young people—even CEOs of our best companies—have a tunnel vision. An even more serious weakness is the inability of young people to write and communicate their ideas clearly. Hence, I was moved to write these essays on the importance of growing up with a broad, open-minded and tolerant mind.

With the loss of Gandhi's and Nehru's ideologies which had guided us for so long, Indians today feel forlorn and seek an alternative vision. In the absence of another comprehensive ideology in this post-modern, post-reform age, I wish to return to the old-fashioned liberal creed as a guide to day-to-day living. I am not sure that one can ever really return to anything. Those liberal values of the Enlightenment may have come from the West, but they are really universal values. Remember, they also served our nineteenth century renaissance and reform thinkers well. It is humbling to remember that our quest for ideology is not so very different from that of Ram Mohan Roy, Bankim Chandra, Gopal Krishna Gokhale and others. And since communism's collapse, ours is part of a worldwide quest for a guiding ideology. Meanwhile, we could do worse than to have the classical liberal and humane values inform our lives.

I chose the title of this chapter from Flaubert's novel, *L'Education Sentimentale*, because I think that the business of going through life is, in many ways, similar to that of acquiring an education. Prof. Edward Tayler of Columbia University used to lecture his first year students about 'building a self', and I follow up on his idea with some thoughts on how to read and write. The next essay, 'Who Will Roll the Chapatis?' is about gender and the changing role of women in contemporary India. It is followed by two short pieces. 'Dance a Little, Laugh a Lot' begins with my favourite novelist, Marcel Proust, but its purpose is to draw the reader's attention to the insecure person who cares excessively about his neighbours and engages in the disgraceful persecution of the minorities, an unfortunate feature of India in the late nineties. The last, 'Small, Sweet Courtesies' is based on an incident in Devlali in 1998 which led me to contrast our rich private space and our impoverished public space.

## Building a Self

Our hot Indian summer comes with unfailing regularity and for middle-class teenagers this is a time to recuperate from the slogging drudgery of tuitions, coaching crammers, computer classes, Board exams and college entrance tests. The summer job has not yet arrived here, so what does one do for 'time-pass', as we say? My secret recipe for an enviably happy summer is to draw the curtains, turn on the cooler, sit in a comfortable old cane chair and begin to read. Feel your youth like a nimbus, and start to create a self. You don't inherit a self; you build it. One way to do it is with the great books. Take a break at noon with lassi or chaas. Read some more after lunch and, in the evenings, treat your friends to dahi chaat and gossip and talk about the books you are reading. For you never accept a text passively; you interrogate it. Smell the jasmine at night and go to sleep reading. There is no royal road to nirvana but only the many roads, large and small, with innumerable curving paths and a thousand steps and turns leading to education.

Why read? We live in confused times, and the search for answers to the questions of identity and ideology, which began with Ram Mohan Roy almost two hundred years ago, is as real for Indians today. Reading, especially of the classics, I think can help clear the confusion a little bit, teach one to think for oneself, and build conviction. After reading, comes writing, and after writing, criticism. Hence, I divide this essay in three parts, related to the three pillars of a liberal education—reading, writing and criticism.

Begin the summer reading project with the Mahabharata, and feel the brute vitality of the air, the magnificence of chariots, wind, and fires; the raging battles, the plains charged with terrified warriors, the beasts unstrung and falling. Like the brilliant first scene in the Oscar-winning *Gladiator*, see the men flung face down in the dust, the ravaged longing for home and family and the rituals of peace, as the two sets of cousins, bitter enemies descended from King Bharata, fall into rapt admiration of each other's nobility and beauty. It is an apocalyptic war poem, with an excruciating vividness, an obsessive observation of horror that almost causes disbelief. Since you are unlikely to read it in the original Sanskrit, look for R.K. Narayan's readable translation, and, if that is not available, try C.V. Narasimhan's version.

Feast also on the great books of the West. Begin with Homer's *Iliad* and *Odyssey* in the Lattimore translation. Follow it up with the great tragedians—read Aeschylus's *Oresteia*, Sophocles's *Oedipus* and *Antigone* in the Grene translation and Euripides's *Electra* in the Vermeule translation. Then a bit of history—read Thucydides's *History of the Peloponnesian War*. Finally, philosophy—read Plato's *Symposium, Apology* and *The Republic* in the Hackett translation, and end with Aristotle's *Nicomachean Ethics* in the elegant Ross translation.

The magic of an American undergraduate education is that it breathes life into the humanistic classics. Whether your field is chemistry or engineering, you are required to read the great books and learn that life and literature are inseparable. With a good teacher like Tayler you learn to read as though your life depended on it, and you are carried along on the crest of excitement and high adventure of ideas that will resonate throughout your life.

Indian students are not so lucky, alas. Not only does our traditional insecurity about jobs push our youth early into careers, our silo-like curriculum does not permit cross-fertilization of disciplines. Now, isn't this what our mandarins in the education ministry ought to be thinking about? They ought to be thinking about how to breathe life into the syllabus so that education is not merely memorizing a bunch of facts.

To experience the romance of a liberal education, I recommend David Denby's *Great Books: My Adventure with Homer, Rousseau, Woolf and Other Indestructible Writers of the Western World*. In 1991, thirty years after graduating from Columbia University, Denby went back to college and sat with eighteen-year-olds and read the same books that they read. Not just the ancient classics that I have mentioned but also modern ones. Together they read Goethe, Kant, Milton, Cervantes, Marx, Conrad, Woolf and others. Denby was certainly a most unlikely student: forty-eight years old, film critic of *New York* magazine, a husband and father, a settled man who was nevertheless unsettled in some way. Was it just knowledge he wanted? He had read many of the books before. Yet nothing in life seemed more important to him than reading these books and sitting in on those discussions.

Denby's book is an account of his journey, sometimes perilous, sometimes serene, through the momentous ideas he consumed with such hunger in middle age. He took the two required 'great books' courses, devised earlier in the century at Columbia, which spread to the University of Chicago and, in the forties, to other colleges in America. If it were up to me, I would require all Indian undergraduates to feast for at least half a year on the great books of the East and the other half year on those of the West.

Our current system is producing too many people with narrow minds. The single-minded pursuit of jobs means that they do not possess the intellectual equipment to deal with the world. Since values are in flux, reading the classics is one way to rebuild our normative universe, allowing us to rise above the confines of our immediate environment and what is accidentally provided us by our family and friends.

If summers are the time to read, the monsoons are the time to write. Like rich monsoon vegetation, college students seem to sprout around my house and they are not shy to ask for advice about courses and careers. To all of them I commend a tiny eighty-five-page paperback called *The Elements of Style* by William Strunk and E.B. White. I tell my young friends that no matter what their field of study or vocation, they will come out ahead if they learn to write well. As far as I know there is no better book on writing English. Astonishingly for a composition rulebook, it made the *New York Times* bestseller list in 1962 and stayed there for years.

White is the great American essayist, whose literary style is as pure as any in the English language 'Singular, colloquial, clear, unforced, thoroughly American and utterly beautiful,' is how William Shawn of *The New Yorker* described White's writing. Strunk was White's unheroic, bespectacled professor of English at Cornell, 'who taught several generations of Americans to write better than they might have done'.

This little book cuts through the vast tangle of English rhetoric and presents the best case that I know for clean, accurate and vigorous expression. Each of its rules is in the form of a direct command. 'Use the active voice,' orders one of the rules. 'Omit needless words' decrees Rule Thirteen. Obediently, I have been trying to omit needless words since 1967. In sixty-three sharp words the little book describes the nobility of brevity: 'Vigorous writing is concise. A sentence should contain no unnecessary words, a paragraph no unnecessary sentences, for the same reason that a drawing should have no unnecessary lines and a machine no unnecessary parts. This requires not that the writer make all his sentences short, or that he avoid all detail and treat his subjects only in outline, but that every word tell.' The book follows up with some advice on how to cut deadwood. 'The question as to whether' is pruned to 'Whether', and 'This is a subject which' is trimmed to 'This subject', a gain of three words out of a possible five. 'The fact that' is a real villain and 'should be revised out of every sentence in which it occurs.' In spite of the fact that' should be excised in favour of 'although'—a gain of four words.

Soon after he became prime minister, Winston Churchill wrote to the First Lord of the Admiralty, 'Pray Sir, tell me on one side of one sheet of paper, how the Royal Navy is preparing for the war.' Churchill knew that if he did not qualify his request he would receive an unreadable 400-page report. Brevity is a great virtue, and nowhere more needed than in India. Our judges write judgements that are too long; our lawyers ramble on; our executives try to impress with lengthy memos; our politicians—well, try to get in a word. Our public affairs would improve immensely if our powers to be silent were equal to our power to speak.

That less can be more is especially true in good writing. I discovered this at Procter and Gamble, a company as famous for its legendary one-page memo as for its products. Its wondrous one-page memo was created out of the same confidence in reason and technology that built America, and is as elegant as Panini's grammar or Euclid's geometry. Based on the reasonable assumption that all managers suffer from an overload of paperwork and files, it is simple, factual and logical. The reader can scan it in minutes and grasp its contents. It has just enough data that a manager needs to make a decision and no more. It is clear, precise, eschews hyperbole, and it actually improves the speed and quality of decisions, and hence it can be a source of competitive advantage.

The one-page memo consists of five short paragraphs, and its first sentence tells the reader what to expect—why should you be interested in what I have to say? The smart writer puts his best foot forward and states upfront the conclusion or recommendation. There is an inherent conflict between the reader and the writer's interest—the writer wants to build a case slowly, leading to a conclusion, but the busy reader wants the conclusion quickly, and is only interested in the rationale later. Since this is not a detective story, a good first paragraph ought to focus on the 'what' and not the 'how'; it must also, of course, offer one or two compelling reasons to believe in the conclusion.

The second paragraph offers background—it is historical, factual, filled with data, and tells the reader why the problem or opportunity has risen. The third para is the detailed recommendation—the 'what' and the 'how', but don't confuse the reader here with the 'why'. The rationale should come in the next paragraph—'here are three reasons why you should accept my recommendation'—and typically one cites precedents, benefits (financial and otherwise) and risks. The fifth paragraph tells the reader that the author has looked at alternative courses of action, and why this is the best. Finally, the last paragraph addresses the next steps and lays out a plan of action that will flow from this decision.

The Maharashtra Administrative Reforms Commission was so impressed with this one-page memo that it recommended it to the government in 2002 in order to make its bureaucrats more efficient. We Indians are verbose, and need to be reminded that human beings were born with two ears and two eyes, but with only one tongue, so that we should see and hear twice as much as we say. Shakespeare too, I think, must have had us in mind when he wrote in *Richard III*: 'Talkers are no good doers.' Hence, he offers us this advice in *Henry V*: 'Men of a few words are the best of men.'

I like the *Elements of Style* not only for its sharp advice but also for its self-confidence and certainty. White tells us that his teacher 'loved the clear, the brief, and the bold'. He scorned 'the vague, the tame, the colourless, the irresolute'. Hence Rule Twelve says, 'Make definite assertions.' To be irresolute is clearly worse than to be wrong. One must believe in right and wrong, as this little book does. Unless one entertains notions of excellence, one's language deteriorates. Unless someone in the republic sets standards of good taste, good conduct and simple justice, governance declines.

One of the pervasive ills of our society is that teachers do not teach and students do not learn. Worse, teachers who do not teach are not punished. Nor are children who do not study. 'Grace marks' is a disgraceful feature of our academic life. Too often the best candidate is not hired. Caste, family connections and political pull, rather than the ability to deliver, determine who rises. For some openings, as many as sixty per cent of the jobs are reserved. The consequences of this are all-too familiar: deterioration of standards, shoddy education, debasement of taste, cheap politics and vulgar art. We are surrounded by amiable mediocrity in India.

This is partly a result of the levelling influences of democracy—a concern with numbers rather than quality. In a democracy, it is hard to persuade people that it is better to have one outstanding graduate than ten mediocre ones, or to say that the government would be more efficient with one-fifth of the people who are paid five times as much. In a democracy, the ordinary person resents superiority in others and will punish eminence at every opportunity. We must make our people accept that inequality is healthy if it leads to excellence. Fortunately, ever since liberalization began, there has been a silent revolution of excellence going on in Indian industry. Because of competition, industrialists have realized that their company is only as good as the superior men and women in it.

High performance takes place in an atmosphere of expectation. If parents, employers, citizens expect it, it will occur. Athenian orators in the fifth century BC were the best in the world because their listeners demanded it. In the eighties, Japanese products became the world's best because Japanese consumers demanded it. We must expect high performance at all levels. An excellent carpenter is infinitely more admirable than a mediocre scientist.

In these unheroic times in India, I find solace in E.B. White, who pursued excellence relentlessly. He was a sceptic and preferred to view life from a deliberately mundane and irreverent perspective. Like Montaigne and Thoreau, he examined life's everyday details with loving attention. He started his writing career at *The New Yorker*, where his 'Notes and Comments' formed the opening section of each issue. Soon he became America's 'best known anonymous journalist'. His casual, pithy approach to a paragraph defined brevity and wit for a generation of aspiring stylists. White's advice in *The Elements of Style* is to write in a way that comes easily and naturally, but not to assume that because you have acted naturally your product is without flaw. And as it is almost impossible to avoid imitating what one admires, 'Never imitate consciously, but do not worry about being an imitator,' he advises.

Many of us write by ear, often with difficulty and seldom with an exact notion of grammar. This should not put us off this book. Nor does White's plain style mean that his writing is bland. White's essays are filled with images of circularity and eternity, which combine effortlessly with those of the passage of time and decay. Describing a young circus rider, White reflects that 'the enchantment grew not out of anything that happened or was

performed but out of something that seemed to go round and
around with the girl, attending her, a steady gleam in the shape of
a circle—a ring of ambition, of happiness, of youth.' But, White
sadly observes, soon the young girl would grow up, 'wear makeup',
the illusion of timelessness created by her graceful ride around the
ring would be shattered.

◿

I cannot remember any of my teachers making me feel that a book
could acquaint me with the mystery of life. But some literary critics
certainly did. One of them in particular, the great American critic
Edmund Wilson, always pushed me to the edge of the human
experience. His extraordinary essay, *Toward the Finland Station*,
described the evolution of socialist literature and ideas from
Michelet's discovery of Vico to Lenin's arrival in St Petersburg. On
each page, Wilson describes how great social moments or tiny
individual fortunes are palpably connected to the irrepressible
world of ideas and literary fiction. It is a great bequest to the art
of thinking and inventing with the help of a pen.

The second man of letters who influenced me was Lionel
Trilling, a professor at Columbia University in New York. His
book, *The Liberal Imagination*, first appeared in 1950 and had a
wide impact on the intellectual life of the post-war years in the
United States and Europe. Trilling was not a liberal in the
economic sense, but he certainly was one in the political sense. He
staunchly defended the great quality of tolerance and the importance
of law as an instrument of justice—virtues we desperately need in
these unsentimental times in India. He also had a Victorian faith
in ideas as the engine of progress, and a conviction that great
literary works are the substance of civilization.

For the generation of Trilling, literary criticism had a great deal
to do with the central questions of human life. It saw in literature
the legacy of the ideas, myths, beliefs and dreams that make society
function, and of the private frustrations that explain individual

conduct. Trilling believed that liberalism had power over life. In one of his essays in *The Liberal Imagination*, he appeared worried that teaching literature might lessen the work of art. He recalled his teaching days at Columbia University when he asked his students 'to look in the abyss' (in the works of Eliot, Yeats, Joyce or Proust). They did so very obediently, took down their notes, and then commented: 'Very interesting, isn't it?'

Trilling despaired that the academic process hardened literature, made it rigid and banal and turned the tragedy of human beings, who are bigger than life, into mere abstract knowledge. It thus stripped them of their ability to 'change' the reader's life. When literature is primarily an object of study it tends to lose its soul and its power. That is the gloomy truth of the matter. Trilling's essay on the teaching of literature is disturbing. Although I am not a student of literature, I can certainly identify with his dilemma. How do you acquaint students with the great works except by teaching them? There is something devious in taking these works of the imagination—the distillation of profound individual experience—and reducing them to a teacher's notes. Teaching methods are inevitably schematic and impersonal. Reducing literature to scholastic exercises and homework degrades it, and then having to grade or mark it adds insult and injury. These works are often the affirmation of real human sacrifices. They are private and it seems a desecration to analyse them in class. They must be read alone, experienced, in the discreet concentration of a reading lamp; and they must be measured by the effect they have on the inner life of the reader.

Edmund Wilson was not a professor in a university and he did not have to face Trilling's dilemma of a teacher. But as a professional critic he exercised a teacher's influence that was far wider than a university classroom. He wrote articles and reviews for magazines and newspapers, and some of his best books—such as the one on the manuscripts found near the Dead Sea—were written for *The New Yorker*. Writing for a wider public did not mean that he had to 'water down' his ideas or be less rigorous or daring. Rather, it forced him to be always responsible and intelligible.

Those are qualities that are relevant to us too. We seem to have an incurable fear of ideas and tend to translate issues into a knee-jerk reaction, reducing all reflection to mere emotion. Since we do not read, the education of our sympathies and perceptions is left to what is accidentally supplied by people in our immediate circle. When we read, however, we learn to rise above the confines of our immediate environment. From those heights we get a broader view of the human experience, of history, of how others have tackled problems that beset us. We may not grow wiser as a consequence, or happier, but we learn to become more tolerant. We are never the same again.

It is a matter of fulfilling our capability and potential. As human beings, we owe it to ourselves not to sell ourselves short. We are the only species in the world with a developed and reflective intelligence. One of the great rewards of that intelligence is language; and one of the greatest gifts from our ancestors is the discovery of writing. To be human is to read. The greatest tragedy, bar none, of our past fifty years in independent India is that half our citizens did not learn to read and were thus denied the opportunity to realize themselves as human beings and participate in the peculiarly human adventure called civilization.

At least those of us who did, owe it to ourselves to read as much as possible, and to read literature. For imaginative literature reflects all human experience and it is also capable of shaping this experience. When we think that we are sinking in chaos, or in serious doubt about where we are headed, or when an excess of complacency surrounds us, it is literature and critics who will stretch our experience, interpret it and make it relevant for one's own generation. Wouldn't it be nice, I sometimes think, to have one such critic like Edmund Wilson or Lionel Trilling to help us interpret our extravagantly chaotic experience of living in contemporary India?

## Who Will Roll the Chapatis?

They say that the measure of a civilization is how it treats its women. If this is true, then we are certainly becoming a more civilized nation day by day, and panchayati raj has something to do with it. Around the world, women have never been freer and this has to be one of the great achievements of the twentieth century. The consciousness of women's oppression came to us from the West, but women's organizations in India passionately took up the rallying cry. Their prize has been one-third of the legislative places in village and municipal governments and one-third again as heads of these governments. We have come a long way from *Manusmriti* to Madhuri.

We have witnessed, in the nineties, the great spectacle of almost one million women panchayat members begin to govern our villages, almost a quarter of a million of whom are chairpersons. Studies have also shown that women are increasingly exercising a benign influence over local affairs and the panchayats headed by women are consistently outperforming those headed by men. Nevertheless, there remains a huge gap between aspiration and reality—the sobering truth is that millions of women either die in childbirth or are never born, and thousands are victims of domestic violence, rape and dowry deaths.

In this essay on the changing role of women, I begin with an encounter with a young girl and her middle class mother which set me thinking about how boys and girls grow up differently. I move on to some observations on love and marriage provoked, curiously enough, by the Valentine's Day mania that has begun to grip our cities. Then I look at an American grandmother's search for meaning in self-improvement projects in a private, individualistic society, and compare her life to that of my mother in India. At the end, I return to where I began and what gives this essay its title. I offer some anecdotal evidence of how panchayati raj is changing women in the villages.

A few years ago, as a result of an unbelievable mix-up, I found myself at a party of middle class youngsters in Delhi, mostly between thirteen and seventeen years of age. Instead of making a quiet exit, I decided to stay and make the most of it. The first thing I noticed at this teenage party was that the boys and girls were in separate corners. The boys were bragging and talking about adventurous things. The girls were giggling, speaking about clothes, gossiping about boys, and nervously sucking on Pepsi straws.

By and large, it did not seem very different from the usual background noise of my adolescent days. When I was growing up, I remember that my mother used to be concerned about the right career for her son. When it came to her daughter, she only thought about her clothes and the type of man she would marry one day. Like every middle class mother, she hoped that her daughter would make the right sort of friends—the 'right sort' being defined not by their character, but by their social position. She unconsciously used the Indian yardstick, *log kya kahenge* (what will people say?) and it was important to measure up to that yardstick.

As I looked at the girls at the party I suspected that they too had been brought up believing that 'what others think of you' is what matters. One of the girls, seeing me out of my depth, came up to talk to me. Her name was Rekha. We chatted about this and that until I thoughtlessly asked her, 'What do you plan to do?' I realized my mistake because she became nervous and defensive. She mumbled something, and I felt that I might have lost a chance to make a friend. However, I quickly made amends by turning the conversation to pleasanter things. As we talked, I became convinced that one must never ask this question of a young person. What I really wanted to ask her was, 'Who are you? What do you want to make of your life?' But this question was never asked. Yet, I think it is so important for a youngster, especially a girl, to face this question. Boys, in any case, grow up having to think about these things, but girls do not. They never quite face reality in our sheltered middle class homes.

I read somewhere of an American study of junior high school

students (thirteen to fifteen years old) which suggested that boys and girls change more than their hormonal levels as they grow. It showed that adolescent girls become submissive and less confident—less likely to speak in the classroom. This seemed consistent with what I had observed about Rekha and her friends. The following day, I found myself at the right party, lunching with the parents of these same boys and girls. Between helpings of masur dal and boondi raita I met Rekha's mother. She said that Rekha had spoken about me. 'What did she say?' I asked. 'Oh, that you are a nice man,' she said. 'Is that all?' I asked. 'Yes,' she said. Before I could get anything more out of her or get to know her better (something that I would have liked), our hostess swept me to another room, in order to 'catch up on old times'.

'How do you know her?' asked my hostess, pointing to Rekha's mother.

'I don't. I met her daughter, Rekha, last night,' I said.

'It's really awful that her husband gets drunk every night and beats her up,' she said.

'What about Rekha?' I asked.

'He beats her too,' she said.

'I mean, why doesn't she do something about it?'

'What can she do?'

I looked across the room at Rekha's mother and I felt a great sadness. Listening to my hostess talk about the other women at the party deepened the sadness. Many of the women in the room, I could guess, had callous, boring marriages to pot-bellied men with wandering eyes. One of them was divorced and she lived close to a daily fear of slipping into poverty. Hope had begun to elude most of them. Why did I feel that yesterday's giggling, starry-eyed daughters were doomed to become today's cynical and brittle mothers?

I wanted to remind Rekha that we lived in a new millennium and ask how was she going to lead her life in the twenty-first century. I wanted to say, 'You don't want to grow up into a helpless victim like your mother. I hope you will marry a fine young man, but you mustn't have the illusion that the nice young man in Rajender Nagar with a white Maruti will take care of you and determine your happiness. You have to be ultimately answerable for your own life. No one else can do that. In order to be answerable you have to take charge of your life, "paddle your own canoe", as the Americans say. You must believe that you can act upon your life, and not have life act upon you. Thus, you will become an autonomous woman who is spontaneous, self-reliant and responsible. Thus, you will be "inner-directed", rather than "outer-directed", in David Riesman's famous characterization.'

If there is one thing that holds a woman back in middle class Indian society, it is her reluctance to face the reality of money. Very simply, money must be made. You have to earn a salary or run a business. That requires hard work, making decisions, and single-mindedly pursuing those decisions. It is the only way you will be free in the long run. Then, if you are caught in a bad marriage or are divorced (which I hope you won't be, Rekha), at least you won't be trapped or become a prey to pressures, or be enslaved by society like your mother. You will think less of *log kya kahenge* and more about what you must do.

⤽

Expectations from marriage are beginning to change in Indian society, and so are the relations between men and women. Oddly enough, the recent Valentine's Day mania has brought romance out of purdah, and that too is a liberation of sorts. It is easy to dismiss it as commercially induced madness—a manifestation of the global lifestyle we are importing. In fact, the St Valentine's feast originated in the market square economies of the medieval West. It is associated with the coupling of birds and return of spring, thanks to Chaucer's famous poem, *Parliament of Fowls* (1382). Now this love festival seems also to have touched a basic human need in our repressed middle classes.

We, too, have our love festivals in India. During Karva

Chauth, a wife fasts for her man. A brother and sister confirm their love at Rakhi. Holi provides a licence for men and women to shed their inhibitions. In ancient times, the Kamundini Mahotsva offered homage to Kama, the love god. Krishna Leela, in medieval times, celebrated extramarital love, but our bhakti saints transformed it into the surrender of the soul to God. The tribals in Bastar celebrate premarital love during ghotul. But nothing in our urban culture today celebrates romantic love.

Indians have always known that marriage is all about predictability, but the West has forgotten this wisdom. Anna Quindlen, the American columnist, reminded me about this in a wonderful piece she once wrote for *The New York Times*. Once every three months, she said, her husband would suddenly notice what she was wearing and exclaim, 'I don't like that nightgown.' Each time he said this, she says, she would feel a magical thrill inside her because she had realized that some things in life are immutable. The touchstone of marriage is security and nothing makes you feel more secure than knowing exactly what the other person is going to say.

The nightgown is also a metaphor for the difference between men and women and what they expect from marriage. It is tempting to think that women want a secure, comfortable and enduring relationship, while men seek excitement and sex. That is certainly the conventional wisdom. Yet, it is too easy. Women too want excitement in their lives—including young Indian women in this post-liberalization age. But both men and women wish that excitement did not mean having to lie and cheat and live a life of deception.

In India, we have always understood that marriage is a conjugal compromise, transforming a fugitive desire into a lasting emotion. A mutual desire—either physical or mental or both—is, however, not enough. Whether it is an arranged marriage or a love match, the essential thing is that both persons think it permanent. Hence, civilizations founded on polygamy have always given way to those based on monogamy.

Nothing in this world is perfect, not even love. It is just as difficult to live with a husband as it is with a lover, because men and women are different. It is hazardous to admit this in this age of women's liberation when women are equally well educated and perform the same jobs very efficiently. The reality, though, is that women are more preoccupied with maternity and love, and men with action. Men are faithful to ideas; women are faithful to human beings. D.H. Lawrence claimed that man's religious soul drives him beyond woman to his supreme activity. Men realize that 'wedlock is padlock', but they dread loneliness more than bondage. So, they get married and want their wives to be mistresses when they are young, companions when they are middle-aged and nurses when they are old.

To some extent, marriage does destroy love; this is a fact that we may have to get resigned to. At certain times in our life, in adolescence and around the time we are fifty, we seem to want to be in the mood for love. But desire is short-lived. How does one make it last; that is, how does one turn an instinct into an institution? The answer, I believe, is to accept that in marriage, as in government, perfection is not possible. We must learn to gradually replace love with friendship, passion with good humour, and rebuild a marriage every day. The game is never won.

⤙

Indian women are living longer and like their counterparts in the West they tend to outlive their husbands. How they live their lives in old age is beginning to engage our attention. I thought about this when I came across a charming account by an eighty-five-year old American grandmother, Hila Colman, in the *New York Times*. I was struck by the contrast between her life and my mother's in India, who is about the same age.

'As a child,' Hila Colman wrote, 'I was content to have my time planned for me: school gym on Monday, piano lessons on Tuesday, dancing classes on Thursday, and so on.' But when she grew up and went to high school, she said she wanted more time to herself. What with the homework and the push for extra-curricular activities ('which would look good on my application for college'), there was no time. By the time she got to college there was a sudden interest in boys and clothes and other pressures. She still dreamed of an occasional lazy afternoon stretched out on a hammock, but it never happened. Perhaps, she thought, it would come when she got married.

After marriage, there was no rest either. She had to clean the house, cook the meals, launder the clothes, shop for groceries, take care of two young boys, in addition to working long hours on her writing. She bought a hammock, but it never met her back. On her eightieth birthday her family and friends gave her a party. They congratulated her and said with a straight face that she looked no more than sixty. 'I thanked them,' she wrote, 'but I thought to myself that I was no beauty at sixty, so why should I want to look like that now?' She looked backed on her life. It had had its good and bad moments, but it had not been peaceful or leisurely.

Now in her eighties, she found that she was again 'being hit from all sides with things I must do, food I must eat, ways I must think to stay forever young.' The suggestions included going to classes 'where I'll meet people and exercise my brain, perhaps study'.

She dismissed all these possibilities because she wanted her old age to be different from her youth. She wanted to experience the luxury of not having anything to do, of sleeping late and going to the post office to get her mail. Living alone in the country, she says, 'I find this to be the high point of my day. I enjoy stopping to visit friends, to gossip, to argue our local politics. I am in no hurry.' This is the time she wants to enjoy the quietness of just being, of stopping to look and feel and think of indulging herself. 'Time for myself at last,' she says.

Hila Colman's story contains many of the nuances and the ambiguities of American life. Forever optimistic, Americans are constantly searching for youth, wanting to improve themselves. All this keeps them so busy they have no time to sit back, relax and reflect. It is not Americans alone who face these dilemmas of modern life. They merely point the way for what others' lives will become one day. A woman in Hyderabad might face the same dilemmas, and if she doesn't, her daughter surely will.

When I read Hila Colman's account, I thought of my eighty-five-year-old mother, who lives in an ashram on the banks of the Beas. Her routine is a mosaic of *satsang*, meditation, *seva* and the daily comings and goings of life. After she lost my father, there has been much coming and going of relatives and for months she has remained busy with the routine of condolences. She, too, raised a middle class family, with its hectic demands, and there was no time to relax all those years. But the difference between her life and that of Hila Colman is that she was never into frenetic self-improvement. Neither was she constantly searching for youth. Nor does she ever think of having 'time to herself', which she would regard as selfish or excessively individualistic. She might even think of it as a lonely life. My mother is content in being swept away by the daily rhythms of the collective Indian way of life. Which of the two, I wonder, has found the right way 'to build a life'?

A decade ago, during the debate on the constitutional amendments relating to decentralization, we constantly heard this refrain: if women get on to the panchayats, who will roll the chapatis? Who will look after the children? Well, no one talks like that any more, as Bishakha Dutta's book on the panchayats in Maharashtra reveals. Today, women members of panchayats travel long distances, sometimes escorted by male relatives. A survey by the Delhi-based Centre for Women's Development Studies (CNDS) in Madhya Pradesh, Rajasthan and Uttar Pradesh finds that 65.5 per cent of women representatives regularly attend panchayat meetings. It also contradicts the common assumption that the women representatives belong to locally influential families with political connections.

Another study by Susheela Kaushik of the CNDS of six states confirms that women representatives are mostly OBCs and forty per cent belong to families with incomes below the poverty line.

In the summer of 1994, Basanti Bai, a Dalit, made history by becoming the first woman sarpanch of Barkhedi gram panchayat in Sehore district in Madhya Pradesh. Her family remembers the days when the upper-caste villagers repeatedly threatened her and registered fake complaints in the police station. After she resigned, no one in the village would give her work and she had to go outside to look for it. Eventually the village realized its mistake—she had been an excellent sarpanch—and they voted her back in the next election. Today, the village hand pump is a proud testimonial to her.

In Chhattisgarh, Chhindia Bai of the Baiga tribal community was also elected sarpanch under the reserved quota. She was illiterate but determined. Chhindia Bai's children taught her to read and to sign papers and cheques. Now the village talks about how she got the old ponds deepened during the last drought. Ganga Devi Rawat, sarpanch of Khawada in Tehri Garhwal, on the other hand, is educated up to high school. Despite pressure from her extended family, she steadfastly refuses to sign false accounts or pay commissions and cuts to government officials who sanction development funds. 'This hand and this signature are no longer my own,' she says, and credits the NGO, Chetana Andolan, for supporting her.

Fatimabai, a sarpanch in Kurnool district in Andhra, wears a burkha and can neither read nor sign her name. She lacked confidence at first, but later managed to do what no man had done for her village. She metalled the access road, built a schoolhouse, repaired the public water tap, registered land ownership pattas, and physically led the village to clean up a large tank. Above all, she refused to lease the village pond to her biggest supporter; instead, she held an open auction, which yielded Rs 1 lakh for the panchayat fund.

In West Bengal, Kamala Mahato, the panchayat pradhan of

Bandoan in Purulia district, reports that she has had ten wells dug for drinking water and irrigation, and has implemented an income-generating scheme for women under the Integrated Rural Development Programme. In north Bihar, thirty-five-year-old Draupadi of Bucha village in Khagaria district was kidnapped by her landlord employer in August last year. Not intimidated, she came back to fight in this year's panchayat elections under the slogan, 'Down with the feudal order!' In Hardia in the same district, Poonam Devi contested the panch's post against her husband's wishes, who himself wanted to be a candidate for the post. 'He refused to bear my campaign expenses, but I pooled some funds from my parents,' she cheerfully told reporters.

But there is a darker side, too. In Madhya Pradesh, Kusum Bai, the OBC sarpanch of a gram panchayat in Khandwa district, defeated another woman candidate, whose husband, along with three others, gang-raped her. Two days later, completely traumatized, she tried to commit suicide. A tribal woman sarpanch in Pune district in Maharashtra, who also happens to be a primary school teacher, was beaten up by the rival male candidate (and his hired goons) simply because she had won the election and he had not. Nirmala Devi, a zilla parishad member in Chandauli district of Uttar Pradesh, won the last election with the highest number of votes in the state. 'The victory would have been real if my supporters and co-workers had accepted the sweets I handed out on winning the election,' she says. 'They didn't, because I am a Dalit.' P. Sainath's survey of 104 Dalit-led panchayats of Tikamgarh in the Bundelkhand region of Madhya Pradesh shows that after the first year, Dalit sarpanches have been ousted by a variety of methods.

Nevertheless, the overwhelming evidence suggests that the Indian village is changing. Studies confirm that women leaders do a better job on the panchayat because they focus on the right priorities—installing water pumps and wells, constructing toilets, village roads, schoolhouses and appointing good teachers. The women surveyed report that the power equation too has subtly changed in their families and they receive a new-found respect from the community since the advent of panchayati raj. Those who were elected have realized that they need to acquire an education or at least literacy skills. Inspired by the example of Mayawati, the Dalit leader of Uttar Pradesh, they are keen to see girls in their village attend school regularly.

Govind Nihalani's film *Sanshodhan* sums up the picture. In it a woman member of the panchayat in Rajasthan mobilizes the village to build a primary school and successfully foils the local Thakur landlord who is bent on stealing the school funds. It is a simple political film, which shows how the elite will try to subvert the democratic process when it goes against their interest. They try to pack the panchayats with their relatives and friends, but eventually they fail and have to reconcile to sharing power.

❧

The stubborn persistence of child malnutrition in India is truly one of the tragedies of our time. Many of us have long agonized over this preventable problem, and we continue to ask, why do half our children not get either enough or the right food or adequate care? Even in sub-Saharan Africa only thirty per cent of the children are malnourished versus fifty per cent in South Asia. And this twenty-point gap exists despite our much higher levels of per capita income, education and even safer water access.

One-third of the babies in India are born with low birth weight compared to one-sixth in sub-Saharan Africa. This is heartbreaking given the dramatic improvements in our agriculture, advances in literacy and great strides in economic growth. For more than twenty years, India has even 'sustained the greatest effort in history to improve nutritional standards', according to UNICEF, through its Integrated Child Development Service Programme. So, it is not for lack of effort. Nor is it due to poverty, which has been steadily declining.

What accounts for this puzzle? In 1996, India's famous

physician-nutritionist, the late Professor V. Ramalingaswami (with others) wrote a groundbreaking article on this anomaly called 'The Asian Enigma'. After considering different factors, including access to food and income and our vegetarianism, he concluded that the lower status of women in South Asia might be the reason.

The link between women's position and child nutrition seems plausible. In many Indian homes men eat first; women have to make do with leftovers. And this is perhaps why eighty-three per cent of women in India suffer from iron deficiency anaemia versus forty per cent in sub-Saharan Africa. A malnourished mother will give birth to a baby with low birth weight—the single most important predictor of child survival. Moreover, the pressure of domestic work often forces a mother to delegate to older siblings the irritating chore of feeding solid food to her baby. If women had more control over family income and decisions they would devote them to better pre- and post-natal care and to their children's needs.

So far this was the theory. But in mid-2002 an extensive empirical study by the International Food Policy Research Institute and Emory University seemed to confirm the Ramalingaswami hypothesis. The study brought together data from thirty-six developing countries, spanning over 100,000 children under the age of three and an equal number of women. It measured a woman's position in the home in various ways—whether the woman works for cash, her age at marriage, and the difference in age and education between husband and wife. The study concludes that the lowly position of women in the family compared to men is the single most important reason for the gap between South Asia and sub-Saharan Africa in children's nutrition, followed by sanitation (e.g., the lack of latrines) and urbanization (slum living). A woman's low place in society also prevents the active use of health services by women and children.

While reading this report I wondered why is the position of women in India so much worse than that of women in other societies? I also questioned whether the tragedy of children's well-being is only a woman's issue, or is it a family concern where men play a crucial role. I suspect there are no easy answers, but they are worthy subjects for further research.

Women everywhere suffer from a lower status, but in India it appears to have devastating consequences. The policy implications are clear: if we want to reduce child malnutrition, we must combine our child programmes with efforts to improve the situation of women in our society. To succeed in the knowledge-based economy, we need healthy children who will become tomorrow's innovative adults. If we ignore gender inequality, we will continue to produce stunted children, wasted lives and untold misery.

## Dance a Little, Laugh a Lot

From the status of women I move to a different sort of education—learning not to be too concerned with others. In Paris of the twenties, there used to be a charming newspaper called *L'Intransigeant*. It was known for its investigative stories, rich city gossip and penetrating editorials. It was in the habit of dreaming up big questions and inviting its readers to respond. One such question was, 'How would you live your last few days if you knew the world was coming to an end?' A literary gentleman wrote that the news would drive the masses to the nearest church or the bedroom, although he himself would climb a mountain and admire the scenery. An actress said that people would actually improve, become honest and shed their silly inhibitions. Another reader declared that he would play a last round of golf and follow it up with a final hand of bridge.

One letter-writer was my favourite novelist, Marcel Proust, unquestionably the most unusual Parisian of his time. He had spent the past fourteen years lying in a narrow bed under a pile of expensive woollen blankets, beside a badly lit lamp, writing one and a quarter million words called *In Search of Lost Time*. The novel instantly became a classic, and a French critic compared Proust to Shakespeare, an Italian reviewer to Stendhal, and an Austrian princess offered him her hand in marriage. The British ambassador called him 'the most remarkable man I have met—he keeps his overcoat on at dinner'.

Proust's letter to the newspaper suggested that the imminence of death would wake us up from the slumber of 'our moral life, where negligence deadens desire'. Life would suddenly seem wonderful, and he, for one, would visit the new galleries of the Louvre, throw himself at the feet of an unnamed woman, and take a trip to India. Four months later, Proust caught a cold and died—without doing any of the three things. His recipe for happiness, however, was brilliant: shed our pretensions to immortality, renew our taste for life, discover new possibilities and reassess our priorities, and live life joyfully. Nietzsche, as usual, put this thought more dramatically in *Thus Spake Zarathustra*, 'We should consider every day lost in which we have not danced at least once. And we should call every truth false, which was not accompanied by at least one laugh.'

I am reminded of Proust because I spent many depressing days in the late nineties reading about the terrible persecution of Christians in our country. I am convinced that the world is divided into two types of people: the minority who are dedicated to happiness and the majority who are dedicated to unhappiness. Those in this happy minority are 'inner-directed', know what they want, and are content with getting on with their lives. They do not bother with what their neighbours think or do. Most of the successful CEOs and creative people that I have met belong to this category.

In contrast, those in the unhappy majority are 'outer-directed', and are not excessively concerned with others. They define their identity in relation to others and believe they can only be happy by making someone else unhappy. The misguided followers of both the Hindu and Muslim fundamentalist groups belong to this group. My advice to Hindu nationalists is to get on with building a great country and forget the minorities. Nietzsche's advice to the Bajrang Dal and Vishwa Hindu Parishad would be to 'dance a little and laugh a lot'. What a wasted life, hating others when you could spend it living with plenitude and producing happiness for others. Even illusory happiness is better than sorrow.

The ghastly murder of Graham Staines in the nineties shook us out of our complacence. The Staines were missionaries, and what they were doing was merely bringing a little happiness to the most wretched in our country. I have seen Christians working in the remotest places, living a selfless life, and bringing education and health care to the poorest. I wonder, how many religious fundamentalists of either the Hindu or Muslim varieties engage in genuine charity? Now the home ministry is contemplating stopping the Rs 20-odd crore that comes from Christian charities abroad. Every rupee out of this is spent with care and love, in contrast to the hundreds of crores wasted in the government's poverty programmes.

The critics of the Christian missionaries in India complain that they not only engage in charity but also convert people to their faith. I ask, what is wrong with that? After all, freedom of thought and religion are guaranteed by our Constitution. If the marketing of ideas by Christians is more successful, it means merely that they are doing a better job than the Hindus or the Muslims. The persecution of the Christians by the Hindu fundamentalists only means that they suffer from an inferiority complex. They lack confidence in their own way, and its ability to hold people. I, for one, have enormous faith in the ability of Hindu civilization to survive, and hence I do not care too much about what others do. The self-styled guardians of Hindu glory should learn from and follow the wise advice of Albert Camus, 'To be happy, we must not be too concerned with others.'

## Small Sweet Courtesies

Laurence Sterne's happy phrase, 'Hail ye, small sweet courtesies of life', brings back a pleasant memory. In September 1998, Ashok Desai, the amusing economist–columnist, and I were invited to Devlali to spend a day with a group of serious-minded young people. Devlali is an old-fashioned cantonment town, quiet and clean, with an artillery school. During the monsoon it greens up like the rest of the Deccan and the effect is magical—like nothing on earth.

After a pleasant day in this 'time warp', we took a three-wheeler to the station for the Panchwati Express back to Mumbai. Just as we turned onto the main road our scooter seemed to die. While Ashok and I fretted, our driver was unperturbed. Calmly, he hailed the first autorickshaw that came along. Since it carried two hefty jawans who, like us, were on the way to catch the train, we did not think that they would stop. But they did! Without fuss or debate, our driver transferred some petrol to his vehicle, we nodded to the jawans, and within five minutes, we were on the road again.

I looked at Ashok with a smile. 'Do you think this could have happened anywhere else in the world?' I asked. 'It could,' he said wisely, 'But in India it does, always.' The Devlali incident reminded me of another. One summer my cousin's car got stuck in a landslide on the road to Manali. They hailed a truck driver, but he was unable to pull the car out of the slush. By now a small crowd had collected. Soon a Sardarji came along on a motorcycle. Taking charge, he assigned a person to each wheel, and with one strong heave they lifted the Maruti out. My cousin was delighted and he offered him a generous tip, but the Sardarji refused. With a hurt expression on his face, he said, 'If this had happened to me, my brother, I would have expected you to do the same. In these parts, these are merely courtesies of the road.'

'Courtesies of the heart,' I said to myself, for isn't courtesy the outer garment of goodwill, which pervades so much of life in villages and towns across India? Francis Bacon used to say, 'If a man be gracious and courteous to strangers, it shows that he is a citizen of the world.' Courtesy may not be unusual in our rich, private lives, but it is remarkably absent in our impoverished public life, which is littered daily with horror tales of callousness, corruption and downright venality. We spontaneously look to our neighbours for help, but not to the local policeman on the beat. Why is it that the same warm, caring human being becomes a monster once he dons the policeman's garb or sits in the politician's or the bureaucrat's chair?

H.L. Mencken, the American humorist, had an answer. He used to say that we ordinary people make the mistake in believing that there are two types of people in public life—the good and the bad—when in fact, there is only one. And it is the duty of all citizens in a democracy to be vigilant and relentlessly minimize the power of the public official.

Corruption is thus not our unique privilege. As Mencken says, power corrupts. It corrupts everyone, everywhere. Neither is it a question of our character, despite the conventional wisdom. The problem lies with our system and our institutions. We have created a big government and given our officials great powers. More important, we have given them powers to discriminate on the basis of discretion. The answer to our venal public life partly rests with liberalization. Liberalization is about making the government more effective and accountable by taking away the discretionary powers of bureaucrats and politicians, and replacing them with transparent rules. Had we had transparent rules we would have been spared many of the sordid scandals of the nineties that have diminished us all as Indians. Our public officials are opposed to economic reform because they will lose their power to give licences and take bribes. The public sector is a cow that they have milked for over forty years, and why should they now allow it to be privatized and taken away?

After fifty years, we are a nation disappointed with itself. Here was a nation created by idealists and it had the world cheering for it. Today we may be good as individuals, but as a nation we are not. We have lost our way, partly because we adopted the wrong economic model, and like a parasite it has eaten into our body politic. Only by relentlessly pursuing administrative and economic reforms can we expect to regain some of that lost promise of goodness, maybe even restore some of the 'small sweet courtesies' to our public life.

# 6

## Playing to Win

*They who lose today may win tomorrow.*
—Cervantes, *Don Quixote* (1605–15)

Foreigners sometimes remind us that Indians are a bright people. They can be analytical and articulate. But foreigners are too polite to add that Indians can also be 'over-smart', and this creates its own problems. They think and argue too much, see too many angles, and don't act enough. It makes hiring and recruiting talent particularly difficult, for all Indians come out sounding well in an interview. How then do you separate the doers from the talkers?

Having said this, one must also remember that national stereotypes, such as this one, can be dangerous and are usually wrong. This has been one of the plainest lessons from the history of the violent twentieth century. Hence, I usually rely on institutions and economic laws to explain human behaviour rather than national character. However, the gap between thought and action is so pervasive in Indian life that I tend to throw caution to the winds and I begin to despair and wonder if the weakness in execution is, in fact, a deficit in character.

My experience as a consultant to a dozen Indian companies during the past decade is that while many have acquired a reasonably robust strategy, they implement poorly. I am also associated with a venture capital fund that has invested in fifteen Indian companies in information technology, and its experience is the same—the successful firms are not the ones with the best business model but those with executional ability.

McKinsey, the respected management consultancy firm, has found the same. In a survey of thirty-five major companies and interviews with more than 600 executives, it has concluded: 'while many Indian companies perform well on strategy, they are lagging in execution'. McKinsey conducted similar studies around the world, and its international data show that the best performing companies in the world distinguish themselves from mediocre ones in their ability to execute. High performers, such as General Electric, Sony and Singapore Airlines, consistently implement better, and this is ultimately reflected in their market share and profitability.

Our bias for thought and against action may explain why there is not a single Indian company with a global presence, although we rank among the top five countries in the size of our scientific talent. I am inclined to think that it may also be the reason why so many Indian companies are floundering ten years after the reforms. There are outstanding exceptions, to be sure. Reliance Industries owes its consistent success partially to its awesome project management skills, which allows it to build plants faster than anyone else. A few years ago, I was on the jury to select the best among forty-odd of Aditya Birla's companies and I observed the same executional excellence in company after company. No wonder Hindalco, for example, has become a world-class aluminium producer. It is the same with Jet Airways. Ask its passengers and they will tell you that it is always on time. Finance companies HDFC and Sundaram Finance have consistently demonstrated outstanding service levels for decades. A jewel of a company in Bangalore, Himatsingka Seide, is able to command Rs 8,000 per metre for its luxurious silks in Europe and the United States because it consistently delivers exquisite, defect-free fabric according to schedule.

Why do these companies have the ability to execute when the majority does not? It begins at the top, I believe. The leaders in high-performing companies, I have observed, are not content with laying broad policies but insist on getting into the messy details of the business—monitoring day-to-day performance, removing obstacles, staying close to employees and motivating them. They reward managers who act and take initiative, and punish those who play safe and behave like bureaucrats. They set clear, measurable goals and create small implementation teams so that people become accountable. Reliance's top management, for instance, monitors daily the number of kilometres of optic fibre that its telecom teams lay on the ground, and motivates them to improve their performance the next day. Thus, they get ordinary people to do extraordinary things.

Successful executives follow the British scientist Jacob Bronowski's advice that the world is not understood by contemplation but by action: 'the hand is the cutting edge of the mind'. Good executives, I have observed, do few things. But they make sure they are the right things, and they do them brilliantly.

While it may be tempting to blame character for the performance of our companies, the real culprit is poor management skills. Fortunately, these skills can be learned, especially when there is intense rivalry in the market place and survival is at stake. Our problem in India is that we have only had real competition in our economy after 1991. So, perhaps, it is early. The lesson for our business leaders is to honestly face up to poor execution as the cause of their troubles. While no businessperson likes competition, the irony is that it is only in an environment of intense competition that managers tend to learn skills such as these. The next time you are tempted to ask for protection, think of this.

It is more than a decade since the reforms began, and most Indian companies are still floundering. With some prominent exceptions, they have not achieved the sort of competitiveness that would have given them the confidence or the skills to succeed in the global economy. In this chapter I draw upon my experience of thirty years as a practising manager and subsequently seven years as an adviser to companies, and I wrestle with the knotty question of how to make Indian business competitive. During my business career I worked in five countries, and based on this background, I discuss the role of strategy, implementation and beliefs in building sustainable competitive advantage.

There is no reason for wholesale pessimism about Indian companies. Nor is their plight an excuse for our policy makers to turn protectionist. True, it has been a slow dance since 1997 and confidence is naturally low, but ups and downs are in the nature of capitalism. Since the wonderfully optimistic years between 1992 and 1997, the spark has gone out of Indian industry (barring one year, 1999–2000, when growth did pick up).

Those who think that Indian brands are disappearing should take note of Titan watches, which is stronger after the entry of Timex. Maruti may have lost market share, but it is putting up a good fight against the best car companies in the world. Bajaj may be struggling in the two-wheelers market, but this has more to do with a shift in the market from scooters to motorcycles than competition. Although Hero Honda became the largest maker of motorcycles in the world in 2001–02, Bajaj also regained market share. Even Thums Up is well and alive within Coke's stable. Taj and Oberoi continue to expand their world-class hotel chains. Ranbaxy's generic drugs have crossed $100 million in sales in the U.S. Bharat Forge has achieved a 60 per cent share of the U.S. frontal axles market for trucks. Then there are two new brands who are demonstrating world-class skills and performance—Haldiram's namkeen and Barista's coffee. Haldiram put up a solid fight against Pepsi's Lehar brand while Barista is single-handedly changing the habits of Indian youth. Finally, outstanding software exporters like Infosys and Wipro are beginning to change our image abroad and our self-confidence at home.

When I returned to Richardson Hindustan Ltd in 1981, after being away for five years in Mexico and Spain, I found that it was in a real mess. I discovered that the Indian company wasn't making any money, the morale of the employees was low, labour-management relations were bitterly adversarial and turnover in the management ranks was unacceptably high. While my priority was to increase profitability, I lost no time in dealing with the labour and the morale situation. To help change the prevailing attitudes, we mounted an attitude-change programme—first for managers, then for supervisors and finally for workers. Next, we took steps to raise profitability. The final step was to identify and commit to new opportunities for future growth.

The turnaround was quick and dramatic, both in results and attitudes, and it surprised us all. How did it happen? There were a number of factors—including luck—but I think the most important was a change in values. The same people who had orchestrated the mess with a different set of values created a different sort of corporate culture and delivered outstanding results. And Richardson Hindustan went on to become a model subsidiary in the whole of Richardson Vicks worldwide. When Procter and Gamble took over our company around the world in 1985, they singled out the Indian subsidiary for this achievement, and unlike the other Vicks subsidiaries we did not lose a single employee after the takeover.

I spell out below three core values that guided us at Richardson Hindustan: 'respect for the individual', 'existing for the customer', and 'continuous innovation'. Most employees are cynical about 'company values', but I think if you asked the thousand or so persons who worked at Richardson Hindustan between 1981 and 1986, they would tell you that these values made a difference.

*Respect for the individual* The starting point is one's view of human beings. If you think people are basically trustworthy, you will trust them, make them feel trusted and they will respond accordingly. Ultimately, this is what we learned as children—that people behave according to how they are treated, and you should 'do unto others as you would have others do unto you'.

This has powerful implications in an organization. For example, if you believe in this, you will instinctively learn to delegate. Delegation too has to be learned; sometimes you can easily over-delegate. You must delegate with the sense that you are a coach, that you must help the other person in his performance. When you do this, you empower your subordinates and you delegate autonomy. When employees become autonomous, you find that decisions are pushed down to the lowest level of competence. This prepares the managers of tomorrow and breeds a culture where teamwork becomes a way of life.

When you respect the individual you share information. Information is power, and one of the things I learned to do was to constantly talk about the company and what we were doing at the various forums of workers, junior managers, while lunching with factory executives, and so on. Constantly engaging employees in conversations about goals and values in an unpatronizing way shows that you respect them.

It is odd that we are proud of computers that think but are suspicious of people who think. We are not so much concerned with the top performers—they will do the right thing and go up regardless. We are concerned with the average performers, who have the ability to do the right thing but often do not. They make hundreds of small decisions every day which, if made in the right way, could benefit the company enormously. How, then, can we motivate the average employee to do the right thing—to motivate the telephone operator to answer the phone on the second ring rather than the sixth, or the loader to gently load a packing case? The key, I think, is to share with everyone the common goals and to respect each other in a company.

Respecting individuals leads us naturally to investing in them. If you believe individuals can grow then you will also invest in them—in training, in upgrading skills (both human and technical skills). I am convinced that this is one of the greatest failures of Indian companies. Since an enterprise is only as good as its people, you can understand why Indian companies tend to perform poorly. I am reminded of advertising guru David Ogilvy who used to say,

'If you surround yourself with people better than you are, then you will build a company of giants. If you surround yourself with people inferior to you, then you will build a company of dwarfs.' I cannot overstress the importance of creating an environment where people develop their full potential; otherwise good people do not stay. Evaluating a manager on his or her record of developing subordinates fosters this kind of environment.

Respect for the individual also implies constant and transparent recognition of achievement. The biggest motivator in a company is achievement. They say a person won't sell his life to you but he will give it to you for a piece of ribbon. An environment that consistently rewards achievement and fresh thinking will breed professional restlessness, and it is the same one where the best and brightest thrive.

*Existing for the customer* The only job of a business, I believe, is to create and retain customers. A successful manager has to be obsessed with satisfying customer needs. The irony is that all the money a company makes is made outside the company, and almost all the time that company people spend is spent inside the company. Time spent inside the company is usually spent battling over turf, whereas spending time in the field makes one realize that the real battles are fought outside, against your competitors and in winning the hearts of your customers.

Why is this so? One reason, I think, is that we don't see customers when we come to work. We only see other employees and we get busy building empires or arguing over whose department is more important and whose office is bigger. In order to bring employees closer to customers, I made a start in my company by getting every employee to spend time meeting customers and retailers. We did this not only to remind ourselves who paid our salary, but we also got a payoff in terms of good ideas to improve our products and services.

The greatest benefit of this belief in staying close to customers comes in R&D. When scientists regularly visit the bazaar they realize that they are not working for science but to improve the lives of ordinary people. When R&D becomes customer-focused, the rewards come in very rapidly. Little improvements in some areas—even in packaging—have a major impact in customer satisfaction and on the bottom line. Ultimately, you succeed in business because you sell a product that is better than your competitor's. If your efforts are directed at making a product better, and doing so constantly, you will win. No matter how much advertising or good marketing you may do, if your product does not deliver what is promised, you will not succeed. This very simple idea begins with the belief that we exist for our customers.

*Continuing innovation* Corporate excellence is the result of a continuous quest for ways and means to improve and innovate, to promote a sense of urgency and a willingness to try new things. A style of management that is more open, more participative, more consultative and less authoritarian, I believe, promotes ideas at all levels and encourages innovation. This, of course, is not easy, as many senior managers are unwilling to relinquish power. In order to create an environment of continuing innovation you need to give people responsibility early in their careers. Begin by delegating wisely, allowing people to make mistakes and learning from them. Second, create an open system of communicating. This will stimulate fresh thinking and a free exchange of ideas. Third, appraise people on the good ideas they come up with and execute during the year and reward them accordingly. Finally, prefer action to thought. We have this great idea that innovative people sit in a room quietly contemplating, and this is how new ideas will be born. In fact, innovative ideas emanate from action—from experimenting, through making mistakes.

These have become my three basic beliefs related to the business world. The ultimate test of beliefs is in their practice—for only when they are practised do they become values. People in business have to realize that their future depends on being able to define a set of beliefs. When these values are broadly shared in a company, they become its core values. Well-defined values help individuals in an organization know the boundaries of freedom and provide a practical guide to day-to-day decision-making, managing others and setting high standards of performance. They enable us to work in harmony and eventually give the business an unassailable competitive edge.

≈

I began this essay by pointing out that the mundane ability to implement day in and day out is more important than strategy, and outstanding companies are built not so much by great strategy but by great execution. Nevertheless, the right strategy can be extremely powerful. The starting point in choosing a strategy is to understand that the competitive advantage of a firm arises from its distinctive capabilities. These capabilities are based partly on the continuity of relationships that the firm builds with its suppliers, customers and employees. Its competitive advantage is, thus, the product of history and is not easy to duplicate. It emerges from within the company, from a recognition of its strengths, and is never imposed from the outside by consultants or created by corporate communication programmes. These relationships are unique and the search for generic strategies for corporate success is doomed to failure. This is also the thesis of British management expert John Kay's book, *Why Firms Succeed*.

This is an important lesson for Indian firms as they have been seriously seeking to build competitive advantage in the nineties. But creating strategy is not just a matter of calling in a big-name consultant, chasing the latest fad in business strategy—be it 'time-based competitiveness' or Total Quality Approach (TQA)—then pressing a button, and bingo! Creating competitive advantage takes years of painstaking effort and few Indian companies have had the patience or the inclination to do so. It requires the ability of the top management to get into the messy details of the business, without losing the focus of the big picture. I have found that many Indian businesses are hopelessly unequal to this task. Till 1991, their talents and their attention were directed (rather, misdirected) by the licence–permit raj. While they were busy negotiating our Byzantine bureaucracies, their competitors in other countries were crafting relationships with suppliers, distributors and customers.

In the sixties, Honda, Kay tells us, captured a third of the American motorcycle market in less than five years. It did not have great vision; it simply did what it did best—making simple, inexpensive motorcycles. But its success lay in unglamorous attention to building long-term ties with its distributors, customers and suppliers. Similarly, Nike's global success came not only from its brand equity, but also in the way it orchestrated its relationships with its manufacturing sub-contractors in East Asia and its independent retailers around the world. Much the same is true of Liz Clairborne. Both companies stand as interpreters of the consumer's needs between retailers and manufacturers, and it is the structure of these relationships that is each company's distinctive capability.

The lesson for Indian companies with global ambitions—for example, Ranbaxy, Tata Steel, Dr Reddy's, Bharat Forge, Infosys—is that success will not come from imitating the successful, but in identifying and nurturing one's own distinctive capabilities. If there were effective generic recipes for corporate success, then all companies would adopt them, and they would cease to yield returns for a particular company.

Thus, what differentiates a successful company is more important than what it has in common with other successful companies. This is a disappointing conclusion for managers and companies looking for quick, opportunistic fixes. But it is a hopeful conclusion for those Indian companies—and there are some—who are focused on the long term, who are well under way in building a network of relationships within and around their firms, and realize that success comes not from doing what others do well but from doing what others cannot do or cannot do as well.

Success, argues Kay, should not be measured by market share

or an organization's size, but by its added value. 'Added value', he defines, is the amount by which the company's output exceeds the input of raw materials, payroll and cost of capital. Corporate strategy aims to maximize this value, and it should begin with the question: how can we be different? Kay identifies four ingredients: innovation, reputation (especially in the form of brands), strategic assets and, most important, the relationships between the company and its suppliers, employees and customers.

Kay's conclusions are not new. Although British, he belongs to the tradition associated with the Harvard Business School—the work of Kenneth Andrews, C. Roland Christensen, Edmund P. Learned and others in the sixties—which focused on organizational uniqueness. Harvard has always believed that strategy is inherently situation specific: every industry and every company is different. Not surprisingly, it is committed to the idea that the only way to learn business strategy is by the case method. Its underlying premise is that a successful firm must match its distinctive capabilities to its environment.

In contrast to this tradition are those who claim that there is a single universal variable on which all strategy can be based. The Boston Consulting Group (BCG) pioneered this second tradition in the early seventies with the celebrated concept of the 'experience curve'. BCG proposed that competitive advantage was defined by a single variable, cost. Cost depended on learning, which increased proportionally with cumulative experience, and which, in turn, depended on relative market share. A firm's strategy, then, was based on a single variable: increasing relative market share. The experience curve gave rise to a growth/share matrix, which characterized the different businesses in a diversified company by growth and relative market share. The resulting designations—cows, dogs, stars, etc.—provided the prescription for strategy. These two approaches represent the pulls and pressures in creating business strategy that operate to the present day. The work of management expert Michael Porter is, in a sense, a reaction to and a synthesis of both these traditions.

I have often pointed out that that there are only three ways that a company can create sustainable competitive advantage. It can compete on the basis of superior costs or superior products or superior service. There is no fourth way. Most Indian companies, I find, were following the cost/price strategy in the nineties, and this made them vulnerable to devaluations by competing countries. As they learned painfully during the East Asian crisis, their cost advantage disappeared overnight.

It is unrealistic to expect Indian companies to become technology leaders. This is not because Indian scientists are not capable, but because Indian companies will take time to mobilize the power of science and create a technology-driven culture. The companies of South Korea and Taiwan still do not have a technology edge. Eventually, some will become innovation-driven, but it will take us ten to fifteen years to get there after sustained investments in R&D.

I suggested, therefore, in my previous book, *India Unbound*, that the right strategy for Indian companies is the third—to differentiate themselves by offering unparalleled service. This is a far cheaper strategy than to invest in R&D or in cutting prices. In the competitive global market, the quality and price of most products have narrowed to the point where it is mainly service that distinguishes companies. A survey in the United States found that sixty-eight per cent of customers are lost not because of quality or price but because of service. Commitment to a service strategy means that you hire new employees on the basis of their attitude and train them on skills. Most companies do the opposite. No matter which of the three strategies you adopt, however, you have to deliver a threshold level of quality, price and service in order to exist. But in order to gain advantage over others, you must choose one and stay with it.

A strategy based on superior service can build upon the proven capability of Indian traders in the competitive bazaar economy. Anyone who has shopped in a sari store or eaten in an Udipi restaurant can vouch for it. The employee in a typical sari store opens a hundred saris within five minutes in an attempt to sell a single one. Similarly, the waiter in a typical Udipi restaurant or dhaba delivers the customer's thali in two minutes. Among larger companies, Jet Airways is a good example of superior service—to the delight of passengers who have suffered for years at the hands of Indian Airlines.

## How to Build Global Brands

Because I spent most of my career in a multinational company, I am sometimes asked, 'How do multinationals build global brands?' Young Indian entrepreneurs are especially curious to know the formula for global marketing success. They harbour the popular belief that you start with a successful brand name in a domestic market; next, you standardize the product, the packaging and the advertising; then, you push a button and you are on your way to capturing global markets.

I believe, this is a mistaken idea. If it were so simple, why would so many powerful national brands have floundered in the global market? For every success, there are many failures. The truth is that each local subsidiary of a multinational corporation subtly adapts and modifies the standard package from headquarters, 'nationalizes' the product, and makes it into its own national brand. In order to succeed, local managers employ a deep understanding of the habits and attitudes of local customers and, in the process, they invest a great deal of local passion into the brand.

Behind Coke's brilliant success in Japan lies a mastery of the tremendously complex Japanese distribution system. Behind the success of Lux in India lies an understanding of the power of film stars. Behind the success of Toyota in the United States lies a better understanding of the complex and changing segments of the American car market. Behind the success of Ariel detergent in Mexico exists a storehouse of insights about Mexican laundry habits, including the unrequited desire of every Mexican family to own a washing machine.

'Think global and act local', goes the saying, but that's only half the truth. International managers must also think local and then apply their local insights on a global scale. The fact is that truths in this world are unique, individual and highly parochial. They say all politics is local. So is all business. But this doesn't keep either from being global. In committing to our work, we commit to a here and now, to a particular place and time; but what we learn from acting locally is often universal in nature. This is how globalization takes place. Let me illustrate from my own experience in the Indian subsidiary of Procter and Gamble. Indian managers of this global company proudly built one of the largest businesses in the world for Vicks products for colds and coughs. A measure of their success is that three out of four Indians stated in a survey in 1986 that Vicks Vaporub was an 'Indian brand', when, in reality, it is sold in 134 countries and is the most globally available brand in Procter and Gamble's stable.

Over a quarter-century, these managers acclimatized and adapted this global brand to the Indian environment. They tapped into an efficient low-cost distribution system perfected by Marwari traders over more than a hundred years. They successfully introduced a low-cost small tin to meet the needs of a poor country. They discovered that people caught as many colds in the monsoons as in the winter, and they modified their advertising copy and media plan to meet this need. Moves like these helped to make them successful. But they also illustrate the importance of tapping into roots of pluralism in our world.

The enormous success of Vicks, however, made the Indian managers arrogant, and they slowly forgot that they were dealing with a global brand—that the product, positioning and packaging of Vicks Vaporub were basically the same around the world. Thus, when a proven new advertising idea came out of Mexico in the early nineties, they were initially contemptuous of it and dismissed it. They suffered from a disease we called NIH, or 'not invented here'. Eventually, they were pushed to try this new idea and, of course, it worked brilliantly, helping to build volumes for many years. This is the power of globalization, and at Procter and Gamble we learned this lesson again and again, whether through Pantene shampoos or Whisper/Always sanitary napkins or Ariel detergents.

If multinational companies attempt to impose standardized solutions too rigidly, they risk demotivating local managers. They will not find sufficient creative challenges left in the business if all the solutions come packaged from headquarters. On the other hand, if an idea has worked in one part of the world there are good reasons to expect that it will work again. Hence, it would be foolish not to at least test it in other countries. This is, after all, one edge that a multinational company has over a local company. You have to strike a balance between the global and the local.

At least five global brands that I know used to successfully run fairly standardized advertising around the world. The most extreme was Marlboro cigarettes, which made five to six cowboy commercials in the United States and ran them everywhere. Thanks to Hollywood and John Wayne movies, Marlboro had tapped a latent wish for open spaces and American individualism among urban consumers to its advantage to become the global brand leader in sales. Kellogg's Cornflakes, Kodak film, McDonald's and Benetton also used to run common advertising in varying degrees, but they deployed local casting and local situations.

Business truths are invariably local in origin, but they are often expressions of fundamental human needs that are the same worldwide. Local insights with a universal character thus can quickly become global ideas, though only in the hands of flexible, open-minded managers who can translate such ideas into new circumstances with sensitivity and understanding. Thus, the admonition to 'think local and act global' is only half the answer.

## Good Managers

I worked in six countries in my career as a practising manager, and I have concluded that managers in India or abroad are not very different. This is not surprising, for the managerial task is basically the same in all countries. What works may sometimes differ, but even in those cases there are more commonalities than differences. Good managers everywhere, I have observed, are confident and instinctively believe in positive outcomes—what management gurus call a 'win-win' resolution.

Even though good managers are very competitive and have victory ingrained in them—the determination to be first—they have learned to temper their desire for victory with making sure the other person gets something in return. I think this comes from having what is called an 'abundance' mentality—that there is enough to go around. They think that life is not a zero-sum game, and there is plenty for everyone. They not only focus on market share but they also understand that the market itself will grow. Bureaucrats, on the other hand, find it difficult to understand the idea of market growth, and they generally operate with a scarcity mentality.

When working with individuals within the organization or with suppliers, customers and associates without, good managers adopt a positive, mature attitude that leads to long-term success. As they succeed, they gradually win the trust of the people that they work with. They learn to listen and remain open to new ideas, and this reinforces the trust. They pay attention to little things, such as keeping a promise even if it means some inconvenience, and they are straightforward and apologize when they are wrong.

Confidence in a manager is a powerful thing and it can be the source of great competitive advantage. It alone may not solve all our stubborn socio-economic problems, but it does provide 'an essential source of renewable energy', according to Harvard professor James Austin. A manager who is a purveyor of hope is a powerful leader of men. Time and again, we have seen smaller companies beat larger companies because their managers had the positive will to succeed. Over the years in the United States we have seen Toyota and Honda gain market shares from General Motors, CNN beat CBS, British Airways win over Pan American, Sony going ahead of RCA. The giants had stronger reputations, deeper pockets, greater technological riches, bigger market shares and more powerful distribution channels. There were many factors behind the success of the smaller companies, but the chief one was a 'winning attitude', a blind confidence that 'we can do it'.

Good managers begin with trust. I have observed that the typical manager does not trust the average employee. Once you begin to trust people and give them responsibility, they will surprise you. The job of a manager is to get ordinary people to do extraordinary things. The best managers create a feeling in the organization that, at the end of the day, people say 'we did it'. A good leader is thus like mortar between the bricks; he should not try to be one of the bricks. For this, you need to create an open culture, where people are free to disagree, where they try lots of new ideas and are not afraid to fail. A motivated organization where people behave like owners can be a great competitive advantage.

I have always believed that bringing in a new person into your company (or recruiting) is one of the most important jobs of a manager. Yet most managers are not trained in the art of interviewing people. In selecting a new entrant, I have always looked for 'fire in the belly', which is the trait that is the most powerful determinant of future success and the most difficult to perceive in an interview. You can tell if a candidate is intelligent and has a good mind in an interview, but how do you gauge if she is hungry for results, or that she will deliver the goods? I think you can, in fact, uncover this if you discipline yourself in the interview, stick to one event in the candidate's life and probe deep enough to see how she went about delivering the result of which she is so proud. Given a choice between a bright thinker and less bright but hungry doer, I have always preferred the latter.

Good managers instinctively develop the people under them. They are aware that their company will only be as good as the training it imparts to younger people. The best way to train and develop people is on the job. And it has to be each manager's responsibility to train his subordinates. His evaluation and his success must depend equally on how well he does this as on how he does in delivering results. Outside courses and classroom training are infinitely less important than creating a culture of training within the company.

The most important decision that a manager takes is what *not* to do. I have found that the best managers do very few things. But they make sure these are the right things. Then, they do them brilliantly. Finally, they enjoy doing them. Success and happiness lie in absorption and mastery over a small area of life.

## Three Cheers for Software!

The stubborn persistence of our software exports is a source of embarrassment to some of our armchair intellectuals, who have been regularly predicting their crash. Instead, they kept growing by an amazing fifty per cent a year during the nineties, and even in 2001–02, the worst year in the industry's history, they grew about thirty per cent. Any other industry would die for this sort of consistency, and so would our cricket team.

Critics of the industry contemptuously described its work as 'body shopping' and wondered how could such lowly activity last. Then they said that it was the Y2K bug that was keeping it afloat. Well, the bug went away, but our software industry refused to slow down. Next they said the American recession would surely stop it. The recession did hurt, but not to the extent that everyone predicted. Finally, they said that September 11 would be the industry's death knell, but the industry quickly recovered from this crisis as well.

What accounts for the industry's resilience, I think, is that India has emerged as the only serious candidate for outsourcing software. The Philippines is not an option. Ireland has outpriced itself. Israel competes in a different segment. China is at least three to five years away. The only thing that might stop India is a full-scale war with Pakistan, which would raise the risk of outsourcing to unacceptable levels in our customer's eyes.

The major American companies doubled their outsourcing budgets between 2001 and 2002, according to the Forrester survey. Another report says 'that 185 of the Fortune 500 companies are now doing offshore work with Indian companies'. Giga, another industry watcher, expects offshore outsourcing to grow twenty-three per cent in 2002. All the major software suppliers in the United States (including Accenture and EDS) have announced that they are coming to India, which raises the prospect of fairly vigorous acquisition activity.

All this, however, does not convey the pain suffered by the industry during the global recession at the start of the new millennium. The best companies saw their benches grow, prices and margins diminish, engineers laid off, buildings emptied, expansions delayed and hopes destroyed. But from the pain has emerged a stronger and more sophisticated industry. What are the lessons that our software companies have learned from managing in these times?

First, larger, brand name companies will do better in tougher times; weaker, smaller ones will not survive. Second, it is paramount to stay close to the customer. Some Chief Executive Officers (CEOs) of the software companies have physically relocated to the United States. Where they haven't, they now spend greater time there, supported by a strong (usually American) head of sales. Both Wipro and Infosys have increased their physical presence in North America. Their pay-off too has been immediate—they are getting their best ideas for new products and services from their customers.

Third, while it is important to target new customers, the bigger rewards come from harvesting existing ones. Hence, 'key account management' has become a powerful tool. Companies are placing teams of engineers at the customers' disposal to show them newer ways to save costs, improve returns from existing investments, introduce newer applications.

Fourth, vigorous interaction with customers allows a company to demonstrate 'domain expertise'. Infosys has hired a medical doctor to enhance its credibility with its health care customer. An airline customer feels more comfortable talking to a former airline employee, who now works for NIIT. The customer feels 'my software supplier understands my needs', and this removes some of the pressure from the sensitive subject of pricing. It leads to longer term contracts and dedicated offshore centres. Domain knowledge, if captured and retained, is wonderfully aggregative—what you learn from one customer adds value to the next.

Fifth is the power of alliances. For example, Mastek, a software company in Mumbai, has formed a 50:50 joint venture with Deloitte Consulting, which has close to $2 billion in worldwide revenues. A Deloitte executive runs this joint venture, and Deloitte's customers derive comfort from outsourcing their work to someone they trust. Thus, our companies are becoming sophisticated. They are rising in the value chain by offering enterprise resource planning (ERP), applications maintenance and Internet services. They have broken into retail and distribution, professional services, communications and utilities. They have come a long way from the 'coolie days' of Y2K. Those companies who sneered at Y2K work now realize that they lost an opportunity because it opened the door to many large customers.

⌒

Close on the heels of software is another services revolution, which will be much more labour intensive. It is remote services based on the outsourcing of business processes by foreign companies to Indian companies in order to save costs. It also exploits the improvement in global telecommunications. These business out-sourcing services range from medical transcription, accounting, debt collection to digital map-making.

An extraordinary thing happened in the summer of 2002, whose significance seemed to escape almost everyone. While the nation was engrossed in petrol pump scams, Shivani's murder and other weighty matters, Wipro, the software company in Bangalore, quietly bought Spectramind, a call centre in Delhi, from ChrysCapital, a venture capital fund. The call centre was valued at Rs 606 crore and this landmark event sent a strong positive signal to the global financial world that India may finally be coming of age.

How does a call centre create so much wealth for the nation in thirty months? The answer comes in three acts of a play. Act One: Ashish Dhawan, a twenty-eight-year-old graduate from Harvard Business School, quits his enviable job in 1999 with the bluest of the blue-chip investment banks on Wall Street, Goldman Sachs. He and his partner, another young Indian, succeed in raising $65 million in America, and they create a venture capital fund, ChrysCapital, to invest in businesses where India has a competitive advantage. They come to India full of hope, invest in lots of dotcoms and lose lots of money.

Act Two: Raman Roy, the head of General Electric's (GE) call centre, meets Ashish Dhawan and based on ChrysCapital's commitment to back him, he decides to leave his job to become an entrepreneur. Spectramind is thus born. Dhawan backs Roy not only for his experience at GE, but because Roy has customers in hand—one of them is American Express, where Roy had earlier worked. Dhawan too helps in convincing some of his corporate contacts in America to outsource business to Spectramind. Roy persuades some of his key collegues to join him at Spectramind in exchange for a share in the ownership of the company. In thirty months, Spectramind has a dozen Fortune 500 customers, a second centre in Mumbai, and 3,700 employees.

Act Three takes place in Bangalore, where Wipro is seeking other avenues for growth after the global software slowdown and is attracted to business process outsourcing (BPO). Wipro likes BPO because, like software, it can be delivered through the telephone line; software customers can become potential customers of call centres and vice-versa; one can also leverage one's domain expertise (such as in finance, insurance, retail sectors) between the two services, and strengthen one's hold on the customer. Wipro finds Spectramind and quickly realizes that it has found a jewel whose competence would take years and hundreds of crores to duplicate. So, it buys Spectramind from ChrysCapital to give itself a jump-start.

There are many lessons in this story. First, it demonstrates that BPO call centres are a robust business. No wonder it has been growing seventy per cent a year and is now worth $1.6 million to the nation, employing more than 100,000 people. McKinsey's projection is also beginning to make sense; BPO has to grow only twenty-seven per cent till 2008 to deliver $17 billion in revenues and employment of a million people. Spectramind's example shows that the starting point in this business is to win a customer and that needs full-time sales employees overseas. Ideally, the CEO of the company should be based overseas close to customers.

The second lesson is that venture capital can play a wonderful role in nurturing entrepreneurs, but it needs an exit door in order to deliver returns to the investors. When ChrysCapital sent cheques to its international investors from the proceeds of the Spectramind sale, India's image soared in world capital markets. Third, reforms create wealth for the nation. Telecom costs have dropped to one-fourth of the levels three years ago and our telecom infrastructure is improving by the day. This obviously improves the competitiveness of our call centres, and makes India an attractive BPO destination. Finally, globalization can create enormous wealth for a poor country. GE, the American multinational, came and pioneered the call centre business in India by transferring its business processes from around the world. In the process it has trained 10,000 Indians to collect debt, authorize credit, process insurance, do payroll accounting—all remotely over the telephone line.

It seems to me that the export of software and IT services are to India today what textile exports were to Britain in the early nineteenth century. If you were a Londoner in the 1820s you would have seen lots of textiles going off to India, but you wouldn't have seen an industrial revolution. Similarly, I think we can see these technology exports, but we cannot see a services revolution that may be transforming India.

Like the rest of the world, we are becoming a services economy. In the nineties, services have exploded and now account for more than fifty per cent of our GDP, while industry and agriculture each roughly accounts for a quarter of the nation's wealth. Some argue that we seem to have skipped the industrial revolution, when the industrial segment should become the overwhelming and the driving force of GDP. If this is true, then we may have lost an opportunity to create a vast number of higher productivity jobs that come with the exports of labour-intensive manufacturing of simple products, as Europe and East Asia discovered to their happy surprise at the point of their take-off.

What is this strange animal called 'services' that is driving our economy? In part, it is the usual banking, trading and retail activities of the bazaar, but, increasingly, new services are emerging. Private schools are mushrooming in villages and towns across the country. MBA or management education is a growth industry. Private clinics are cropping up in many small towns. Computer lessons have become as ubiquitous as STD booths, with NIIT having reached thousands of towns. Villages in Punjab and Haryana are dotted with beauty parlours.

Whether we are going to skip the manufacturing revolution and leap into the services age is unclear. What is clearer is that an entrepreneurial revolution is under way, and this is what we predicted when we began to liberalize our economy. From the bazaars of Amritsar to the high-tech firms in Bangalore, entrepreneurs began to transform India in the nineties in ways that we did not quite understand.

It is to Joseph Schumpeter, the Austrian economist at Harvard, that we owe our contemporary use of the word 'entrepreneur'. Schumpeter wanted to be the world's 'greatest horseman, greatest lover, and greatest economist'. He claimed that he succeeded in achieving two of the three ambitions—he and horses just didn't get along.

Schumpeter took an old word from the economics dictionary and used it to describe the secret of the capitalist system. Capitalism is dynamic and brings growth, he explained, because the entrepreneur introduces technological or organizational innovations, which bring new or cheaper ways of making things or ways of making wholly new things. These innovations create a flow of income, which cannot be explained either by the contribution of labour or capital. The new process enables the innovating capitalist to produce the same goods at a lower cost, and this cost differential raises his profit until other capitalists learn the same trick. Schumpeter's great insight was that this profit is not due to inherited or God-given advantages but it springs from the will and intelligence of the innovator or entrepreneur.

Secondly, the new money flow is not permanent 'rent' but transient profit. The innovator is not a 'normal' businessman, following established practices and norms; nor is he a representative of a social class. He is someone who introduces discontinuous change in economic life, combining the element of production or service in a new way. On the heels of the innovator, says Schumpeter, come a swarm of imitators, and soon everyone wants to invest in the new idea. Banks get busy making loans to the imitators, everyone begins to talk of a boom and there is a rash of capital spending

As with all booms, however, supply soon shoots ahead of demand; soon there is huge excess capacity. With competition, prices are quickly forced down and gradually profits begin to decline, as business once again becomes a routine. And as profits disappear, so does investment, and this leads to a bust. Schumpeter's entrepreneur falls as well, squeezed out of his share of income, ironically, by the very dynamic of the process that he set in motion. Schumpeter calls this process 'creative destruction'.

The individual that emerges from his vision is a romantic, almost tragic, figure. Entrepreneurship is not a profession or a position that is handed down from one generation to the next. He is not a glamorous leader like a general or statesmen. Nor is he a respected member of the business class. Yet, he craves for social esteem and respect. In *The Theory of Economic Development*, Schumpeter says, 'When his economic success raises him up socially, he has no cultural tradition or attitude to fall back on, but moves about in society as an upstart, whose ways are readily laughed at, and we understand why this type has never been popular.'

Why then does Schumpeter's entrepreneur carry out his precarious and often thankless task? Schumpeter adds, 'There is the dream and the will to found a private dynasty—then there is the will to conquer, the impulse to fight, to prove oneself superior to others, to succeed for the sake, not of the fruits of success itself, but of success itself. Finally, there is the joy of creating, of getting things done, or simply of exercising one's energy and imagination.'

But how times have changed! In Schumpeter's days in the first half of the twentieth century, old wealth used to look down contemptuously on new money. The newly rich have always been objects of derision. Satyajit Ray's brilliant film, *Jalsaghar*, offers only one example, but nineteenth and early twentieth century novels from around the world are liberally littered with this social prejudice. Now, however, perhaps for the first time in history, the new millionaires are looked up to with pride and even reverence. For they are a new meritocracy—entrepreneur-professionals, who are creating value by innovating in the global knowledge economy. Hence, we look up to Narayana Murthy, Azim Premji and the heads of the top twenty software companies. In September 1999, *Business Standard* published a list of hundred Indian billionaires in which eight of the top ten were first generation entrepreneurs. Six had made their fortunes in the knowledge industries. Most did not inherit wealth, nor did they have a family name. They reflected a new social contract of post-reform India where talent, hard work and managerial skill had replaced inherited wealth.

Even though the valuations of the new companies have dramatically come down since the crash on Nasdaq in 2000, and the wealth of these new entrepreneurs has diminished, they have shown that Indians can build vibrant, globally competitive companies. They have inspired both new entrepreneurs and energized some of the young in the old family business houses to shed a few of their hopelessly diversified and uncompetitive commodity businesses and begin to create shareholder value by reinventing their enterprises. It will take time, but the churning is taking place, and eventually some globally competitive companies will emerge from amongst them.

Our economic reforms are based on the unspoken premise that if conditions are favourable, entrepreneurs will make their appearance. Economic historians have long debated the many causes of this great transformation, but it was Schumpeter more than anyone who recognized the Promethean role of the entrepreneur. Our nineties also brought about a significant change in attitudes. Young Indians are no longer embarrassed about wanting to be rich. Hence, the nineties brought a vast number of stories of 'rags to riches' and once again to rags, because, not surprisingly, most of the new ventures failed.

The important thing is that the economic reforms did release bottled up energies and created a new confidence and a feeling that 'we can do it'. Vikas Kedia is only one example of that new mindset. In the spring of 2000 the twenty-three-year-old MBA from the Indian Institute of Management, Bangalore, turned down a campus offer of a job paying $100,000 (Rs 45 lakh a year at the time) with the Mitchell Madison group in order to pursue his own dream. After that, he worked sixteen hours a day in his thirteen feet by thirteen feet room getting his start-up idea ready. With the dotcom bust he never got venture capital funding, but the fact that he was willing to take the risk speaks volumes for the entrepreneurial spirit of India's nineties.

## *It Is Easier to Make Money than to Give It Away*

American industrialist Andrew Carnegie used to say, 'Anybody who dies rich dies disgraced.' John D. Rockefeller Sr. took his words to heart and he set about transforming Standard Oil from the largest money-making machine into the greatest money-giving machine in history. By the time he died, he had given away the equivalent of $6 billion at today's prices. In the nineties, Bill Gates announced plans to donate most of his $79 billion fortune in Microsoft stock before he died. All this sounds a bit strange to us in India because we are unaware that philanthropy is part of the unspoken contract underlying the American dream.

'Anyone can give away money,' said Gates when he announced his philanthropic plans, 'but the point is to give sensibly.' How should an Indian who wants to make a difference go about giving sensibly? Most Indian companies and businessmen traditionally make ad hoc donations to temples, schools and hospitals. They passively accede to requests rather than actively seeking out worthwhile projects. They prefer to endow buildings to perpetuate their name rather than build up human capabilities. They give 'fish' to the poor rather than teaching them 'how to fish'. They manage charities on a part-time basis using their own staff rather than funding professional non-government organizations (NGOs) who have experience and expertise. It is ironic that these same companies employ highly qualified professionals to conduct their businesses but do not think twice about letting amateurs oversee their non-profit activities. In short, charity in India has not graduated into serious philanthropy.

The average business leader in India, I am convinced, has a social conscience and would like to do something for the community. However, he or she usually doesn't know where to start. Fortunately, a new breed of professionals has come up in India who view philanthropy as an instrument of economic development and social change. They have coherent long-term perspectives based on a deep understanding of poverty. They make feasibility studies, conduct pilot projects, monitor field activities, and make detailed assessments to ensure that the money is well spent. Some of these professional bodies are 'clearing houses' and they include the Centre for the Advancement of Philanthropy, the Indian Centre of Philanthropy, the National Foundation for India, Society for Service to Voluntary Agencies (SOSVA), ActionAid and Partners-in-Change, among others. They have built up a computerized database of donors and donees and help to link them together. They know which charities will make suitable partners for which businesses.

At the same time, dozens of excellent NGOs have emerged in India in the past two decades, headed by outstanding young social entrepreneurs. Their success has encouraged hundreds of young people to care about society and seize the initiative. For philanthropy to flourish, our government also needs to reduce controls. It is our good fortune that thousands of idealistic young Indians have joined NGOs, but it is heartbreaking to see them spend so much time battling government controls. Today, there are more than 20,000 NGOs who spend roughly Rs 4,000 crore a year through several lakh employees. Inevitably, such a large operation has also led to abuses.

Because Indians do not support these professionally-run NGOs, most of them have to depend on foreign generosity. To receive foreign funds, NGOs need clearance under the Foreign Contributions Regulations Act (FCRA), which was enacted during the Emergency to prevent money going to Jayaprakash Narayan's movement against Indira Gandhi. Today, the FCRA is mainly used by bureaucrats to extract bribes. It has not stopped a single terrorist from getting foreign funds, which was its purpose. Isn't it time that we abolished the FCRA in the same spirit as we have scrapped FERA? The liberalization of controls will give a huge fillip to philanthropy in India and it will certainly improve the lives of thousands of idealistic youth.

The economic reforms of 1991 have begun to create new wealth in our society and will do much more in the future. Some of the new millionaires, especially in the technology areas, are already beginning to demonstrate a commitment to philanthropy. Ultimately, it is wealthy individuals and business leaders who will make a thousand flowers bloom in this field. However, real success will come from effective partnerships between business and NGOs. For this to happen, the people who work in the NGOs also need to show greater sensitivity and a more enlightened attitude towards the business world. Today, their attitude is one of contempt. They have to understand that businesses create enormous jobs and wealth for society, by doing what they do. Also, business people have to justify charitable donations to their auditors, shareholders and to the tax authorities. They have to appreciate that any expenses which do not further the revenues and profits of an enterprise are, strictly speaking, not legitimate.

It is not easy to donate intelligently. George Bundy, head of the Ford Foundation, used to tell Henry Ford II, 'Henry, your job is easier; it is only to make money. My job is tougher—it is to give your money away, wisely.'

*This column above generated an unusually large response from readers, some of it from business people and companies asking for the addresses of the philanthropic 'clearing houses', and I give this information below: (1) Indian Centre for Philanthropy, C-8/8704 Vasant Kunj, New Delhi 110070, Phone: 6899368, 6121917, Fax: 6121917; (2) National Foundation for India, India Habitat Centre, Zone IV-A, Lodhi Road, New Delhi 110003, Phone: 4641864/65, Fax: 4641867 (3) Centre for Advancement of Philanthropy, Mulla House, 4th Floor, 51, M.G. Road, Mumbai 400001, Phone: 2846534 (4) Society for Service to Voluntary Agencies (SOSVA), Shardaram Park, 'A' Wing, 3rd Floor, Pune 411001, Phone: 622555, 621287, Fax: 626130 (5) Mr Anil Singh, Voluntary Action Network India, B-52, Shivalik Colony, Malviya Nagar, New Delhi 110017, Phone: 6426369.*

# PART THREE

## *Public Space*

*As soon as public service ceases to be the chief business of the citizens, and they would rather serve with their money than with their persons, the State is not far from its fall.*

—Rousseau, *The Social Contract* (1772)

# 7

## *Learning to Live, Living to Learn*

*The schools of the country are its future in miniature.*
—Chinese Proverb

We are a nation so disappointed with itself that we have become immune to good news. So when it does come, we either ignore it or cynically dismiss it with a shrug. Census 2000 is an example—it brought the happy news that literacy in India had jumped from fifty-two to sixty-five per cent during the last decade. This is a major achievement, for it means that the growth rate of literacy doubled during the nineties from 0.7 per cent a year historically to 1.4 per cent. It also means that millions of children have been liberated from the bondage of ignorance, with the greatest gains having come from rural areas, the backward Hindi states and among girls.

Having said that, it is also worth remembering that the census measures literacy of a very rudimentary sort, and it hides more than it reveals the gigantic failures of our government school system. There is no easy answer to the puzzle that literacy should have gone up while government schools remained so miserably wretched. So, how did this happen?

The essays in this chapter deal with various aspects of education. I begin with the miracle in Madhya Pradesh and its Education

Guarantee Scheme that became a model for many states in the nineties. The second essay, entitled 'If Indians Can, Why Can't We?' deals with another sort of miracle—the mushrooming of private schools among the poor, which has been precipitated by the failure of our government schools. The next deals with Kerala and points to the equal importance of fostering markets as well as social investment. Finally, I try to draw lessons for education policy from our cricket mania.

The literacy achievement of the nineties, I am convinced, was more the result of demand than supply. Parental motivation has been rising, as mothers and fathers are increasingly realizing, even in the most backward villages, that education is the passport to their child's future. On the supply side, there was a combination of initiatives. First, the District Primary Education Programme (DPEP) has made an impact. This internationally-funded initiative has encouraged the practice of making teachers accountable to local communities. The concept of para-teacher (*shiksha karmi*), has also become popular and we now have an astounding number—around 500,000—para-teachers, who are helping overcome the problems of money and chronic teacher absenteeism, the scourge of primary education in rural areas in the Hindi heartland.

Second, mushrooming private schools of varying quality, in towns and villages across India, are increasingly meeting people's aspirations. The state-run schools, especially in the Hindi belt, have grown so rotten that people have taken matters into their hands and pulled their children out of government schools and put them into indifferent private schools, where the teacher at least shows up and some teaching does take place.

Third, outstanding individuals in some states are making a huge difference. Mass literacy in Madhya Pradesh, Rajasthan and Andhra Pradesh climbed twenty percentage points in the nineties. In Madhya Pradesh, for example, literacy rose from forty-four to sixty-four per cent in the nineties. Compare this to a six points gain in the sixties, eleven points in the seventies and six in the eighties. Female literacy in the state also climbed an impressive twenty-two percentage points—from a lowly twenty-eight per cent to fifty per cent. Madhya Pradesh and Rajasthan have begun to replicate Himachal Pradesh's education miracle, which saw a huge jump in literacy in the eighties, and soon they might stop being contemptible Bimaru states (a word constructed from the names of Bihar, Madhya Pradesh, Rajasthan and Uttar Pradesh and meaning sickly).

Chief Minister Digvijay Singh made the best move of his life the day he announced the Education Guarantee Scheme in Madhya Pradesh. Inspired by insights gained from voluntary organizations, he encouraged some audacious officers to implement a daring programme that empowered local communities to provide primary education. What makes this scheme different from its predecessors is that it begins at the grass roots and not with the education bureaucracy. Equally significantly, it has been evolving, getting better year after year.

The process of setting up a school in this scheme begins with at least twenty-two parents signing up to 'demand' a school. The village panchayat then comes up with a space for a classroom, and, together with the parents' committee, identifies a local resident to be a teacher. The block panchayat verifies that the demand is genuine and the teacher is qualified. The district administration then transfers the funds to the village panchayat, provides free books and teaching materials and trains the teacher. This is a time-bound process and the school is up and running in three months.

The strength of the scheme is that it is rapid, affordable, accountable and community centred. It recognizes the urgency of time—children cannot be kept waiting for what is their birthright. It is economical—it costs Rs 18,000 annually per school, plus the cost of mid-day meals. Compare this to the Rs 3,000 *per child per year* that the government spends on formal schools. The para-teacher is paid less than Rs 1,000 per month (compared to roughly Rs 4,000 paid to the regular teacher) but the panchayat is encouraged to supplement this. The para-teacher is also a local person and accountable to the village, and this helps to get over today's biggest problem—teacher absenteeism in the formal government schools.

The programme being community centred means that parents want the school, are willing to provide a space for it, and supervise it. The teaching material is relevant to life in the village, and it tries to enthuse the learner, unlike the idiotic rote learning models of the formal schools.

In the beginning, critics called this programme mad and impudent. However, they are silenced today for the results have been overwhelming. By the end of the nineties, more than 26,000 such schools had opened. During its heyday in 1998, schools were opening at the rate of forty a month. Of the students enrolled in these alternative schools, forty-five per cent were girls and sixty-eight per cent were tribals and Dalits. The total cost of establishing these schools was also incredibly small—around Rs 20 crore, including the cost of mid-day meals.

Some of the criticism is also valid. Critics see in this scheme a conspiracy by the state to off-load the burden of primary education to the village panchayats. They rightly point out the flaws—too often sarpanches are tempted to appoint their daughters and nieces as teachers. Critics also worry that alternative schools might institutionalize dualism between two types of schooling systems. Moreover, an unscrupulous politician might make para-teachers permanent. These are real concerns.

The critics, however, overlook the richness of the achievement. Tests administered by independent experts of the Indian Institute of Management, Ahmedabad, found that children in these non-formal schools run by para-teachers consistently outperformed those in the formal government schools. The experimentation with the curriculum in these schools, such as the 'joyful learning' package developed by the voluntary organization, Eklavya, is making a significant difference in young children's development.

Having said that, the Education Guarantee Scheme faces huge challenges. Where the community structure is feudal and rotten, it works very slowly. To get around the problem, the pioneers of the scheme have gradually handed over the running of these schools from the politicized panchayats to the *gram shiksha samitis* (village education committees) or parents associations. Now parents play an active role in selecting the teacher and monitoring the school. Another problem initially lay in the poor training of teachers. But this has also been corrected, and teachers in these schools are re-trained for fifteen days every year.

Madhya Pradesh is clearly teaching us many lessons about primary education. Another one is that there is clearly a huge demand for education at the grass roots. The state education bureaucracies had been lying to us for decades, saying that parents were apathetic and this was the reason for high dropout rates and poor attendance in our schools. The truth has turned out to be different. Parents always wanted to educate their children. The children, too, wanted to go to school if they thought that teachers cared.

The state's experience shows that the commitment and attitude of the teacher is far more important than qualifications or salary, or even the school facilities. A few teachers in every society will always be committed to excellence, but for the majority, this commitment is fostered by accountability. In our present formal schools, teachers get away without teaching because they know that no one is looking. They are responsible to bureaucrats in the education ministry in distant state capitals, and poor villagers are intimidated by them, and powerless to enforce good behaviour. The teachers' unions have ensured that our centralized, bureaucratic school systems will not change. We can only expel this evil in the short term by hiring teachers locally and by making schools accountable to parents. This is precisely what Madhya Pradesh has achieved.

The news from the latest census is encouraging and we have reasons to feel good. What the census does not reflect is a change in attitudes to primary education in India. Some state governments are becoming allies of non-profit organizations, and together they are mobilizing and empowering local communities and people. Having recognized that they cannot reform their own bureaucracies, chief ministers like Digvijay Singh, S.M. Krishna of Karnataka and

Chandrababu Naidu of Andhra Pradesh are working around the old apparatus to reach out to the people and empowering them. When it comes to education, Digvijay Singh has bypassed his teachers' unions and education bureaucrats and is slowly devolving power to villages and parents.

## If Indians Can, Why Can't We?

The English have been surprised by Professor James Tooley's observations that India can teach Britain something about education. This is an unusual spin over the usual foreign expert who patronizingly offers us advice on how to improve ourselves. Indeed, when Tooley wrote about this in the *Times Education Supplement*, his editor was so perplexed that he inserted a photo of a cow in front of an impoverished school in Bihar with the caption, 'Education in India has a lot to teach the British'—implying, perhaps, that the good professor had lost it.

The professor of education from Newcastle has been documenting a 'self-help' revolution in Indian towns and villages as education entrepreneurs are opening private schools and creating opportunities for the poor to rise. Most Indians would agree that private schools are indeed mushrooming across India, although they worry about their indifferent quality. But it may be one of the factors behind the doubling of the growth rate of literacy in the nineties. Tooley argues that India's blossoming spirit has much to teach Britain's poorer inner city areas.

Most of us were shocked when, in 1998, the government-sponsored *Public Report on Basic Education in India* (PROBE) disclosed that teaching was going on in only fifty-three per cent of government schools in the villages of Madhya Pradesh, Bihar, Uttar Pradesh and Rajasthan. Teachers were absent in one-third; many had brazenly closed their schools and were busy running shops. Some teachers were found drunk and a few even expected pupils to bring them *daru* (liquor). A few were asleep; others engaged the girls in domestic chores, including minding their babies.

Given this, is it surprising that parents are turning to private schools in more and more communities? PROBE also confirmed that village private schools, in contrast, had 'feverish classroom activity' and more dedicated teachers. The reason, it said, was that teachers were accountable to managers (who could fire them) and to parents (who could remove their children). Research shows that these private schools charge modest rates—from Rs 35 to Rs 50 per month in villages and Rs 65 to Rs 100 in towns. They are also popular because they teach English.

In the slums behind the Charminar in Hyderabad, a private school exists in every alley. Five hundred such schools belong to the Federation of Private Schools, and they are mainly working among poor communities. They are run on commercial principles, charging Rs 750 per year, and they do not depend on state subsidies or private charity. Typical parents include rickshaw pullers and vegetable and fruit sellers, and many schools offer free seats to roughly twenty per cent of the poorest students. Tooley has observed this same phenomenon of the rapid growth in private schools in the poor communities of Thailand, Colombia, Tanzania and Chile. Cheap, private schools, it seems, are doing more for the poor because state education has let the poor down.

What does this mean for our education policy reform? Obviously we have to fix the shocking state of our government schools. But we must also nurture and encourage these rapidly growing private schools. Today, private schools face great hostility because we have not got used to the idea that education can be commercial. Indeed, the infamous Unnikrishnan judgement of the Supreme Court prohibits 'commercialization' of education. The bureaucracy exploits our society's prejudice and it has created a virtual licence raj in education, which makes it impossible to start a new school without paying a bribe. Education entrepreneurs face a plethora of regulations, which limit competition, create artificial scarcity and allow existing schools to exploit parents.

Their major problem continues to be 'recognition' of these schools. To obtain recognition, schools are required to have, for example, playgrounds, among dozens of other requirements. That is all very well, but private schools for the poor cannot afford these middle class luxuries. Indeed, the Prime Minister's Economic Advisory Council has recognized this problem and has recommended that 'education must be liberalized and all entry–exit restrictions and bureaucratic hurdles faced by [private] schools and colleges should be abolished'.

Instead of flaying the state for the umpteenth time for its failures, we should ask hard questions: Given the shocking state of government schools, can we trust the state to deliver education? If we can't trust it to produce bread, how can we trust it with the minds of our young? However, in our vast country only the state has the resources for universal primary education. Hence, the solution is 'state-aided' schools. The government must give up running schools and become a non-interfering funds provider. Running schools is best left to education professionals, voluntary organizations and 'edu-preneurs' on a contract whose renewal is based on performance. Indeed, there are organizations today which already run parallel schools (inside government schools during off hours in some cases) and they are delivering excellent results. Once this happens, new schools will emerge, creativity will blossom and parents will have choice. The miserable state schools will also improve when they are forced to compete, and if they do not, parents will pull their children out and they will either have to close down or be sold off.

This idea will take time to get accepted, but the thinking middle class can make a beginning and become more understanding of these new private schools. It is odd that our judiciary, with the enthusiastic support of the middle class, is up in arms against private education. It thinks that schools are profiteering at the expense of parents. The Justice K.S. Duggal Committee on private schools, set up after a Delhi High Court order, has condemned the 'exorbitant fees paid by harassed parents'. The Karnataka government has banned donations to private schools and colleges following a High Court order and introduced price control on school fees.

This only shows that our middle class is economically illiterate. The honourable judges, with due respect, are also wrong. The fact is that schools run by the government are so uniformly bad that private schools are the only recourse for the middle class. However, there are not enough private schools. And the oldest law in economics says that when demand exceeds supply, prices will rise. We have in the past fifty years painfully learned that the answer to rising prices is not to control them but to increase supply. Price controls are self-defeating—they destroy quality, inhibit the growth of supply and only expand the powers and wallets of bureaucrats.

Private education is not a public good. If you do not like a school, you can remove your child from it. Private schools operate in the market and they are subject to competitive market forces and they also have a right to a decent profit. The real issue in private education is not of equity but of quality. Parents, after all, choose to pay for a private education in preference to a practically free state education. Rising fees of private schools are the result of a mismatch between supply and demand. If there is profit in education, new entrepreneurs will enter the market, and eventually supply will catch up with demand. When that happens, there will be stiff competition for pupils among rival schools. Schools will quickly realize that in order to retain students or attract new ones they will have to either improve quality or lower fees. Hence, the market can, to a great extent, solve the problem of high fees. We do not need price controllers.

Among the millions of boys and girls who dash off to school every morning go not one but several future prime ministers, Supreme Court judges, dozens of chairmen of major corporations, vice-chancellors of universities, secretaries to the government, eminent scientists and men of letters. How do we make sure that the very best of these children rather than mediocrities will rise to the top to lead us in the future? The answer is quality education. The wealth of a nation consists in the number of superior men and women it harbours. In a competitive world where global market share is increasingly determining winners and losers among nations, we have a responsibility to ensure that our leaders have the ability to engage and win in the global contest. The sad truth is that these leaders are unlikely to come from state-run schools. Not because students in government schools are less bright, but because they do not receive a proper education. Quality education needs autonomy from the state. The middle class is thus fighting the wrong battle. It should fight to free education from the shackles of bureaucracy, rather than fight for price control.

At the same time, the state has responsibility to fund primary education. Hence we ought to fight to make life easier for state-aided schools. Fighting for high standards does not mean that one is elitist. The best schools and colleges must and do offer a part of their seats on scholarship to bright but poor students. This is the model in the United States, where alumni generously fund scholarships for outstanding men and women of ability.

Philosopher Alfred North Whitehead once said, 'In the conditions of modern life the rule is absolute, the race which does not value trained intelligence is doomed.' In the nineties, we have witnessed in India a revolution in our attitude to men and women of ability. Earlier, we were extravagantly wasteful of talent. Today, ask the head of any major company and he or she will tell you that their biggest problem is to find executives with leadership ability. Only a sound education equips a person to be a leader. So, the answer is to vastly expand our net for talent.

## Does Sen Make Sense?

A few years ago, I met a charming mother of two from Kerala. The subject of Amartya Sen came up. 'You must be pleased,' I said, 'that he has put Kerala on the world map.' I was surprised by her answer.

'He doesn't understand the tragedy of being a mother from

Kerala. All our young people have gone away. There are no jobs in Kerala. What's the point of having the highest literacy rate in India? You work hard to bring up your young and then they are forced to leave you. Is this what life is all about?'

I was left with a vague sense of unease. She was suggesting that while Sen emphasizes education and health, he underplays the importance of creating dynamic markets, investment and economic growth. Children leave Kerala because there are no jobs there. There are no jobs because the state is hostile to private investment. No sensible entrepreneur invests in Kerala because of an adversarial labour and government.

However, for her to blame Sen, I thought, was not entirely fair. After all, her children were not deprived in the same way as the desperately poor and illiterate in the Hindi belt that Sen is concerned with. At least the Keralites have a choice. Education has empowered them to find a living elsewhere, if not at home. Having said that, I also believe Sen would sympathize with her dilemma. Her sadness was genuine and Sen, I think, would be the first to admit Kerala's weaknesses.

Sen has said many times that Kerala is not an ideal model, despite its impressive literacy achievements. India also needs economic reform, better-functioning markets, less public sector and more globalization. Thus, we are engaged in a bogus debate in India between efficiency and equity, growth and redistribution, and globalization and national sovereignty. Almost everyone in the world now agrees that a successful nation needs both dynamic markets and social investment and good governance to end poverty.

I was first attracted to Sen by the elegant way he had developed the philosophic notion of human capabilities and placed it at centre stage in policy debates. He had argued that the wealth and poverty of a nation is not measured only by the growth of income per head, but real development was about expanding the opportunities for individuals in society. This meant increasing the freedom of citizens to pursue what they value by expanding their capabilities. Enhancing a person's capability is to increase one's choices about the kind of life one wishes to lead. A poor person lacks opportunities and is not capable of doing many things. A poor person is thus 'capability deprived' and less free. Merely going to primary school opens one's horizon and makes one employable in new areas. Secondary school adds to these choices and higher education further multiplies one's capabilities. That half our population is illiterate means that half our people are still unfree more than fifty years after Independence, and do not have a chance of fulfilling their capabilities.

Nevertheless, Sen is responsible for the hype around Kerala. Because of his advocacy we have come to believe that Kerala is a model of successful government policies in education. We avidly read V.K. Ramachandran's essay on Kerala's achievements in *Indian Economic Development—Selected Regional Perspectives*, edited by Jean Dreze and Sen, and we believed that the communists at least educated the people. We concluded that the answer was for the state to raise its spending on education and everything would look after itself. Thus, our battle-cry throughout the nineties was to lift India's spending on education to six per cent of GDP.

The truth, we have discovered, is more complicated. In digging deeper we have now found that the real reason for Kerala's success lay not in government policies but in community action. The initial spark for the spread of education began more than a hundred years ago with the Christian missionaries who set up the first modern, open-to-all schools in the old state of Travancore. This spurred the Nair community, led by Mannathu Padmanabhan, to set up a vast number of community schools. The backward Muslims and the Ezhavas did not want to be left behind and they followed the example. Kerala's community initiatives also led to the state's famous reading room movement and libraries came up in the smallest villages.

After Independence, the left parties unionized the teachers, brought the schools under state control, and forced the government to pay their salaries. But even today sixty-five per cent of Kerala's 12,400 schools are in private hands. The lesson from Kerala is that success in education usually comes from private and community efforts, and not from the state. Americans have learned the same lesson. Their best schools are in communities where parents are involved and parent–teacher associations are strong. Even a few volunteers can make the difference. Wherever this American idea of community initiative has been tried, such as in *gram shiksha samitis* (village education committees) in Madhya Pradesh and Andhra Pradesh or by voluntary organizations in other parts of India, it has made all the difference—despite enormous opposition from the bureaucracy.

We have learned from painful experience that the state is highly inefficient in providing education, just as it is inefficient in producing steel, watches, power or banking services. The Indian state spends Rs 3,000 per child per year in primary education, but a third of our children are illiterate. Government teachers earn Rs 5,000 to Rs 15,000 per month but a shocking number of them do not show up in classrooms. The ones that do are uninspired and pour rote learning into students. The reform of Indian education has to begin with the conviction that schools have to become accountable to parents and neighbourhoods instead of to bureaucrats. We have to fight for the autonomy of our schools and make teachers responsible to parents.

Since the state has failed as a producer of education, its role should change to one of enabler. Libertarian Parth Shah in his *Agenda for Change* suggests that the state should completely get out of classroom teaching and NGOs or panchayats or the private sector should run schools and charge fees. The state should give parents coupons worth Rs 3,000 per child per year—what it spends in educating each child. The central idea is competition among schools and choice for parents. If their neighbourhood school is bad, parents should be able to move their child to a competing school. Some schools will charge the basic price of, say, Rs 3,000 a year; others will charge more and offer higher quality education; and some parents will be willing to supplement coupons with their own funds. Thus, schools will compete for students and become innovative in providing better education. Parents will be empowered, teachers will be forced to become 'customer friendly' and Indian education will come into its own.

This may sound radical, but the idea of putting parents in charge of the Rs 3,000 per child per year that the government spends on education today is sensible. The key is that one does not need to increase spending to dramatically improve the quality of education. But will our parents return the compliment and get involved in parent–teacher associations? I think they will because all parents want their children to get ahead.

There is a concept in yoga called one-pointedness (*ekagrata* in Sanskrit.) Successful governments, like successful companies, have an uncanny ability to be one-pointed, while seeming to do hundreds of things in the routine of the day. There is a vast unfinished agenda of reform, but if I were to select only one item, and make it the one-pointed purpose of our government, I would unhesitatingly choose education reform. Eliminating illiteracy will do more for the average Indian than almost anything else. An educated workforce will give Indian companies competitive advantage in today's workplace, which demands a 'knowledge worker'; it will raise the backward castes far more than reservations by making them employable. It will lead to better governance as the voter becomes more responsible. It will liberate Indians, for, as Epictetus says, 'only the educated are free'.

## Cementing Kerala with Haryana

Indians, they say, do not win cricket World Cups because 'we don't have a winning spirit'. Others think that we lack a 'killer instinct'. Forget this twaddle, I say. A competitive culture is inbuilt in children. They worship sporting heroes and love victory. Give them a ball, a bat and a space and they will mark out a pitch with their shoes and they will play to win. Give them less homework and banish them from coaching classes. It is about a simple chance to have a go.

There is a ratty municipal playground near my house where the children of the neighbourhood come out and play. At any time there are two or three cricket games in progress, usually with a tennis ball. One day there was a breathless hush on this ground— four balls left, six runs to make and the last man in. Pure of heart, a ten-year-old schoolboy walked to the wicket. The young hero flashed at the first ball. The second ball he smote for a four. He hit the third ball uppishly, but the catch was missed. The last ball was a beauty but our young hero was not daunted—he hit a straight drive in the manner of Rahul Dravid, and it fetched him three runs and the match. The joyful grin on his face as he walked towards his father said it all.

Winning World Cups or beating Pakistan are good to talk about but they are not the point. It is not the lack of the 'will to win', nor the deficit in 'killer instinct', but the lack of opportunity for our children to go outdoors and tire themselves out. We do not have enough scrubby open spaces in our towns and there are too few playgrounds in our schools. We need teachers who show up, and a slack in the school day, which motivates schoolteachers to organize games after hours. We need to give our children a break from the intolerable burden of rote learning. The experts are wrong when they say that we must spot talent at birth and 'fast track' it through elite cricket academies. The truth is that talent will emerge at different speeds through informal kickabouts and tennis-ball cricket games. Ad hoc games, at school and close to home on dusty bits of hard ground, will do more to lay the foundation of great sporting careers in talented children.

The high-minded complain about the commercialization of cricket. They lay the blame, yet again, on the economic reforms and the culture of television and greed. Rubbish, I say. It is not Gandhi or Nehru or even democracy that holds India together. It is our cricket team that we can watch on television for free because advertising pays for it. Each time Tendulkar hits a straight drive for a four he cements Kerala with Haryana and Ranchi with Kolhapur. What if he grunts *yeh dil mange more* for Pepsi? Tendulkar has come to be the metaphor of India. Whether he scores a century or gets out for a duck, his performance reflects every Indian's tenuous grasp on success and happiness. With every square cut he gives our millions a vital lesson in what it means to be an Indian. Cricket in India is more than recreation for the masses. It is about human possibilities. It is a means to upward mobility and it furthers the social revolution created by the ballot box by giving the sahibs and non-sahibs common heroes.

Fifty years after Britain left our shores, this game of the English village green has found new energy in the hot and dusty plains of South Asia. Lords may still be the Mecca of cricket, but the future history of the game will be written in the huge stadiums of our subcontinent. Without question, the genuine enthusiasm of our crowds provides the real fun of international competition.

Lastly, something for our swadeshi-wallahs to note. The last World Cup demonstrated that the global economy is a two-way street. While the non-Western world has been strongly shaped by Western ideas, the West is today adopting and adapting to non-Western fashions, faces and ideas. They could also remember the fear on English cricketers' faces as they faced India at Edgbaston in 1999, and wondered if they were, in fact playing an 'away game'.

# 8

## The Ambiguous Village

*When tillage begins, other arts follow. The farmers therefore are the
founders of human civilization.*

—Daniel Webster, 1840

'Teenage lovers hanged to death as hundreds look on,' read the
bold headline of a page five report from Alinagar in Uttar Pradesh's
Muzaffarnagar district on 6 August 2000. It told the tragic story of
Sonu, a Jat girl, and Vishal, a Brahmin boy, who lived across the
street from each other and had been in love for months. Their
families had tried to break off the relationship because they were of
different castes, but when Vishal's father caught the young lovers
'in a compromising position in a field nearby,' he summoned the
families and the village elders. The panchayat held an impromptu
meeting and 'ordered a death sentence'. They took the couple to
the roof and hanged them.

The next day, the police arrested the families and many
villagers who had taken part in the event. The parents, while
consoling each other in jail, said without remorse, 'We had to do
it for the village's honour.' The police chief added, 'They will be
let off, of course, because no witness will come forward. But then
this sort of thing is not uncommon around here,' and he recalled
three such incidents during the past year.

I was aghast, and I thought, who needs the tragedies of Shakespeare or Sophocles? How, indeed, does one begin to make sense of the Indian village? B.R. Ambedkar, one of the founding fathers of our Constitution, shocked many in the Constituent Assembly in November 1948 when he remarked: 'What is the village but a sink of localism, a den of ignorance, narrow-mindedness and communalism?' Some British administrators, however, held a more generous view. Charles Metcalfe, the Governor-General in the 1840s, called our village communities 'the little republics'. Lord Ripon, the Viceroy in the 1880s, thought that the Indian village 'contained a reservoir of intelligent and public-spirited men', and he proposed local boards of elected village representatives. With that, he struck the first blow for local self-government.

Mahatma Gandhi was a man of the city but he had the most romantic view of the countryside. He dreamt of building a modern India around self-governing village republics: 'My idea of village swaraj is that it is a complete republic independent of its neighbours for its own vital wants and yet inter-dependent for many others.' Marx too, curiously enough, was struck by the independent nature of the Indian village, with its blend of agriculture and industry. But, like Ambedkar, he condemned it as closed, stagnant and a victim of nature. He felt that it 'restrained the human mind within the smallest possible compass, making it the unresisting tool of superstition, enslaving it beneath traditional rules, depriving it of all grandeur and historical energies'. Jawaharlal Nehru also disagreed with Gandhi, saying that 'a village, normally speaking, is backward intellectually and culturally and no progress can be made from a backward environment'.

As in all such things, I believe, like Aristotle, that the truth lies somewhere in-between. The majority of the villages, I am sure, are deeply unjust, many are chronically divided among factions, and some are tyrannical to the Dalits and the backward castes. But even if a quarter are decent, just and peaceful, then we ought to lend our wholehearted support to the revolution that is quietly bringing self-government to our villages. Rajiv Gandhi fought courageously for panchayati raj in the eighties, and this culminated in the Seventy-third Amendment to the Constitution in the nineties. It is, in the end, some sort of irony that Rajiv Gandhi was willing to ditch his grandfather's socialist vision and embrace Mahatma Gandhi's vision of village governance.

Yet, the truth is that many are sceptical and almost no one in power is enthusiastic about village democracy. The urban middle classes are too preoccupied with their own problems and the village seems to have receded into a remote memory. When they do think about it, it is in terms of caste wars and feudal attitudes, fuelled by stories in the media about Sonu and Vishal. The political class and the bureaucracy oppose panchayati raj because they will lose power. The villagers themselves lack confidence and education. Only in a few states like West Bengal, Kerala and Karnataka—where people have practised local democracy for several decades—have expectations risen, along with skills and confidence. People have seen corruption decline, a new class of village political leaders has come up, and they are bringing in better schools, drinking water and primary health clinics.

So, it is a matter of time. As villagers in the other states gain experience, they too will gain assurance and determination. Plenty of heart-warming stories come every day from the villages of Himachal Pradesh, Rajasthan, Madhya Pradesh, Maharashtra, Gujarat, Andhra Pradesh, and the newsletter of Delhi's Institute of Social Sciences, *Panchayati Raj Update*, meticulously documents them. They show how the people are beginning to stand up to the members of their state and central legislatures, the local functionaries, and the upper-caste landlords. Self-government is not a panacea. We have learned this lesson with much pain in the past fifty years. Governance is only as good as the people who come forward to govern and manage to win elections. The Indian village, like life itself, will remain an ambiguous mixture of the good and evil, but participation in governance gives people a voice and a sense of responsibility even though their capacities may be low.

## Democracy Comes to the Village

Former Prime Minister P.V. Narasimha Rao unleashed the two most important revolutions of the nineties—the liberalization of the Indian economy and the ushering in of local self-government—but in neither case did he seem to realize the historic nature of his acts. He acted under compulsion, and because he was without deep convictions, he did not take credit for his acts at the polls, and, not unsurprisingly, he was not re-elected. The political revolution began on 24 April 1993, when the Seventy-third Amendment came into force.

During the decade, almost everywhere villagers voted and created panchayats. The virtuous states—Kerala, Karnataka, West Bengal and Madhya Pradesh—held local elections promptly, repeated them after five years, and local self-government has increasingly become a reality there. But most other states were kicked and dragged into holding the elections. Some like Bihar and Andhra Pradesh were forced to do so by the Supreme Court. In the virtuous states, panchayats received varied levels of funding and, in a few cases, they even began to raise revenues locally. They sat periodically to decide on whether to build water tanks, village roads or schoolhouses. In Kerala, they began to make their own development plans at the district and village levels. In Madhya Pradesh, teachers were made accountable to the village panchayats—they could now be transferred for absenteeism or poor performance. In Karnataka, forty-three per cent of the local legislators are women and the three 'Fs' (functions, functionaries and funds) have reached many villages

Overall, however, it is a mixed record. Panchayats work better where voluntary organizations are present. Where leaders were committed to decentralization—E.M.S. Namboodiripad in Kerala, Jyoti Basu in Bengal, Ramakrishna Hegde in Karnataka, Digvijay Singh in Madhya Pradesh—there is considerable progress. In the states that had devolved power before the constitutional amendments were enacted—West Bengal, Karnataka and Kerala—local self-government is vibrant. There panchayat members have had more experience and people's expectations are also higher. In most other states, the situation is pretty dismal.

Local self-government faces three formidable enemies: state politicians, bureaucrats and feudal elements in the village. The members of the legislative assembly (MLAs) and members of Parliament (MPs) don't want to lose 'the pot of honey' which they have enjoyed for decades, as they siphoned away the funds from anti-poverty programmes. The local functionaries, likewise, don't want to lose their power to steal. The upper-caste landlords cannot stomach the rise of the lower castes and of women. A landlord in Melavalavu in Tamil Nadu is reported to have said, 'How can I sit next to a dhobi? I'll kill him.' And he did the next day, reports George Mathew of the Institute of Social Sciences. A Dalit was pushed into the fire in Kusumpur village in Uttar Pradesh because she dared to campaign against the upper-caste gram pradhan. The local don of Banuchapra in Bihar threatened that nobody in the village 'would be left with limbs intact if he did not win the zilla parishad seat'.

There are, however, numerous positive stories as well. The point is that like economic reforms, these political reforms will also take time. Merely participating in their local elections has raised people's expectations and their minds are beginning to change. The more than one million women panchayat members are slowly realizing that they are not as powerless as they thought. People who are sceptical about panchayati raj need to remember Amartya Sen's words that people don't become fit for democracy but it is through democracy that they become fit.

～

Meteorologists tell us that we had a decade of splendid monsoons in the nineties, but we know that even in the years of plentiful average rainfall some areas don't get enough rain and there is huge suffering. The good overall rainfall did mean that year after year we were sitting on the largest mountain of grain in the world and yet people went hungry, especially in areas affected by drought. Successive food ministers would shed crocodile tears, insisting that they had offered free grain but 'the states were not lifting stocks'. The states claimed that they were bankrupt and could not afford to pay for transporting and distributing food to the poor.

Most of us in the cities, despite our reputation for callousness, would be happy to see the poor fed, but we are cynical of the government's ability to implement anti-poverty programmes. Rajiv Gandhi's famous indictment rings loudly in our ears that only fifteen per cent of the money for anti-poverty programmes reaches the poor. Whether it is fifteen or thirty, the truth is that a vast sum leaks out. There are two main sources of corruption and inefficiency in our food-for-work programmes. One is in honestly distributing food to the poor in return for a hard day's work. The second is in the movement of grain. Now, there is evidence to show that both leaks can be plugged and there are models of success that we can follow.

The main disease afflicting food-for-work programmes is that the wrong people corner the benefits. Typically, local officials collude with the sarpanch, create bogus rolls and siphon off the food grains. States like Madhya Pradesh have found the answer, where neither local officials nor sarpanches are allowed to decide the anti-poverty project or the beneficiaries. It is the gram sabha or the assembly of all adults in the village that decides. When a food-for-work programme is announced, all villagers assemble together and vote for what asset they want to create in the village. Those who want to work in exchange for food come forward in the assembly. Although the panchayat executes the project, the gram sabha meets again to ratify the panchayat's accounts. Several sarpanches have already been sacked by their gram sabhas for stealing funds and NGOs in some drought-affected districts of the state have confirmed that there has been a marked decline in corruption this year. Hence, people in Madhya Pradesh no longer call their local government 'panchayati raj'—they call it 'gram swaraj'. In Rajasthan, corruption has declined thanks to the 'right of information' movements, as local officials are forced to open government records to the people.

The second source of corruption and inefficiency is in the movement of food. Many welfare experts now advise governments that it is more efficient to give vouchers or food stamps to the poor rather than incur the huge cost of moving, storing and delivering the food to thousands of places. There is evidence from Iraq, the United States and Sri Lanka that vouchers work, and very simply at that. Instead of food, the beneficiary receives a voucher, which she (or he) exchanges for so many kilos of rice or wheat from her normal store (it doesn't have to be a ration shop). The shopkeeper, in turn, exchanges these vouchers for grain when replenishing his stocks. Thus, grains only move through normal retail and wholesale channels. When the state doesn't physically have to move the food, costs come down and corruption diminishes. And state governments can no longer offer the excuse that they cannot implement food-for-work programmes because of lack of funds.

As prosperity has grown in the past two decades, we have discovered that the poor are also eating other food beside grain. So, a grain-for-work programme, if it has to be attractive to the poor, will have to offer far more grain per day's work than in the past. But this is not so bad because it will diminish the grain mountain faster. It does increase the subsidy burden, but it is better than letting the rats get to the grain. A well-designed voucher scheme for the poor can also make our school mid-day meal programmes more efficient, and could eventually eliminate the Food Corporation of India and the public distribution system.

With the two biggest obstacles to food-for-work overcome, can we now expect the morally offensive situation of hunger amidst plenty to disappear? Will our leaders now implement massive food-for-work programmes? If they don't, rats will get to the food. If they do, the poor might re-elect them. So they can choose—feed rats or people. It doesn't seem to be a difficult choice since rats don't vote.

The power of people's participation is also the moral of this tale of two districts. Jhabua, in western Madhya Pradesh, is a success story where forests have been regenerated, bodies of water have sprouted and incomes are growing. All this because people have learned to help themselves. Kalahandi, in Orissa, is a failure, with chronic starvation and cases of parents selling their children to pay for food.

Both districts are uplands and home to tribal people. Both were once covered with splendid forests—mainly teakwood—but these have been dying in recent years. As forests vanished, rains became irregular and village water tanks fell into disuse as the government took over their ownership. Increasingly, the two districts became prone to drought, and people began to migrate for six months a year. In the mid-eighties both districts were in the news when Rajiv Gandhi visited them following reports of food riots in Jhabua and the sale of children in Kalahandi.

The Centre for Science and Environment, Delhi, reports that in Orissa, the soil conservation department has spent more than Rs 90 crore since the mid-eighties to build 1,400 water-harvesting structures. The Central government has poured huge sums for constructing micro-watersheds. But these projects have been poorly implemented and have been plagued by massive corruption charges. Lazy district collectors allegedly don't work and the budgeted funds of the drought prone area program (DPAP) and the employment assurance schemes (EAS) are consistently underspent. Whatever is spent is largely lost in corruption, according to NGOs. 'We get complaints of corruption in watershed activities, but the officials belong to the state (rather than the Centre) and we can't punish them,' says N.C. Saxena, the former secretary of rural development.

It is the opposite story in Madhya Pradesh, where local communities created 706,304 water harvesting structures between February and June in 2001 alone through people's participation, and they will irrigate 52,000 hectares of additional land. The benefits, too, have come quickly. Decent rains in late June and July 2001 filled these village tanks, ponds and earthen check dams (*johads*). Madhya Pradesh is succeeding because it is involving people (and NGOs) in managing water and energizing institutions of local self-government, while Orissa depends on apathetic bureaucrats to do the job.

The people of Jhabua district tell their own story. Residents of Kalakhoont removed three metres of silt from their village tank that had accumulated from the erosion of surrounding hills. The very first rains in June filled the tank and 'the stored water will be enough to irrigate more than sixty-one hectares of land and recharge our old, unused wells,' a villager, Nana Basra, excitedly told reporters of *Down to Earth* journal.

In neighbouring Datod, villagers built a community dam on the seasonal Mod River to irrigate the surrounding villages. 'This is something unheard of in our drought-stricken district,' said Balusingh Bhuria, president of the block panchayat. People contributed a quarter of the cost through their labour, and they were ably assisted by an NGO and supported by the state watershed mission. As a result of hundreds of these efforts between 1995 and 2001, the water table in Jhabua is rising. Satellite pictures confirm that tanks, lakes and village ponds have grown visibly and so has the green cover.

A similar success story comes from the neighbouring state of Gujarat, where twenty-three out of twenty-five districts were again affected by drought in 2000. Here the 60:40 check dam scheme (with 60 per cent contribution from the government and 40 per cent from the villagers) successfully built 13,500 community structures in 2000 and 6,000 more in 2001. But whereas Madhya Pradesh has passed on the ownership of these structures to the gram sabhas and village assemblies manage the water structures, the Gujarat government is threatening to take over the management of these structures in the future because 'water does not belong to the people but to the state'.

For the first time in history, it seems to me, we are dealing with drought and water in a different way. Gujarat and Rajasthan have also reported plenty of miracles of community effort during the last drought, but these states are not pushing power down to the people as single-mindedly as Madhya Pradesh. The Gujarat government, in fact, is notorious for sabotaging panchayati raj. The voluntary organizations in Gujarat are worried. 'The check dam scheme will be sustained if people's committees manage them,' says Manu Bhai Mehta of Savarkundla Gram Vikas Mandal. Apoorva Oza of the Aga Khan Rural Support Programme also worries that 'without ownership, farmers might not maintain these structures'.

The challenge for the future is to look after these people's water structures, and keep recharging the ground water. Environmentalists tell us that four years is enough for ecological regeneration, and if you maintain a structure for five to eight years then the community will be able to withstand three droughts in a row. That is why I am betting on Madhya Pradesh, even though the people of Gujarat have more initiative and are more commercial-minded. Madhya Pradesh will succeed in the end because it is building sustainable institutions.

## Time for Another Green Revolution

Throughout the nineties, reforms eluded Indian agriculture. Only in March 2001 did the debate begin when the then finance minister, Yashwant Sinha, included seven specific agricultural reform proposals in his annual budget. And he announced some more reforms in March 2002. With industry performing poorly, it began to dawn on people that it might be better to focus on agriculture, where India has a greater competitive advantage.

In the sixties, we used to be called a 'basket case'. We were thoroughly dependent on PL 480 wheat (imported from the United States under Public Law 480), and when the rains failed for the second consecutive year in 1967, we averted a famine only because of America's generosity. B.K. Nehru, our ambassador in Washington, recalls in his autobiography that at the peak a ship full of grain would leave an American port every ten minutes.

How time have changed! Now, we comfortably sit on a grain

mountain year after year. This is not a good thing because it blocks a colossal amount of taxpayer's money and burdens the nation in avoidable inventory carrying cost too. Although we have become a surplus nation, our minds have not changed. We keep raising the support prices of wheat and rice and keep sending the wrong signals that encourage farmers to produce these crops when they are not needed.

Once the green revolution was in place, thanks to Lal Bahadur Shastri's foresight in appointing C. Subramaniam as Minister for Food and Agriculture, wheat production rose 5.5 per cent a year for a whole decade from 1967 to 1977. Food grains have climbed from fifty-four million tonnes to 200 million tonnes since 1950, growing three per cent a year, ahead of our 2.1 per cent population growth. (In contrast, food output grew one per cent annually between 1905 and 1945). On the negative side, the revolution mainly benefited the irrigated areas of the northwest. From the mid-eighties, however, it has moved into the poorer states and has modestly improved rice yields as well. Wherever it has gone, it has shown a great appetite to employ surplus labour, despite increasing mechanization. Hence, sixty-three per cent of Indians still live in rural areas although agriculture now accounts for twenty-six per cent of our GDP. Yet, we have a long way to go.

Where do we go from here? Experts believe that we are on the verge of a second green revolution. With our large arable land and plentiful sunshine, India can become a major global power in agriculture. Our yields are still only a half to one-third of China's. But first, we must change our 'poor, starving country' mentality and regard ourselves as potentially big food exporters. We should begin to view agricultural trade in a positive light, and think of the Cairns group of agricultural products exporting countries within the World Trade Organization (WTO) not as enemies but as allies. Second, we will not conquer the world through peasant farming, but through technology and capital. Remember, the first green revolution was a technological revolution. Third, technology is now with international companies and they will have to play a crucial role. Much of the talk about the harmful effects of genetically modified crop technology is rubbish. We heard the same talk about Mexican wheat in the sixties. Fourth, we have to liberalize agriculture and remove needless controls.

Ashok Gulati, the agricultural economist, has spelled out a clear reform agenda. He has demonstrated that India has a global competitive advantage in a dozen commodities. Among these are cotton, wheat, rice and horticulture and dairy products. The time has come to open these to free trade. We must first scrap the Essential Commodities Act. Free exports and imports will link us to world prices and consumers will benefit from lower prices and farmers from a larger market. Export controls have diminished considerably, as have import restrictions, but high tariff barriers remain.

◦

Inspired by one of Emerson's essays, Mathew Arnold, the English poet, wrote in the nineteenth century about the 'seeds of godlike power'. He was thinking of the human being's great potential for progress, but his happy phrase fits the new miracle seeds that will help India create a 'second green revolution'. The seeds are a product of biotechnology. Farmers love them because they don't have to spend on costly pesticides—they are resistant to pests—and they raise yields and income by thirty to fifty per cent. Consumers like them because the food is less toxic and more nutritious. Many seeds are also nutritionally enhanced. For example, you won't feel guilty eating the new potatoes because you will get protein in addition to starch in your diet. No wonder, the seeds cover 44.2 million hectares in thirteen countries on six continents. Eight of these countries are industrialized and five are developing. In the past five years, genetically improved crops have grown twenty-five-fold in acreage—a dramatic rate of adoption for any new technology. Tragically, India's farmers had to wait six long years before being allowed to experience this miracle.

In March 2002 they were finally allowed to step into the world of biotechnology when the government allowed commericalization of Bt Cotton. The new cottonseed is especially popular because it is resistant to the dreaded bollworm, which attacks seventy per cent of India's cotton crop and destroys thirty-five to fifty per cent of it every year. In 2001 many farmers committed suicide because of this. Meanwhile, forty per cent of the US and twenty per cent of Chinese cotton crop is planted with Bt cotton. For other crops foot dragging continues. Proagro's mustard seeds have been tested to death for seven years and they have not yet been approved.

Chinese bureaucrats, in contrast, take a more practical approach. They saw that Bt cotton was being extensively used in several countries and that it had cleared the rigorous requirements of the United States Food and Drug Administration. So, they decided not to re-invent the wheel, but to merely check Bt cotton's bio-safety in their soil and climates. Eighteen months after trials, Chinese farmers had begun to enjoy its fruits while Indian farmers were committing suicide. Our two largest cotton-growing competitors, the United States and China, have thus taken a lead over us. When global agricultural markets open up—and that day is not far off— our rivals will be better positioned because their costs will be lower and their yields higher.

As with any breakthrough, genetically improved seeds have plenty of critics, especially in Europe, including Prince Charles. They are creating a scare in people's minds without a shred of scientific evidence. Since most seeds are the discoveries of international companies, there is also the usual anti-MNC prejudice. European NGOs have funded Indian NGOs in order to stop transgenic seeds here and they are spreading plenty of disinformation. They have even taken the Indian government to court for approving the Bt cotton trials. One of the leading anti-MNC activists, Prof. M. Nanjundaswamy, instigated 3,000 farmers in Karnataka on 3 January 2001 and they uprooted Bt cotton planted in trial plots in two locations. According to scientists, the European stand is emotional and based on unknown future risks, not on data. But these vocal critics slowed our bureaucrats and made them timid.

Remember, India has only two per cent of the world's arable land, one per cent of the world's rainfall but sixteen per cent of the world's people. Indian farm yields are only half or one-third of our competitors. The hybrids of the first green revolution have stopped giving productivity gains. Remember, also, that our first green revolution was not an accident. Bold individuals created it. Had they waited for endless trials, it would not have happened. In comparison, our second green revolution so far is a sordid tale of apathetic, timid bureaucrats, misguided activists and eco-terrorists who are robbing our farmers' future.

⌒

Marcel Proust used to say that if one goes on performing any action, however banal or stupid, long enough, it automatically becomes 'good and special'. A simple walk down a hundred yards of a village street is 'wonderful' if it is made every Sunday by an old lady of eighty. Similarly, a businessman I knew in Mumbai worked diligently but unimaginatively in a set routine. When he was alive, everyone said, 'What a wonderful man!' When he died, his business collapsed, and people said, 'Ah, he kept things together, and look what's happened now.' This rule of Proust also applies to many of our sacrosanct but wasteful habits. Every year, we waste ten to twenty per cent of our food harvest because of bad practices. Even if only ten per cent of grains is wasted, that alone is twenty million tonnes and worth Rs 15,000 crore each year. If only half were saved, we could become a major food-exporting nation.

Is there a more efficient way to organize our post-harvest activity? As it happens, a steering committee of the food ministry has found an answer. The inspiration for the new system comes from Australia and involves mechanizing bulk grain handling. The gist of the idea is simple. A farmer today carries his produce to a mandi, where it is packed into bags and sold through a system that involves a long chain of middlemen. In the new system, farmers would be able to sell directly to silo operators, who, in turn, would transfer the grain in specially designed trucks and wagons to scientific silos and store them in an insect, pathogen and bacteria-free environment. From there, the produce would move to consumers in cities in the same hygienic transport.

Flour manufacturers would buy grain from silo operators. Even the government would procure its needs for ration shops from the silos. The silo operators would recover the capital cost of silos and wagons through their margins, which are unlikely to be greater than the combined margins of today's long chain of middlemen. The nation will save by avoiding waste in transit and by eliminating a large number of middlemen. We would all gain by replacing the inefficient and corrupt practices of the state agencies by a competitive system of scientific storage and movement run by entrepreneurs. Over time, these savings will translate into lower prices, grain surpluses and exports.

The first step in this direction has been taken with the government inviting bids for the construction of silos. It remains to be seen how successful it will be. Middlemen are bound to resist the new system, for they also act as moneylenders to farmers. But don't shed tears for them. They are enterprising people and they will find many entrepreneurial opportunities in the new system—they could become service providers to silo operators, or financiers of the new trucks and wagons, or silo operators themselves.

⁖

Praise was showered on Yashwant Sinha's budget in March 2001, and deservedly so. There was much to laud and everyone has his favourite measure, but I was happiest that agriculture has finally entered the reform agenda. By investing in agricultural reform we will get a 'bigger bang for our buck', as the Americans say. The timing is good because no one seriously worries about food security.

Agricultural reform is a big agenda and there is no point talking of globalization or the WTO when the Indian market is not free. Our farmers are victims of archaic laws that prohibit them from selling their produce freely within the country, traders face limits on how much they can buy and stock, mills face levy burdens on rice and sugar, prices are distorted by politicians. All this is incompatible with a modern, successful economy, but the biggest change we need is in our mindset.

No country became a successful agricultural power through peasant farming. Farming is not a 'noble profession'; it is agri-business. Ask any peasant—his son doesn't want to be a peasant. We must treat farmers as businesspeople. Our green revolution succeeded because we treated Punjab's farmers as capitalists. Our farms need a huge infusion of capital and technology in order to raise yields and to compete globally. Peasants cannot make this investment. Neither can the government, for it is bankrupt. Hence, we must free peasants to lease their lands to agri-business professionals with capital and technology. Only thus will we stage the second green revolution and become an exporter in a world economy.

All our agricultural institutions—extension services, co-operatives, FCI and dozens of others—are stagnant or defunct and incapable of reform. Five ministries interfere in our farmers' lives—Agriculture, Fertilisers, Water, Food, and Consumer Affairs—and there is no coordination, professionalism or result orientation. It takes six months to import a commodity (and by then we do not need it) and five months to export it when prices have plunged. Obviously, we need to trust the individual and the market.

Vajpayee's government has struck a big blow on behalf of agriculture reform, not only through budgetary measures, but by challenging these old mindsets. First came the National Agricultural Policy tabled by then agriculture minister Nitish Kumar. It talked of freeing controls on agriculture, future trading and contract farming. The government has freed inter-state trading by amending the archaic Essential Commodities Act. This will lift storage and stocking curbs, which hurt farmers and diminished their incentive to produce. It has decontrolled cotton. It was trying to chop the FCI's role and decentralize food management, but an official committee on long-term grain policy favours its continuation. Perhaps the boldest move is to remove excise duties on food processing, which could usher in a horticultural revolution and transform our fruit exports.

My favourite measure is agri-clinics or agri-business centres, financed by the National Bank for Agriculture and Rural Development (NABARD) loans, which could unleash thousands of agricultural graduate-entrepreneurs. It leverages knowledge and marks a new era of private farm services—in testing soils, plant protection, seeds, marketing, post-harvest handling, etc. Farmers will pay for result-oriented, private consultancy instead of free, apathetic government extension service. Just as our IIT graduates become millionaires, it is now the chance for our 17,000 youth who graduate from agricultural colleges every year. Each clinic will need, on the average, three graduates and nine technicians, and this could also create vast employment for the educated in rural areas.

I have two criticisms, however. One, we have lost an opportunity for reducing the present grain mountain by not including a vigorous food-for-work programme. And two, there is complete silence on the reform of our mandi or post-harvest system. With ten to fifteen per cent of our food wasted, we must at least begin to experiment with a modern system of silos and mechanized bulk handling, as I have pointed out above.

India is not a tiger but an elephant—hence our reform process is frustratingly slow. No one doubts that with all the lobbies and vested interests it will take time to reform our agriculture. But as a first step, agriculture needed to be placed on the national reform agenda. This Vajpayee's government has done.

# 9

## To Reform or Not to Reform

*Planning and competition can be combined only by planning for competition, but not by planning against competition.*

—Friedrich A. Hayek, *The Road to Serfdom*, 1944

$\mathcal{D}$ay-to-day governance caused us the greatest anxiety in the nineties because the old institutions of the state were decaying and the new institutions for regulating capitalism were too long in the coming. The rot in the older institutions—the bureaucracy, the lower judiciary, Parliament, the police, political parties, public sector services—had begun in Indira Gandhi's time, and it continued unabated. The new institutions for protecting competitive markets after the 1991 reforms—to regulate, for example, telecom, power, insurance and capital markets—were still in their infancy. As the decade wore on, it dawned on us that economic growth was not enough; we needed both growth and robust institutions to become a successful nation.

On the other hand a few institutions did work and, in fact, became stronger in the nineties, and they shone brightly in the political darkness. One of these was the Election Commission. The Supreme Court was another. The Central Bureau of Investigation (CBI) had also regained credibility by the decade's end. Thanks first to Chief Election Commissioner T.N. Seshan, and later M.S. Gill, elections became fairer, and the ordinary citizen could see the difference. For the first time in decades, politicians were afraid, and this fear brought a new respect for laws and a realization that they did not have unlimited power. Imagine, we thought, if Parliament could be similarly reformed and suddenly begin to attend to its legislative task of debating and passing laws rather than incessantly debating the irrelevant and the unreal. Imagine, if our political parties were to hold free internal elections and there were genuine intra-party democracy, we might see a new quality of politicians emerging, who were responsive to the real needs of the people. Then, for a change, one of the world's poorest countries might take an interest in becoming rich.

There are two long essays in this chapter, both to do with our economic reforms. In the first I look at the reform of our institutions. The second essay, 'All Boats Will Rise', seeks to show that the reforms are not anti-poor.

## Reinventing Our Institutions

Mancur Olson, the American social scientist, warned us that reforming institutions would not be easy. He said that democratic societies tended to foster special interest groups, which subverted the dynamism of society and the market. Writing in 1982, Olson compared the experiences of post-war Britain with Germany and Japan. Narrow interest groups were destroyed by the war in Germany and Japan and they had to begin from scratch. In Britain, however, a powerful and dense network of trade unions and professional associations created 'institutional sclerosis' that dragged down the economy for decades. Germany and Japan created miracles of economic growth in the post-war decade, while the British economy remained slow, and even sick, in some years. Olson hoped that a public educated to the harmful effects of special interests might begin to resist such behaviour. This is what eventually happened in Britain. Sick and tired of its unions and its stifling regulatory institutions, the English voter brought in Margaret Thatcher to right the balance.

In India, we began to right the balance in 1991, and partly because we have not had a strong reformer at the top like Thatcher, the reform of our institutions has been frustratingly slow. In the essay 'Our Crumbling Institutions', I looked at four institutions—the bureaucracy, railways, SEBs and the judiciary. Here I return to two of these—power and the railways—and also examine the reform of state television, telecom, civil aviation and water.

Does the government own a newspaper? No. Then why should it own a TV channel? This is the question that I asked bright and articulate Arun Jaitley, soon after he took over as Minister for Information and Broadcasting in 1999. He replied that the bureaucrats in his ministry believed that the government had to own Doordarshan to provide public service broadcasting. I explained to him that there are far more effective and cheaper ways to deliver public broadcasting. It costs us Rs 1,000 crore a year to keep Doordarshan afloat, and if the government bought airtime on the private channels—Zee, Star and Sony—it could beam an awesome amount of public service broadcasting for a fraction of the cost. With Rs 200 crore, it would become the biggest spender on television by far, and such an important power to reckon with that the private channels would certainly do its bidding.

Because of competition between channels, public service programmes would instantly improve. Added to the pleasure of watching them would be the warm feeling that comes from saving Rs 800 crore. If the Prime Minister had an important announcement for the nation he could easily make it on the private channels through a pre-legislated system. The United States government does not own a channel, yet the president routinely broadcasts to the people. In fact, Americans complain that they get too much of the president on their TV screens.

If, on the other hand, the government owned a newspaper, no one would read it. The government realizes this and delivers public messages to newspapers through press releases and advertisements. It could easily do the same without owning stations and airing unwatchable programmes at colossal public expense. Doordarshan represents much that is ugly about our public sector. It sometimes invites me for an interview, and when I show up, I find that often no one is there and the studio set is covered in a thick layer of dust. Gradually the camera and lights people straggle in. The last time I went I borrowed a duster and dusted off my chair. The interviewer arrived forty-five minutes late. He had not studied the subject, and so the interview was hesitant and dull and it left a bad taste. The following day, the private New Delhi Television (NDTV), which produces news and public affairs programmes for Star TV, invited me for an interview on the same subject. This interview was in a clean studio and it began bang on time. More important, it was lively, because the interviewer had taken the trouble to do her homework.

Until the mid-nineties, our government channel was the clear leader in revenues if not in ratings. Its advertising revenues were five times the combined revenues of all satellite and cable channels. At the end of the decade, Doordarshan's revenues were only about one-third. This is despite the fact that it reaches twice the number of homes. The private cable and satellite system reaches about thirty-five million homes while Doordarshan reaches around seventy million. 'This must be the fastest dethroning of any leader in any market,' says newspaper editor T.N. Ninan. With thirty-five million more homes than the private channels, why should Doordarshan earn less revenue? Clearly, something is terribly wrong and Doordarshan needs complete restructuring, an attempt Jaitley made but could not follow through because of a change in portfolios.

Like zero-based budgeting, restructuring must begin with first principles. The first question that must be asked is why the government should own television (and radio) stations when it doesn't own a newspaper? Over the years, the nation has invested Rs 55,000 crore in Doordarshan. This is not a mean amount—it is equal to three per cent of the GDP. If we had sold it off during the new economy boom of the late nineties, we may have got back that full amount. If we sell it now, we may not get back the whole amount, but we will recover some part, according to investment bankers. The reason is not because of the value of its massive assets, but its monopoly access to thirty-five million homes.

In the end, the government was not persuaded to sell Doordarshan, partly because it had other, more pressing privatizations to look into. But Jaitley did the next best thing, before he was shifted. He sold off Doordarshan's time in large blocks to independent companies and this did help to repair its finances.

In contrast to Doordarshan, we made significant progress in bringing about expansion and efficiency in telecommunications. Again, it was no thanks to the erstwhile Department of Telecommunications (DoT), which, in fact, did great harm to India's image as a reformer. Ever since the first reforms were announced in telecommunications in 1994, it consistently sabotaged all efforts to bring in competition, and it became a living example of the ugly truth that bureaucracy doesn't work on behalf of the people but only on behalf of itself. Through most of the nineties, it was DoT versus the citizens of India.

When our economic reforms began in the early nineties, experts estimated that it would cost $37 billion (Rs 140,000 crore) over ten years to create a modern telecom infrastructure in India. An investment on such a massive scale would create millions of new jobs and bring in new technologies and skills. Since our government did not have that sort of money, it decided to open the telecom sector to private investment in 1994. The government had also seen how private competition had improved the performance of the other state monopolies—Indian Airlines, Doordarshan and SAIL—and it wanted to replicate that experience in telephones. However, it made the grave error of asking DoT to create and implement a new policy. It was like asking Bajaj Auto to bring in Honda and Suzuki to compete with itself in scooters. We should have entrusted the job to an independent body.

Predictably, DoT came up with a flawed policy that was designed to fail. It was based on selling licences for cellular services at extortionate fees to private competitors, which would lead to high tariffs for consumers and result in the eventual failure of private companies. Certainly, the private sector was also to blame for bidding unrealistic fees, especially one irresponsible company which destroyed the field for everyone. As expected, private providers were in serious financial difficulty by the end of the decade, and the Prime Minister, in frustration, had to take away the telecom reforms from DoT. He changed the minister, and passed on the authority to the Group of Ministers on Telecom headed by Jaswant Singh, who finally gave us a pragmatic policy that has transformed the telecom scene.

Apart from wanting to preserve its monopoly, DoT was also wrong in thinking that cellular phones were toys for the rich. It initially set extremely high mobile phone tariffs, which only the rich could afford, and it is not surprising that there were very few subscribers. Most other countries did the opposite. They saw mobile phones as an opportunity for the poor and those in the remote areas. Hence, in China, Bangladesh and the Philippines the cellular phone became an instrument of development. The Telecom Regulatory Authority of India (TRAI) spent the rest of the decade lowering the high initial tariffs.

DoT's third mistake was to open local telephony before long distance (STD/ISD). The latter is easier to implement, needs less investment, and it would have provided the country a chance to learn from the experience of other countries. Nevertheless, when the local service was opened up, our hopes rose and we thought that we would soon be able to choose between two telephone providers for our fixed phones. But these hopes were soon dashed for the reasons that I have mentioned. In a few cities, private services did start and there the threat of competition did stimulate DoT. In Indore, for example, you could get a new telephone connection from DoT on the same day and choose from twenty-two telephone models.

To give the devil its due, during the nineties, consumers were surprised to see a visible improvement in DoT itself. Under the threat of competition it had energized itself and multiplied telephone connections from five million in 1990 to almost thirty million by the end of 2000. Better still, its service also improved. DoT is rightly proud of these achievements, but it should remember that in China telephones grew by twenty million in eighteen months alone—from eighty million to 100 million in 1997–98.

By 1997, the government had realized the damage that DoT was doing and it did what it should have done in 1994 when the telecom reforms began. It set up the TRAI to regulate the industry. It staffed it with upright individuals who stood for the consumer's interest. TRAI quickly set up transparent systems and began to force the pace of reform. It brought down cellular tariffs, lowered STD bills, challenged the wicked idea that the cellphone owner should also pay for calls received and proposed competition in domestic long distance telephones. However, DoT, in its cussed way, kept defying the TRAI at every step. Nowhere in the world is the regulator taken to court on every order that it passes.

Meanwhile, the world also changed. The Internet came. Technologies for telephones, television and the Internet began to converge. Phone bills around the world began to drop dramatically, and the regulator in India also responded with significant tariff drops. Vajpayee's government responded to the change by breaking the Videsh Sanchar Nigam Ltd's (VSNL) Internet monopoly in 1998. This was a great moment, and we realized that at last there were modern minds in the government, who understood the enormous potential that information technology held for transforming our future. However, DoT remained true to character and it dragged its heels, not giving gateways to private companies for thirteen months.

With the world moving rapidly and DoT putting up hurdles at every turn, it became obvious to the government that DoT was incapable of meeting the challenges of the future. So, as I have already pointed out, the Prime Minister took the responsibility for policy away from the department, and in 1999 we finally had a sensible New Telecom Policy. It turned out to be the most important reform executed by the BJP-led government. As a result, DoT was soon corporatized. VSNL was also privatized. The principle of revenue sharing replaced the concept of extortionate licence fees, and the infant private telecom industry's health quickly improved. As mobile call charges began to drop, the number of cell phone users exploded, and the device is on its way to becoming a genuine instrument of development.

The TRAI was also divided into an appellate and a tariff-setting body. But there remains a huge flaw—the implementation of the new telecom policy remains in the Department of Telecom Services' (DTS) untrustworthy hands. Also, TRAI is financially dependent on the DTS, and this will undercut its independence. Worse, the courageous members of the original TRAI were sacked. True, the Secretary of DoT was sacked at the same time, but that is poor consolation to Indians who want their nation to succeed in the Information Age. When ordinary men fall it is sad; when honourable men do, it is tragic. As it is, there are too few persons in Indian public life that invite admiration these days. Some of them were at the TRAI, and their sudden dismissal came as a great shock. Again, it was DoT that was behind the mischief.

～

If our telecom future is secure, the outlook for our railways is precarious. Every Indian seems to have one impossibly romantic railway memory. Mine is of a journey from Kalka to Simla as a five-year-old, when I feasted for the first time on the snow-tipped crests of the Himalayas, and I recounted it in my novel, *A Fine Family*. Our railways are a mirror to contemporary India, showing some that is good in us and much that is bad. They weave the nation together and have made the poorest Indian mobile—for Rs 50 you can travel 200 km. They are cheaper than anywhere in the world because extortionate freight prices subsidize passenger fares.

Yet, seventy million Indians (mostly in Bihar, Uttar Pradesh and West Bengal) travel without tickets every year.

The railways are the Indian government in miniature—inefficient, corrupt, hopelessly over-manned, utterly politicized, with shoddy, callous service. Their powerful unions resist downsizing or modernization. The faster trains may average 100 km per hour but they are often late. Yet, Indians do not seem to mind because they have no other alternative. Private companies would not dream of transporting goods by rail, not only because of high tariffs and constant delays, but because they would be stolen. Hence, even coal, petrol and diesel are inefficiently transported by road. Politicians make investment decisions, and these bear no resemblance to consumer needs or commercial considerations.

Today, the Indian Railways is in a financial crisis, and if something drastic is not done, it will wither away like the state in Bihar. What are the answers? To become a modern, efficient institution, it has to shed 500,000 overpaid and underworked employees, whose presence demoralizes daily the ones who do work. There are three ways to do this: one, don't replace the people who retire; but this process will take ten years and by then the railways will be dead. Second, retire three out of four persons compulsorily at the age of fifty-five, retaining only the outstanding ones. This too is slow, but it will help create a climate of excellence. The third way is to offer surplus employees the generous voluntary retirement scheme announced by the government, but implement it like the best companies—get rid of the deadwood and retain the good people. I expect we will have to combine all the three ways if the railways are to be saved.

The second solution is to reverse the decline in freight traffic and regain market share lost to road traffic. It is a national scandal that it costs more to send goods from Delhi to Mumbai than from Mumbai to London. Because of uncompetitive freight rates, thousands of trucks bring coal from Bihar to Punjab. In 1996 then railway minister Ram Vilas Paswan and an irresponsible Railway Board caused this damage when they hiked freight rates by twenty-two per cent. Calculations show that freight rates could be reduced by fifty per cent and the railways could still make a profit on freight. It will need more than lower prices to fix the problem, however. To regain primacy in bulk freight, the railways will need new container terminals with new operators, raise speeds of freight trains, improve communications and signalling. Most important, they will need to change their callous attitude to the customer. The threat of early retirement will help, but other incentives and penalties will also be needed to change the monopolistic 'take it or leave it' mindset.

The third and most important way to save the railways is to distance them from the government. The Rakesh Mohan Committee studied the best practices around the world and discovered that the best railways have achieved autonomy from their governments by becoming independent companies with an autonomous regulator. With corporatization, they will need to focus only on their core responsibilities and outsource all other distracting activities—sanitation, manufacturing, rest houses, hospitals, schools, printing, etc. To prepare leaders, they will need to change their processes and style—they will have to reduce over-centralization at the Board level and give autonomy to the operating managers.

The railways are dead set against these excellent recommendations. They rightly point out that mere corporatization will not reduce government interference, and the railways could end up becoming another fourth rate public sector undertaking—they are, at least, third rate right now. The answer, I think, lies in a transparent contract between the government and the railways at the time of corporatizing that will ensure their commercial autonomy. This may not be enough, but if the status quo remains then a grand institution will just wither away, and that would be a shame, indeed!

⤚

Unlike the railways and state television, we have at least *tried* to reform our power sector. However, if we succeeded in reforming

our telephones, we have failed in the case of electricity. For the past
twenty-five years my family has owned a small coconut farm in a
village in Maharashtra. If this does not make me a full-blooded
Maratha, it does make me at least an honorary Maharashtrian in
my neighbours' eyes. Bhiku, our gardener, looks after our *wadi*,
and we have seen his children grow up nicely over the years. I have
always taken a special interest in his eldest boy, and when the
Enron power plant came up I confidently predicted that Prashant
would have a shining future.

The main obstacle to our village's prosperity is perennial
shortage of power, which inhibits commercial activity. Although
the Dabhol power plant has made Maharashtra surplus in power,
our village still does not get power on Fridays and brownouts
define our other days. Across the harbour is Mumbai, where people
get plenty of power and entrepreneurs set up industries, call centres
and software companies, and create thousands of jobs every day.
Who is robbing Prashant of his future, especially when our state
has abundant electricity?

People blamed Dabhol and it owner, Enron, and they expended
enormous negative energy in blaming the foreign devil for selling
expensive power. I did not particularly like Enron's ways, and I also
believe that the Dabhol contract was flawed. But the truth is that
Dabhol's power was not much more expensive than similar new
plants' would have been. Dabhol's power appeared expensive
because the Maharashtra State Electricity Board (MSEB) bought
only half the power that Dabhol could produce and this made the
latter inefficient. If Dabhol could run full blast, then the cost of its
power would be Rs 4.02 per unit. Even a new thermal plant like
the National Thermal Power Corporations's Kayankulam plant
produces power at Rs 4.50 per unit. Dabhol's notorious tariff of Rs
7.80 a unit was a fluke during the month of July 2000 when the
MSEB bought only thirty per cent of Enron's power. The rise in
oil prices and the rupee's depreciation did not help, but the main
problem was the MSEB's inability to buy enough power from
Dabhol. If you buy a monthly train pass for Rs 100 and use it only

once, then your journey will cost you Rs 100; but if you use it one hundred times then each journey costs Re 1. If you create a fixed asset you should use it as much as possible.

We should not waste our energies in blaming Enron but in reforming the MSEB. It seems to behave in this irrational way partly because it is bankrupt. It does not have money to buy Dabhol's power because it sells power below its cost. If a mango seller buys mangoes for Re 1 and sells them for 50 paise, she too becomes bankrupt. The MSEB has thirteen million customers and of these 11.8 million get power below cost. Nine out of ten Maharashtrians pay 42 paise per unit and one out of ten pays Rs 5.40. On top of this, many of its customers steal power. Hence, the MSEB loses Rs 5 crore per day.

Mumbai, however, has plenty of power because the MSEB does not distribute it. Professional private companies like the Bombay Suburban Electric Supply (BSES) and Tata Electric Companies do. They ensure that their bills are collected and they don't let anyone steal their power. Transmission and distribution losses in Mumbai are only nine per cent while they are thirty-one per cent in the rest of Maharashtra. The truth is that if some people have to pay thirteen times more for the same thing than others, then no amount of policing by the MSEB will help. The answer, of course, is to charge customers what it costs to produce electricity. This is easier said than done because no politician has the courage to raise tariffs to farmers and risk losing his assembly seat at the next election. The MSEB must also learn from Mumbai and privatize power distribution.

The crux of the problem facing Dabhol and every other independent power producer in India is that they have the freedom to generate power but they do not have the freedom to sell it. In a power-starved country we should encourage all our power plants to produce as much power as possible (which will lower production costs). Put this power on the national grid, and open the trading of power to private entrepreneurs. Private companies will bid for power from generators and sell it directly to consumers. Those who want high-quality power without interruption will be willing to pay more. So will customers who live in power-scarce areas. Consumers will be able to choose between different suppliers and from a menu of prices. During peak hours rates will rise, but eventually when supply exceeds demand, prices will decline, as they did when the cement industry was liberalized.

So, Prashant, don't blame Enron for spoiling your future. Blame Maharashtra's politicians and the incompetent MSEB. In the next election, you should vote for the candidate who promises to make everyone pay for the real cost of power, who will privatize distribution, and who will sack the MSEB linesmen who steal power. Remember, only insecure people blame foreigners for their own troubles.

It is more than ten years since we began to reform our power sector, and nothing in our country diminishes us more than our electricity situation. It reminds us every day that we are a Third World country. We have lost ten years, and had we made the same progress as we have in telecom, we would have been able to say proudly what a Chinese woman said to me in Shanghai recently, 'I feel I am living in a different country.'

Our biggest mistake has been to forget the central idea behind our economic reforms—create competition in the market, and this will bring choice to the consumer, lower prices, improve quality and service. To create a competitive power market, we have to allow anyone to produce electricity and sell it in the market. If we did this, there would be plenty of good quality electricity for everyone. In our enthusiasm over the Orissa model of power reforms, we began to break up our SEBs and privatize distribution, but we forgot that there must be more than one player in each distribution circle.

For creating competition, we do not need to lay new lines, because each producer of power ought to have open access to the central grid and connect its power to the lines that are already laid. And any distributor, supplier or bulk consumer of power ought to have open access to this power, and by paying a charge for the use of the network it should bring power to our doorstep. This is what we are beginning to do in telecom. We must separate in our minds carriage (the wires or lines) and content (the electricity that runs on the lines).

Two momentous events were happening in the country in 2002, when this book went to the press, and they could still set the country on the right path. One, the Electricity Bill, 2001 was before a select committee of Parliament and it was being debated avidly. Two, Delhi privatized power distribution.

The Electricity Bill accepts the idea of open access in distribution, but it does not specify when this will happen. The original draft bill specified that it would happen in three years, but the monopolists in the power ministry deleted this date. Our well-intentioned power minister, Suresh Prabhu, was trying hard to solve the power crisis when he was forced to resign by his party. He is bright and energetic, but even he could not show the door to the vested interests in the ministry and the SEBs who want to preserve their monopolies. Otherwise, why should they suppress part of the report of the Expert Group that included Montek Singh Ahluwalia, Deepak Parekh, Rakesh Mohan, Jairam Ramesh, K.V. Kamath and Harish Salve? The group studied data from around the world and concluded that our power prices would only come down if we allowed more than one company to sell power to the final consumer. It also cited the example of Mumbai, where competition between BSES and TEC had lowered power prices.

India should look at international experience (the United Kingdom, Australia and New Zealand) where there are multiple providers of power, and this competition has resulted in lower prices and better service to consumers. The European Union has been so impressed with the United Kingdom's Electricity Act of 1989, which has brought down electricity prices by thirty per cent over the last decade, that many European countries are restructuring along similar lines.

Delhi's recent privatization has two tragic flaws. First, the city has been divided into three circles and there is only one company per distribution circle. Thus, a public monopoly has been replaced by a private one. Although the massive theft of power will diminish, prices will not because a sixteen per cent cost-plus return is guaranteed to each monopoly. Delhi's second fatal mistake is to give monopoly status to the state transmission company, which will become the sole buyer and seller of bulk power. We should undo this quickly and allow any distributor to buy power from anyone. Similarly, bulk consumers initially should have the right to buy directly from competing producers or suppliers; this should later be expanded to retail consumers, when the infrastructure is in place. Only thus will the public interest be served.

~

The liberal revolution that is sweeping the world is being fed in turn by a series of technological revolutions. In the eighties, it was the telecommunication breakthroughs that destroyed the old state monopolies in most countries and liberated people from state control. In the nineties, it was the Internet that was leading the world towards a digital economy. Now, we seem to be on the verge of an electricity revolution, which holds the promise of producing power, quite literally, in every backyard.

In a cover story in August 2000, the *Economist* described dramatic breakthroughs in 'micropower' technology, which will allow the generation of clean electricity from small fuel cells and small gas turbines. Because of large inflows of venture capital funds (estimated to be $800 million in 2000) and the involvement of multinationals like GE and Asea Brown Boveri (ABB), micropower could soon become a commercial reality. Experts predict that the world market for these backyard generators will be $60 billion a year in a decade. Localized power generation has finally become economically competitive, partly because there are few transmission losses since power does not have to travel across distances.

The whole world will benefit from the electricity revolution, but India will be one of its biggest beneficiaries, because we have failed to deliver decent conventional power. Before we can be worthy of this revolution, however, we have to do further reform. We have to allow private trading of power, for every 'backyard' generator will produce more energy than it needs. Even today, many of our power plants have surplus power at various times. But the government holds the trading monopoly and it is making a mess of it. A smart trader would hustle, make forward contracts and take risks and a spot and futures market in energy would develop. Power trading entails taking big risks, and bureaucrats are incapable of taking risks. Instead of becoming a trader, the government should run a 'power stock exchange', which allows buyers and sellers of power to transact in an orderly manner.

The promise of micropower should not slow our resolve to implement our current power reforms. Unless politicians learn to say 'no'—to free or cheap power for farmers—and bureaucrats learn to say 'yes'—to liberalizing and creating a free market for distribution, generation, transmission and trading of power—there will be little hope.

From the impossible situation that we face with our power institutions, I turn briefly to the relatively easier and happier scene in air travel. With liberalization, travelling by air almost became fun. There was competition in the skies and Indian Airlines responded with a big leap forward. Meanwhile, Jet Airways came up and it demonstrated how an Indian company could quickly become world-class. Through meticulous attention to detail, outstanding training of each employee and an obsession with 'on time arrival', it became the envy of domestic airlines around the world.

The airplane passenger's life suddenly seemed to have become unbelievably congenial. You could almost coast into the airport without a ticket, and know that you would get on. It was as easy as taking a bus to the next town. This was heaven compared to the bad old days before 1991, when you had to beg, lie, plead on your knees for a seat before the imperious duty officer of Indian Airlines. There continued to be a few irritants, of course, even in this heaven. Occasionally you had to sit on the tarmac for hours awaiting clearance from the control tower. 'VIP movement' was the reason given, and suddenly you were reminded that you lived in a fourth world country, where a junior minister could delay hundreds of busy businessman with impunity. But this too changed by the end of the decade as the government reformed its rules relating to 'VIP movement'.

Dark clouds, however, began to gather in these open and sunny skies. Perhaps it was a coincidence, but it was around the time the new civil aviation minister, C.M. Ibrahim, came to power in 1996. The private airlines started to collapse. Modiluft first went under. So did East West Airlines. Then came the turn of NEPC. Only one serious competitor was left. No one took Sahara seriously and Indian Airlines began to look menacingly monopolistic once again. Instead of encouraging competition, Ibrahim stopped the entry of the Tata–Singapore Airlines venture. It was a big blow to the traveller and a setback to our campaign for foreign investment. Coming as it did on the heels of the Enron affair, it sent out a signal to the world that the Indian government could not be trusted. To top this, Ibrahim also stopped progress on the new Bangalore airport, which was promoted by the Tatas and Singapore's famed Changi airport. With two successive reverses, the government of Singapore turned against us. Singapore may be a small place, but its $77 billion foreign exchange reserves (versus our $25 billion at the time) meant that it had a big clout in the world markets.

Next, out of the twisted mind of the civil aviation ministry came a policy that prohibited foreign airlines from operating domestic flights, but allowed foreign investment. In effect, it allowed Pizza Hut to operate an airline in India but kept out an airline or anyone who might actually know the business, which might help upgrade our aviation industry. The policy seemed suspiciously designed to help Jet Airways and Indian Airlines retain their oligopoly of the Indian skies.

At this point, Tatas called Ibrahim's bluff. They decided to break with Singapore Airlines and go it alone, thus fully complying with the new policy. Ibrahim was cornered, but with the help of his bureaucrats he created more red tape, and somehow once again succeeded in blocking their entry. Curiously, the then Prime Minister had backed the Tata–Singapore Airlines venture as the right thing for the country, but it seems he was too weak to prevail.

The situation for the passengers, meanwhile, deteriorated for several months in late 1997 and early 1998. The flight controllers, sensing a weak government, embarked on a 'go-slow agitation for more pay'. Flights started to get delayed. To top the passenger's woes, the flight controllers were joined by engineers of Indian Airlines. These engineers were amongst the highest paid in India, but they knew passengers were vulnerable on many routes where Indian Airlines was the only carrier. Because these events came together, life suddenly became miserable for the air traveller.

What is the answer to our troubles, and how do we secure our future in the skies? The obvious answer is to scrap the Ministry of Civil Aviation and replace it with an impartial regulator, such as the ones in insurance, telecommunications and power, but this is easier said than done. Even in telecom and power, we have not been able to disband the ministries, even though everyone understands that they serve no useful purpose in a liberalizing economy. Second, we should make Indian Airlines and Air-India truly independent of the government by privatizing them along the lines of British Airways. The civil aviation ministry had blocked this move consistently in the last decade, and when we finally got our act together and were ready to privatize, there were no takers. The situation of the world airlines also deteriorated after September 2001. But we must persist on this path. Third, strengthen competition in the skies by encouraging and not discriminating against private carriers. Fourth, convert our airports into autonomous corporations and gradually privatize them. Besides, of course, getting tough with flight controllers and other public servants who take undisciplined positions.

⌒

Having looked at the usual suspects who figure in our day-to-day life, I turn finally, to the more unusual area of water. 'It has no taste, no colour, no smell, no definition in fact, yet it is life itself,' wrote Antoine de Saint-Exupéry on the wonders of water. What could be more fundamental to life? Yet a third of our people do not have access to safe drinking water, and this is the most damning measure of our failure. And the main reason is the myth that water must be free. Because we get it so cheaply we tend to squander it.

The myth in our collective unconscious harks back to an idyllic past when few people inhabited the earth and they would drink from the streams. Hence, the Biblical saying, 'Whoever will, let him take the water of life freely.' Today we are a billion people and it costs money to bring water to people. Unless we learn to pay what it costs, we will continue to waste it.

The controversy over big dams has focused attention on the charmed liquid. I shall not enter into the dams debate here, but only point out that we need large storage spaces because water flows unevenly in rivers. During the rains, river basins overflow and run off. In the dry months the flows slow down. But people need water round the year, making storage of river water a necessity, especially as our need for water is expected to double over the next fifty years.

There is a saying that we never know the value of water till the well runs dry. The starting point of the political economy of water is to appreciate that we are running out of fresh water and the greatest scarcity in the twenty-first century will be that of water—not of oil or other fossil fuels. The second point is to acknowledge that we waste much of our water today. Despite great shortages in many parts of the country, we do not meter homes or farms; so there is no incentive to turn off taps or pipes. Worse, we charge only a fraction of what it costs to provide water.

Though our local governments spend thousands of crores on water, the main benefits flow to the middle and upper classes while the poor rarely get piped water. Our wonderful old canal systems are in decline because water rates to farmers (like electricity rates) are so low that there is no money to maintain the canals. Because of these subsidies farmers over-pump ground water to grow water-guzzling crops like rice and sugarcane. Cheap water is inevitably overused and this has turned vast stretches of land into water-logged and saline wastes.

Economists have always argued that subsidies are bad. Subsidies distort prices in the whole economy; they send wrong signals to producers, who go on to produce the wrong things. Subsidies also eat away funds meant for investment in infrastructure. Worse, the benefits of subsidies go mainly to the rich and the middle classes. The answer to the water crisis is to price water properly to reflect its true cost. Once this happens, people will conserve it. It will also attract efficient private firms to invest in improving water delivery and give access to safe drinking water to many more, including the poor people. The poor will pay for water—even today they often pay while the rich get it free.

Private supply of water may seem radical, but in France private firms have managed water for more than a century. Britain handed over its water assets to private companies a decade ago. From Indonesia to Mexico, private firms are helping governments to improve bill collections, reduce leakage and expand water supply to the poor. The city of Buenos Aires in Argentina has handed over its waterworks to a private company, which invested $1 billion to upgrade equipment, and this has given water to 1.6 million additional people without significantly raising water rates. Where did the money come from? From cutting out the huge municipal bureaucracy. Country after country is learning that it is easier to get efficiency and good behaviour from private companies than from its own bureaucracy. Besides, governments today do not have the funds to improve water supply. Private companies, on the other hand, have both the money and the management skills.

The answer, then, is to begin the liberalization of water. This means that we must transfer the management of water from populist politicians and corrupt bureaucrats to professional managers. If we begin to learn from the best practices in the rest of the world, we too will begin to give our thirsty the fountain of the water of life.

⁓

My final example relates to the reform of institutions that impact on housing, and where a veritable revolution is under way. When I was young, owning a house was a hopeless dream. Either the company or the government provided shelter to the salaried middle class, and at retirement one scrambled to find a place of one's own and a lower standard of living. But today, this is all changed. Even a young person starting a career can put down a deposit of ten per cent of the cost of a house and can easily raise a fifteen-year mortgage loan, and this explains why the housing finance business has been growing 35 per cent a year between 1998 and 2002, and why there is a boom in middle class housing in Gurgaon, Thane, Powai and many other cities.

This is good news for everyone. A construction boom can become the engine of growth for the entire economy, and especially depressed sectors like steel and cement. Every rupee invested in housing adds 78 paise to the nation's wealth or GDP. House building is also a great generator of employment—a million new houses create 5 million new jobs directly and 7.5 million jobs indirectly. Moreover, owning a home brings social stability, as homeowners tend to be more law-abiding and caring of the community.

It is not often that one can link growth to reforms, but one can in this case. The housing boom is the direct result of a dramatic fall in interest rates in recent years, from 18 to 10 per cent, combined with rising tax deductions on home loans. The repeal of urban land ceilings in many states has increasingly made land available for building and kept property prices low. Legislation is already in Parliament which will allow housing loans companies to repossess houses from those guilty of not paying back their loans. All these factors are encouraging banks to give more loans and owning a house has never been easier or more affordable.

Having said all that, this has been a small revolution, and the dream of owning a home is still distant for most. Of the thirty million middle class families only half a million take home loans each year, which is about the same number of cars that are annually sold in India. For an economy that has been growing steadily for so long, we ought to have experienced a series of construction booms, just as Shanghai, Bangkok, Kuala Lumpur and any number of cities did in East Asia. Like Singapore, these now look like first world cities, and by contrast our Mumbai and Kolkata look like slums. Why is that?

The reason is the same sordid tale of bad, unreformed laws, corrupt and lazy bureaucrats, suspicious of the private sector, and 'a government that is far too big for the little things and far too small for the big things'. First of all, unclear titles keep land away from the market—by one estimate fifty per cent of India's land does not have a clear title. If Thailand could fix this problem, and Andhra Pradesh is also doing it, why can't the other states? Second, municipalities in India require roughly fifty separate permissions in order to develop land, and this takes three to five years, which is enough to break the back of any honest builder.

Third, rent control is a powerful disincentive for new building; it penalizes the young and makes our cities look like slums. Again, the answer is simple: enact Delhi's model rent control law everywhere—it protects the interests of both tenants and owners in a sensible way. Although enacted by Parliament in 1995, traders in Delhi have prevented its implementation. Fourth, stamp duties in India are high—they average 10 per cent compared to around 2 per cent in the rest of the world, and this adds to housing cost and restricts demand. On the other hand, property taxes in India are too low—0.002 per cent compared to 1.5 per cent in the world—and this means little incentive for municipalities to develop urban infrastructure. Fifth, half the states have still not repealed the vicious Urban Land Ceiling Act, which keeps land away from the market and means artificially high home prices in those states.

These land market barriers mean that India's land costs as a proportion of GDP per capita are the highest in the world, and housing construction has stagnated at only 1 per cent of GDP, compared to 6 per cent in Brazil, 5 per cent in Korea and 4 per cent in the U.S. The same goes for housing's share of employment, which is only 1 per cent in India compared to 4 per cent elsewhere. The answers too are blindingly clear. And they are contained in the government's wonderful 1988 National Housing and Habitat Policy. All we now need is for the government to act on it!

## All Boats Will Rise

From the reform of our institutions, I now turn to the impact of reforms on the poor. During the nineties, Indians did not talk as much about poverty. Certainly the strident, leftist rhetoric of the past against the 'kulaks', the 'bourgeoisie', about 'class and property relations', and the 'failed land reforms' diminished considerably. A few pockets of radical violence remained in Bihar and Andhra; the governments of West Bengal and Kerala continued to belong to the left, although their supporters seemed to have lost their convictions (Kerala in 2001 got a Congress government). The trade unions also went on the defensive. Even the Communist Party of India (Marxist) or CPM, the most vocal among national leftist groups, carried less and less credibility and more often than not it was seen as a spoiler and an irritant in Parliament.

There were good reasons for the change. First, the condition of the poor itself began to improve after the economy started growing seriously from 1980. Persons below the poverty line began to decline by roughly one per cent a year, according to Suresh Tendulkar, economist at the Delhi School of Economics and one of our most respected students of poverty. At this rate, roughly 200 million people have risen out of poverty in the past two decades. Although our poverty numbers continue to be as contentious as ever, most people are inclined to accept the 26 per cent poverty figure put out by the Planning Commission in 2000. Despite the progress, it is sobering to remember that the absolute number of the poor in India remains the largest in the world. At the turn of the century, roughly 260 million people live on an income of less than Rs 50 a day, and to them the first Rs 1,000 they earn could make all the difference. All the readers of this book live a life closer to millionaires in comparison to their lives.

Second, the experience of East Asia reinforced the view that economic growth was the best tonic for raising the living standards of the poor. As a result, the nation began to think more seriously about growth and wealth creation and less about distribution. Third, with the collapse of communism around the world many were forced to think of non-statist solutions to the problem of poverty. Thus, our attention shifted to the work of voluntary organizations, especially with regard to community participation. Fourth, liberalization and economic reforms turned the nation's focus to deregulation, efficiency and competition, and away from the poor.

Our thinking on poverty has also undergone a change. In the fifties and sixties, we believed that the cause of poverty was our inegalitarian agrarian structure and we concluded that land reforms and land ceilings were the answers. We did succeed in abolishing zamindari soon after Independence, but we despaired over the uneven and unsatisfactory implementation of other land reforms. We should have known better—there is a limit to the radical change that can be effected in a democracy. Redistributive measures hurt the very class that controls the system, and the rich peasant is at the heart of our democracy—he delivers the votes, and it is unrealistic to expect the people who have power to go against their own interest.

In the seventies, a Gandhian strain became dominant in our thinking and reached a peak during the short Janata Party rule. The core idea was to mobilize surplus rural labour and widespread idleness for productive purposes. The success of Maharashtra's Employment Guarantee Scheme had helped to popularize this thinking, but its intellectual antecedents went back to the wage–goods model of the Mumbai economists C.N. Vakil and P.R. Brahmanand, and others, who had argued that a state-sponsored programme of productive employment in rural areas would raise family consumption, and this would lift the have-nots above the poverty line.

The strategy of Raj Krishna and other economists in the mid-seventies called for providing the unemployed with guaranteed jobs, beginning with the Sixth Plan. Instead of merely breaking stones (as in famine relief), the workers would dig irrigation ditches, improve soil, build small earthen dams and bunds, reclaim land, plant and maintain trees, and set up cottage industries based on agricultural raw materials. What made the idea attractive was the possibility of creating durable social and economic assets and eradicating poverty at the same time. It was such a compelling idea that all our governments subsequently made it the centrepiece of poverty alleviation, although under various political names (the Jawahar Rozgar Yojana being one of them).

Over twenty years, the nation spent a gigantic amount of its hard-earned money—tens of thousands of crores—on poverty programmes. Such were our hopes that even in the nineties, spending did not decline. But they turned out to be one of modern India's colossal failures, and they failed, predictably, because of poor implementation. According to official estimates, only a fraction of the benefits ever reached the poor; the rest were lost in 'leakages' and in administrative costs.

There is now a growing belief among thoughtful people that the best answer to poverty is to give the poor better access to education and health, while accelerating economic growth. Because of disenchantment with delivery, our thinking has shifted again, this time to the lessons learned by voluntary organizations and activists of the panchayat movement. We have realized that people's involvement is crucial to the success of anti-poverty schemes.

                                               ∽

I walked into our neighbourhood chemist's one spring evening in 2001 and the shop assistant gave me a look that spoke a thousand words. He looked me straight in the face and his eyes said 'treat me as an equal'. He sought equality based on dignity and mutual respect, and his boldness, it seems, had already got him in trouble. For the Punjabi woman ahead of me complained to the chemist. She used the nice Urdu word *tamiz*, which roughly means 'courtesy', but in her feudal mind it really meant that the shop assistant was not sufficiently servile. When she left the chemist confided in me: 'This boy is good and efficient, but he is a Dalit from Bihar and his manners seem to put off my customers.'

Walking back I was reminded of George Orwell's description of social equality in *Homage to Catalonia*. There he describes the waiters in revolutionary Barcelona 'who looked you in the face and treated you as an equal'. The Indian middle classes, used to feeling superior to the lower castes, are now going through disconcerting times as Laloo Prasad and Mayawati have given the other backward classes and Dalits a new sense of confidence. We are in the midst of a social revolution that has been created by the ballot box. As economic reforms deepen and prosperity becomes widespread, this will only accelerate.

Poverty may have declined but there exists huge inequality in our society and between rich and poor nations. Leftists claim that inequality has grown in recent times and globalization is its cause. This is plainly false. In fact, for the first time in two centuries global inequality has actually begun to decline since the eighties, and this is mainly because living standards in China and India have begun to rise as growth has accelerated in both countries. China has done far better than India because it has taken better advantage of globalization. Its reforms have gone deeper, its exports have grown brilliantly, and it has received far more foreign investment. Critics of reform and globalization—such as the powerful voices in the Congress, RSS and CPM—should seriously learn from China before they force India to turn inwards and condemn our poor to perpetual poverty.

Soon after the chemist episode, I was at a social gathering in Delhi where everyone was avidly discussing the salaries of six recently minted MBAs from the Indian Institute of Management, Ahmedabad, all of whom had bagged jobs paying over $100,000 a year. This is close to Rs 50 lakh, and I detected much discomfort. The gathering felt righteous and indignant, and people blamed liberalization for the growing inequality in our society. I felt, like American jurist Oliver Wendell Holmes, that their passion for equality was in fact 'idealized envy'.

These two episodes—the equality sought by the Dalit and the inequality created by the management graduates—left me vaguely uneasy. The cause of our discontent, I'm increasingly convinced, is that we confuse inequality with poverty. Everyone, I think, agrees that there should be equality of opportunity. This means that every child should have access to a good school, primary health care, and safe drinking water irrespective of birth and ability, and we should minimize the head start that some children have over others based on caste, gender or birth.

This, however, is very different from an equality of result or an equal standard of living that the Marxists sought. Absolute equality is desirable, but it does not appear possible on this earth because it seems to go against human nature. Humanity has suffered too much in the twentieth century in chasing this ideal. Most of us would happily accept rich people or an increase in inequality among the middle classes provided it leads to even a small improvement in the conditions of the poor and the most disadvantaged. It is more important, I believe, to raise the living standards of the poor than to worry about inequality.

We have to realize that economic reforms are bound to increase inequality that comes from open and free competition, but that does not mean that they will worsen the situation of the poor and the most disadvantaged. It is stupid to believe that every inequality worsens the condition of the worst off. The crores that some will earn are the result of a competitive economy which, in the long run, will accelerate economic growth and eventually reduce the disabilities of caste and gender. Thus the economic reforms are not anti-poor, but they must be accompanied by an equal passion for reforming primary education, health and the delivery of our poverty programmes, all of which will improve equality of opportunity.

The reforms are actually the best chance of the poor to pull themselves out of their desperate circumstances. The objective of the reforms is quite simply to build an open, productive and competitive economy, which will grow faster, create more jobs, and, in time, wipe out poverty. Few will disagree with this objective, for what we have had until the reforms began was an unproductive and uncompetitive system that suppressed growth and jobs while failing to deliver equity. It was a system that combined the worst of socialism and capitalism.

Yet, there continues to be a constant refrain that the reforms hurt the poor. But honestly, whom have they hurt so far? Scrapping licensing has only hurt the corrupt bureaucrat and businessman. It does not immediately affect the poor. Privatization may hurt the overpaid, underworked labour aristocracy in our inefficient public sector; it may actually have to do an honest day's work after years of idleness. Opening the economy to trade and investment will create competition and affect the Indian producer; either he will become more efficient or he will be driven out. None of these are the wretchedly poor.

Reducing controls on the economy will only bring more efficiency, reduce monopolies and liberate new entrepreneurs. It is true that labour reforms will make it easier to lay off a worker based on customer demand, and this does cause job losses and pain, as we have seen in the United States and the United Kingdom. It is always painful when a person loses a job, but mature economies have learned to cope with the problem. Otherwise, how does one explain that workers in the United States no longer want to join unions despite the fact that the country has the most flexible labour markets in the world? Our new economy companies also testify to this fact. They now employ people in the thousands, and they are also known to cut back when there is a recession. Yet, they are not unionized. Admittedly, these are white-collar workers, but I think the same rules apply. Because of enlightened self-interest they have learned to treat their people well. Contrast this to our nationalized banks, where white-collar workers hold the bank managers and customers to ransom.

Nor will cutting subsidies significantly hurt the poor. Economists have been saying for decades that subsidies are the worst way to help the poor because they distort the price mechanism for the whole economy and misallocate society's scarce resources. Instead of subsidies, it is better to give money to the poor (which, of course, has its own problems, for all Indians, including millionaires, will stand in a queue to be counted among the poor).

The reforms, thus, do not hurt the poor. As I have said before, there are two ways in which the poor will rise. The first is through rapid economic growth, and only the market will deliver it. India is one of the few places left in the world where one has to keep repeating that the state must be kept out of the production and trade of goods and services, because private individuals will do it better. The state's role is to encourage the market and provide the basic systems for it to work efficiently. The second way is to provide an opportunity to the poor for education and health. The state does not have to deliver education and health, but it must provide the resources.

While we must continue to deregulate our economy, the focus of our reforms must now shift to human capital formation. The lesson from East Asia is that we don't need to dramatically increase spending on education as a percentage of GDP, but to improve the quantity and quality of primary education. As GDP grows more rapidly via an open and competitive economy, more resources will become available for education and per pupil costs will drop as a constant share of GDP. Rapid growth will also raise the return on labour skills, increasing the demand for education. There is ample evidence that enrolments rise with growth. With rising demand for education, teacher salaries will rise, bringing in better quality teachers. With more primary education for girls, the birth rate will decline, which means that we can spend less on new seats and divert more resources to raising the quality of education.

Income distribution will improve as our economy keeps opening up and growth rises. With lower tariffs, manufactured goods have already become cheaper, which has improved the terms of trade between agriculture and industry, and this will reduce the gap between the majority who live on the land and those who live in towns. The growth in exports will create new jobs, for the home market no longer limits demand. As productivity rises, jobs will become more skilled and add more value, and inequality will further decline.

In the short term, the reforms will have little impact on the poor—let's admit this honestly. In the long run, the reforms will pull up the poor into the middle class. Our middle class was barely eight per cent of the population in 1980. After our economy began to grow respectably in the eighties, the middle class has tripled. According to the National Council of Applied Economic Research (NCAER), it is now around eighteen per cent of a much larger population. NCAER rightly does not use the normative term 'middle class'; it prefers instead the term 'consuming class'. Our middle class is also much poorer. Instead of being car-owning, it is a two-wheeler owning class. Given the right incentive system, the middle class invariably pulls itself up through hard work, self-help and education in a competitive society, and the task of economic reforms is precisely to create such an incentive system. If the reforms are successful, they will make a majority of India's population middle class within a generation and a half.

# 10

## What Slows Us Down?

*It is an easy and vulgar thing to please the mob, and not a very arduous task to astonish them; but essentially to benefit and improve them is a work fraught with difficulty and teeming with danger.*

—Charles Caleb Colton, *Lacon*, 1825

The stubborn persistence of democracy is one of India's surprising achievements. Time and again, Indian democracy has shown itself to be resilient and enduring, giving the lie to the old prejudice that if people live in poverty they are incapable of the kind of self-discipline and sobriety that makes for effective self-government. Yet, it is an infuriating democracy with poor governance and fragile institutions that have not delivered enough prosperity to the people, and the rate of change is too slow.

The centre of gravity of Indian democracy shifted perceptibly to the right in the nineties with the rise of the BJP and the decline of the Congress Party. The historical hold of the Nehru–Gandhi family also diminished. Many Indians who had grown up under the umbrella of the Congress for forty years were worried and they wondered what this new polarization of power might mean. Some thought that it was a good thing, arguing that a modern democracy needed a viable second party and it gave voters a choice. They pointed to the Anglo-Saxon model where the two-party system was the foundation of political stability. The issue that remained unresolved in Indian minds was how the BJP was going to evolve in the future. Would it be able to move into the moderate mainstream, shed its sectarianism, distance itself from the more fanatical elements, and become a sustainable right-wing alternative to the Congress Party?

This chapter is about our political economy, and the frustratingly slow pace of our economic reforms and poor governance are the two themes that run through it.

## Democracy before Capitalism

Democracy and capitalism have emerged as the dominant problem-solving institutions for human beings in modern society. After the collapse of communism, in particular, country after country has been embracing these two institutions. In this great adventure of modern civilization, each nation is trying to adapt these two institutions to find the right mix of market competition, political pluralism, participation and welfare. More than fifty countries are engaged in economic reform as they make the transition from inward-looking, autarchic economies to open, market-driven ones. India is one of these, and among the best placed to make a quick and successful transition to capitalism. Unlike Russia, it has had a highly developed national market, going back to the seventeenth century, which was integrated further when the railways came in the nineteenth century. Unlike China, it has had a robust, indigenous financial system, which was upgraded into a modern banking system in the early twentieth century. Unlike Russia and China, India also had clearly defined property rights, a well-developed commercial law and an English-speaking entrepreneurial and professional class.

Unlike India, democracy followed capitalism in almost every nation. In country after country in Europe, suffrage was gradually extended over the past 150 years, and it slowly altered existing capitalist institutions and practices. This unique reversal explains a great deal about Indian society today, including the failures in governance and the painfully slow pace of economic reforms. As mass political parties and trade unions developed in the West, democracy began to impinge on capitalist institutions and practices. The democratic propensity for redistribution and labour unions started to constrain the productivity and risk-taking spirit of entrepreneurs. This process culminated after the Second World War in the welfare state in the West and in Japan, with social insurance and health care and extensive regulatory frameworks designed to protect against the shortfalls of capitalism. It is possible that had capitalism not been so modified by democracy, it may not have survived.

In India, on the other hand, democratic institutions came up before we had the chance to create an industrial revolution. Even today, over sixty per cent of our people continue live in rural areas, organized labour constitutes less than 10 per cent of total labour, and the middle class, despite tripling over the last two decades, is less than twenty per cent of the population. Because of the unique historical reversal, populist pressures for redistributing the pie built up before it was baked. We set up intricate regulatory networks before the private economy had transformed a rural into an industrial society. We began to think in terms of 'welfare' before there were welfare-generating jobs. The result, as we have seen, has been throttling of enterprise, slow growth, missed opportunities, huge subsidies and a rapacious bureaucracy. It is the price we have paid for having democracy before capitalism—or rather too much democracy and not enough capitalism.

We also underestimate the difficulty of transforming an autarchic, centrally-planned economy into a market-oriented one. The state cannot merely withdraw from activities by privatizing them. Some liberals think that markets are natural and they spring up on their own. Their belief is based on what Adam Smith called 'man's propensity to barter, truck and exchange one thing for another'. Markets, however, do not work in a vacuum. To function smoothly they need a network of regulations and institutions; they need umpires to settle disputes. These institutions do not just happen;

they take time to develop. Thus, reform is not an easy path.

Experience around the world over the last two decades teaches us that markets generate perverse results in the absence of good regulatory institutions. At the same time, we may have reformed our policies but we have not dismantled the huge bureaucracies created by the licence raj, and they keep putting up obstacles to change.

⁓

While it is easy to blame democracy for our failures, there are other reasons behind our poor performance. An important one is our tendency to always place politics before economics on our agenda. The local press in any country, it seems to me, reflects the concerns of its people. During a visit to several countries in Southeast Asia in the early nineties, I noticed that the newspapers carried economic and business news on the front page. In contrast, Indian newspapers stuck to politics. Ten years later, in 2001, I visited China and I was again struck by the same contrast. Whereas economics is at the centre of China's agenda, politics continues to dominate our debate in Parliament, in the newspapers and on the street.

During my visit to Thailand in 1991, I met a successful Japanese businessman and he told me that he had invested in Bangkok because Japanese labour has grown too expensive for making his motor parts.

'Why don't you think of investing in India as well? We too have cheap labour.'

He curtly replied, 'Thailand is a good place to do business—India is not.'

I pointed out that we had done a lot to liberalize the economy.

'Ah, but you have a long way to go. Thailand is way ahead of you. Everything works here. Thailand is also more linked with the world. They have lower tariffs, lower taxes and a disciplined labour. They are rapidly privatizing and the old monopolies are disappearing.'

'But we have a more educated workforce,' I said.

'But I can remove a worker here who does not perform. I can't in India.' Then, he added: 'I suppose the most important reason is that the Thais want us and they want to learn from us. Indians only want to give us advice.'

I asked him how India could be made more attractive to him.

'Your reforms will only begin to work,' he said, 'when you remove your bureaucrats from economic jobs.'

This was a sobering conversation. I came away thinking that the hopes of the common person in India were no different than theirs. Then why is it that economic issues are not at the centre of our concerns? Is it a failure of our democracy? Why do the representatives of our people not respond to the economic aspirations of the people who have elected them?

It is a good thing that in the nineties we began to be exposed to how people live in other countries, thanks to the satellite TV channels. I wish our people, especially our members of Parliament, could see the progress made by the people in the east. I wish we could transport all our members of Parliament to the countries of East and Southeast Asia—especially to China—for a short while. It will open their eyes and make them think twice before they thoughtlessly place politics before economics on the national agenda.

While the ordinary citizen in India obviously cares about food, housing and schools, he does not understand how economic reforms will help improve his life. He does not understand how 'making India a good place to do business' will translate into more investment, more jobs for his children and more prosperity for his family. The average Indian does not understand that Japanese investment will bring technology and work habits with it which will improve the skills of our children; that it will improve the quality of our products and raise our capability to export; that improved exports in turn will allow us to import even more products which will compete with Indian products; and this competition will force Indian companies to further upgrade their products, productivity and the skills of our workers. As skill and productivity climb up, so will wages, and this will result in a higher standard of living and a better quality of life for our children.

This is the challenge for our politics and all our politicians. They have to translate liberal reforms into the language of the common person. Just as Nehru sold socialism to the masses, so must they sell reforms and liberal economics to the voters. None of our political leaders has done this in the nineties. They have tried to reform by stealth and we are paying the price for it today. This is why every prime minister wrings his hands when he is asked why the reforms are stuck.

Our failures are due not only to democracy preceding capitalism and because we place politics before economics on the national agenda, but also because we are poor at implementation. If there is a widespread consensus on economic reforms, as everyone says, why are there such frustrating delays in implementing them? If we are agreed on what is to be done, why don't we just do it? One reason is that we haven't had a true reformer at the top, such as a Deng or a Thatcher. Equally, we haven't had reformers at the head of our economic ministries, particularly those dealing with infrastructure.

Our discourse on reforms is also dysfunctional. We continue to waste our energies in debating 'the what' when we ought to focus on 'the how'. How to reform is a more difficult challenge and it is not for lazy minds. It needs problem-solving ability; and it needs mental toughness. Most of all, it requires acute attention to detail. It is not for drawing room amateurs. We Indians are good when it comes to defining the broad picture, but we fall apart when it comes to detailed planning and tactics, which lead to successful implementation. This is a flaw that attaches both to our public and private sectors. Hence our products and governance are both shoddy. Most of our politicians and businessmen suffer from this disability.

Our political parties are also mentally lazy. The leftists want more money for the poor. No one grudges them the money if it actually reaches its beneficiaries. Why don't the leftist parties apply their minds to redesigning poverty programmes so that the poor actually receive the benefits? The voters will respect them and might even vote for them.

Instead of berating multinational companies, let us learn from them. One of the first lessons that a young manager in a good company learns is that 'God is in the details.' It is not enough to have a broad strategy; success depends on penetrating the details of an issue. One has to be mentally tough in choosing between unpalatable alternatives. It is this attention to detail that allows multinationals to deliver awesome performance—e.g., reducing costs by thirty per cent across the globe within nine months by involving 100,000 people, as Nissan did in 1989.

We commonly make the mistake of blaming our character, or ideology, or even democracy for our nation's failures when the real felon is more pedestrian. It is the unhappy inability to translate thought into action that afflicts our public life with devastating consequences. Nehruvian socialism need not have deteriorated into licence raj had our civil servants possessed better management skills. East Asia grew twice as rapidly as India between 1965 and 1985, not only because of better strategy, but because of better execution; not because it saved and invested significantly more, but because it had the ability to make its investments more productive.

During the last decade every government has wanted to reform the economy. Yet, why have we suffered such heart-breaking delays in implementing the reforms? How to reform requires mental application and the ability to implement. And this is precisely what our public figures—both politicians and civil servants—seem to lack.

Our politicians and civil servants seem to fail when it comes to detailed planning, monitoring, readying alternative courses of action, following through and showing the determination to stay the course that eventually leads to delivering results. An important reason for Narasimha Rao's spectacular success between 1991 and 1993, I think, was his administrative ability, and for this he is not given sufficient credit. He brought in the right people—Manmohan Singh and P. Chidambaram—to head the right ministries. He brought in a reformer, A.N. Varma, as his principal secretary, whose office became the control room for implementing the reforms.

Rao encouraged Varma to create an implementation structure for executing the reforms. This was the famous hands-on Thursday committee of secretaries (of the economic ministries) that I wrote about in *India Unbound*. It coordinated, monitored, gained cabinet consent for and implemented reforms week after week. Varma ran his committee tightly. No one was allowed to travel on Thursdays. The committee met for only two hours, when the reform in question was openly discussed. Varma summarized and minuted the outcome and the reform proposal was taken to the cabinet for approval the same day, and then on to Parliament the following week.

The succeeding governments followed Rao's strategy but without his executive ability. They continued to reform the 'softer areas' and they did not confront the main interest groups. They trod gingerly, either skirting these groups or giving them pain in a slow, incremental manner. This, of course, does not augur well for the future of reform in India. Who is going to bell the cat when it comes to the tougher reforms? The present BJP-led government appears to be serious—it has an ambitious privatization programme and it did announce bold labour and agricultural reforms—but it has not shown the will nor the administrative ability to deliver the results. Because of a strong-willed disinvestment minister, only privatization has moved ahead.

Reforms, of course, do not happen without reformers. Even the most reform-minded minister needs an officer to help build pro-reform coalitions in the bureaucracy, the party and in Parliament. Just as Narasimha Rao had Varma, so Manmohan Singh had Montek Singh Ahluwalia. Chidambaram had Jairam Ramesh, and Vajpayee had N.K. Singh. These minister–officer partnerships have been crucial in making reforms happen. Those who criticize the Prime Minister's Office (PMO) for becoming too powerful forget that in our political model ministries are independent and someone has to coordinate our chaotic government.

Ironically, there appear to be better performers in the states today than at the Centre—for example, S.M. Krishna in Karnataka, Chandrababu Naidu in Andhra Pradesh, Digvijay Singh in Madhya Pradesh. They are quietly transforming their states with the help of handpicked doers from the bureaucracy. One of them is S.R. Mohanty, a civil servant in Madhya Pradesh. As head of the Madhya Pradesh State Bridge Corporation, he has got the country's longest toll road, connecting Indore and Edalabad, going. How he went about it is instructive. Mohanty and his team of three discovered that the Public Works Department (PWD) had a Rs 120 crore road maintenance fund. With the chief minister's support, the team put this money into a sinking fund, and used it to raise Rs 500 crore through bonds with the help of SBI Caps. Having overcome the single biggest hurdle—of financing the infrastructure— the team focused only on three per cent of the state's roads, which carried, however, eighty per cent of its traffic. It announced the projects on Day One; it opened tenders for the Indore–Edalabad segment on Day 25; it got all government clearances on Day 34; it issued a letter of intent by Day 39; and developers began constructing a world-class highway on Day 49. This is implementation.

Implementing the second generation of reforms will need huge administrative skills because of thorny labour, agriculture and privatization issues. The Prime Minister has to surround himself with a proven team of doers with strong networking skills. But, more important, he has to set the agenda and send clear signals about what he expects from his ministers and civil servants. Then he has to monitor progress—he must wake up each morning and remind himself that nothing is more important to his, his party's and India's future than the prosperity of his people, and this will only come from implementing reforms. Remember, good leaders do a few things, but they bring all of their and their organization's energies onto that single focus, and they execute brilliantly. And history does not forget them.

## Can the BJP Become a Conservative Party?

When the reforms were stuck in the nineties, some liberals voiced the idea that India needed a new political party. Amartya Sen called for a right secular party. I am an unrepentant liberal, and I would be thrilled to see liberal forces strengthened in India, but I am also pragmatic in thinking that a classical liberal party like the old Swatantra Party will not survive. And when it dies, liberalism will get a bad name. Over the last decade, we have seen ample proof of the damage that marginal parties have done to the polity. The answer, alas, is to depend on either the Congress or the BJP, our two main parties, to push economic reform. Instead of starting a new party, I would rather that liberal reformers infiltrated either of our mainstream parties and 'subverted' them from within in favour of a liberal agenda.

Economic reforms originally belonged to the BJP (going back to its Jan Sangh days), and its early manifestos clearly advocated it. However, the Congress stole this platform from the BJP under the pressure of the 1991 economic crisis, and engaged in vigorous reforms between 1991 and 1993. However, it stopped reforming after that and seemed to go into a shell of self-doubt. These doubts have continued for ten years, making the ordinary person wonder if there ever existed real conviction in the party in favour of liberalization. This, it seems to me, is an opportunity for the BJP to again re-define itself as the party of reform. It will entail educating its supporters in the basics of liberal economics, but we have not seen this will in the BJP. Nor have we seen the competence to deliver the goods. Thus, a liberal cannot trust the Congress because of its statist tendencies; nor does the BJP inspire any greater faith, despite its rhetoric of reform. In fact, its cultural agenda makes it even more unattractive to a decent, free-thinking Indian. So, what is the choice for the ordinary reform-minded Indian?

History teaches us that a modern democracy needs a vibrant two-party system. With much pain and experimentation, we seem to have got there. We now have two viable parties at the Centre. The bogus 'third force' has been wiped out. Recent experience around the world also teaches us that parties only win elections when they move towards the centre because, in every society people tend to be conservative. The only hope for the BJP, thus, is to shed its fanatical right and for the Congress to expel its lunatic left. Once they do that, the liberal wings of the two parties—the ones who favour reforms—will be automatically strengthened.

As the decade of the nineties wore on, the BJP did show hopeful signs of moving into the moderate mainstream. The media called it 'Vajpayeeism', but many BJP leaders seem to have genuinely realized that their party can only succeed at the polls by widening its popularity and shedding its narrow sectarianism. There is significant opposition from within, and especially from the RSS, as Vajpayee has made the party rethink its identity and urged it to distance itself from the religious fanatics among its sangh parivar supporters. Partly under pressure from his coalition partners, he also made his colleagues realize that rightist parties only succeeded at the polls when they marginalized the fanatics at the fringe. But then Hindu–Muslim violence erupted in Gujarat in 2002 which left more than 800 dead, and voters began to doubt if the BJP could ever become a non-sectarian party.

Neither has the polarization between the Congress and the BJP brought the stability that Indians had hoped for. Neither party was able to win a majority in Parliament in the nineties, and we entered a melancholy era of coalition governments. The inability of the BJP to win a majority is partly the result of it weak performance in the states, partly a suspicion about its sectarian character, and partly its own fuzzy image of itself and what it stands for. The Congress, despite its waning popularity, is more predictable—it represents a viable left-of-centre alternative for the Indian voter, but Sonia Gandhi's leadership is a real issue. If the BJP wants to seize this historic opportunity and become a stable right-of-centre party, then it must sharpen its 'positioning in the mind of the prospect' (to employ a phrase much loved by the marketing fraternity). What better way to do this, I believe, than to position itself as a traditional conservative party of the sort that we are familiar with from the history of Anglo-Saxon countries? It will then have a positive USP, a 'unique selling proposition' (again to borrow from marketing jargon), rather than its current negative anti-Muslim image.

In order to become a true right-of-centre party from an economic viewpoint, the BJP needs to demonstrate greater commitment to free markets and economic reform. The voter distrusts the Congress's commitment, despite Manmohan Singh's historic achievement. No one has attempted to sell the economic reforms—least of all the Congress—as the right thing to do in order to build a vibrant, competitive economy, which will do more for the poor than the tired old socialist and populist solutions. The Swatantra Party attempted this task thirty years ago but its timing was wrong—the nation's centre of gravity was too far to the left at the time. Today, more and more Indians understand that the socialist party is over, that we need to dismantle controls and cut red tape, and that ten per cent of India's organized workers cannot hold the other ninety per cent to ransom. While Vajpayee's government maintained a strong rhetoric of reform, its overall performance with regard to the second generation of reforms was poor. It did not show the deep commitment that was needed to dismantle the institutions of the past, nor has it earnestly sold the reforms to the voters.

Many in the BJP also need to shed their attachment to swadeshi and their allergy to foreign capital. If they want to make

India a good place to do business, they must demonstrate greater commitment to foreign investment and to global free trade. But first, they need to engage in vigorous domestic reform. Given their wish for a strong India, they could begin by making India a common market. With a plethora of octrois, police check posts, differing sales taxes, the ordinary businessperson faces an army of rent seekers in transporting his goods across the country.

With its strong roots in the small trader community, the BJP is wedded to the bourgeois values of thrift, hard work and discipline. These are the same values that conservative parties have traditionally espoused. These are also the values that have made twenty million overseas Indians one of the most successful global communities. Thus, it is not such a big leap for the BJP to occupy the empty space that is available for a party that espouses fiscally conservative, pro-business, free market policies. It must first sell the idea to Indian voters that pro-business does not mean anti-people. This is what conservative parties had to do everywhere. If it succeeds in doing that, then it could become a viable alternative to the left-of-centre Congress.

The BJP is right to believe that national pride can lead to competitive advantage. Pride, however, is the result of performance, and does not come from testing nuclear bombs or bashing Muslims or Christians. Performance is measured by social development and economic prosperity. This, in turn, comes from a single-minded devotion to liberal economic reforms and a dedication to improving the opportunities for education and health of the people.

As a conservative party, it is right and proper for the BJP to be drawn to tradition. But if it wants to become successful at the polls, it should look to the rich tolerant and syncretic tradition of India's past, rather than its own narrow version. A Hindu is, by definition, inclusionary. He worships all deities and his mind is stubbornly eclectic. Buddhism disappeared from its birthplace partly because Hindus started to worship the Buddha as one of their gods.

The BJP should tap into the rational and worldly traditions of

India's past. Many Indians have got it wrong in thinking that India's past is mainly religious and other-worldly. Ancient India was far more balanced. Look at the marvellous animal stories of the *Panchatantra*, the love poems of Vidyakara, the realpolitik of *Arthasastra*, the philosophy of Charvaka, and the great Indian texts of astronomy, mathematics and medicine. Even the ancient religion of the Vedic texts is speculative and not dogmatic. There is high worldly drama in the epics. This India is positive, upbeat and self-confident, in contrast to BJP's India, which suffers from feelings of inferiority and hurt pride from the recent domination by Muslims and British.

Is the BJP, then, capable of transforming itself into a responsible conservative party? This depends in part on whether the Indian electorate is capable of supporting such a party. Mr Vajpayee's record would suggest that the party is evolving. The major discontent of the voter with the BJP is not on account of ideology but of competence. The BJP has been unable to provide the day-to-day governance that the voter desperately seeks. Until it does that there is little point in speculating about its ideology.

## Living with Coalitions

The results of the 1996 Lok Sabha elections, when no party got a majority, cast a shadow of gloom over the country. The mood of the nation quickly turned to one of uncertainty as our worst fears of a hung Parliament were realized. People were terrified by the expression 'hung Parliament' because the failed coalition governments of 1977 and 1989 were still fresh in their minds. The prospect of a National Front–Left Front ragbag coalition and a return to autarchic economic policy began to haunt industry. These had been the fairest and cleanest elections in memory, and the Supreme Court had brought down a dozen corrupt politicians. The states had begun to assert their independence. With the Gandhi dynasty absent, politicians had become modest, as is appropriate in a democracy. Moreover, the previous five years had been the best five years in our economic history. People were confident as they went to cast their vote, but this cautious optimism receded when the verdict was announced.

These melancholy fears also reflected our Anglo-centric world-view. The democratic ideal held out to us is of a stable two-party system as practised in the United States and the United Kingdom. We should look instead to the experience of other multi-party democracies. On the European continent, coalitions have been a routine feature of public life in the past fifty years. Yet, these nations have continued to prosper. The biggest and richest, Germany, has been ruled more or less continuously by coalitions in the entire post-war period. And the average coalition lasted thirty-seven months.

Switzerland, which has a higher per capita income than the United States, has institutionalized coalitions. It is a plural society like India where the political parties vigorously represent the interests of the three major language groups (French, German and Italian) and the two religious groups (Catholics and Protestants). It is traditional for the four largest parties to come together after an election and form a coalition. Poland's economy too has boomed in recent years despite numerous coalitions. Thus, workable coalitions can be formed on stable foundations. In our case, unfortunately, we cannot escape the truth that coalitions are extracting a heavy price by slowing down the reforms.

'Coalition' comes from the Latin word *coalitio*, from *coalescere*—'to grow together'. It reflects the primordial human situation of interdependence. Coalitions in politics are not fundamentally different from joint ventures in business. Two firms, even competitors, will sometimes join hands to pursue a common objective. A joint venture is successful only when it merges the different strengths of its partners.

Skill is the key word. The coalitions of 1977 and 1989 failed because our politicians lacked the skill. They had not learnt the nature of interdependence and could not subdue their egos and ideologies for the sake of the coalition. Business people, on the other hand, have an instinctive sense of mutual dependence because every business transaction involves a buyer and seller. Unless both gain from the transaction it doesn't go through.

The 1996 electoral verdict threw up much more than three national combines. It reflected also geographical diversity and regional aspirations. This is not surprising in a plural and heterogeneous society. If America is a 'melting pot', India is a 'salad bowl', in sociologist Ashish Nandy's words. Our identities are sharply defined despite a shared national ethos. A truly national coalition should be able to accommodate the aspirations of the Dravid parties in Tamil Nadu, the ambitions of the Lingayats of north Karnataka and the Akalis in Punjab. It is somewhat the way a company manages the aspirations of a wholesaler in Tamil Nadu, a software supplier in Karnataka or an after-sales service provider in Punjab.

What are the foundations of a successful coalition government? First, it must be for the long term. Only then will there be commitment from its members and stability for the government. It must not be expedient; otherwise it will not last. Second, it must be created in a transparent manner. There must not be secret deals; otherwise horse-trading will destroy it. Third, it must be authentic and not inconsistent ideologically. This means an upfront agreement on a minimum programme and, equally, an understanding on what it will not pursue. The lack of ideology in the current elections suggests that we have a large area of shared beliefs and a consensus on vital social and economic issues. During the past five years, the nation has decisively shifted to the right, and this must be reflected in the ethos of the combine.

We may be learning to live with coalitions, but the disappointing fact is that we had too many governments and too many prime ministers in the decade of the nineties—six prime ministers, to be precise, and five governments. This is too much democracy even for a people who are addicted to democracy. People do not like instability, and when Mr Vajpayee's government was pulled down by a single vote in 1999, they were visibly upset. I must confess that I was outraged. I am not a supporter of the BJP, but I felt that something terrible had gone wrong.

Here was a properly constituted government and it was toppled on the most frivolous grounds. That Vajpayee was returned to power later that year is less significant than the pain, the cost and the distraction to the nation in having to go through a second election so soon after the previous one. Part of the Congress Party's continuing unpopularity in the subsequent years, I am convinced, stems from this backlash.

Then we have all these small politicians, with small reputations and small parties, thinking they are emperors of India, because neither of the two major parties is able to manage a majority. What do we do with these Jayalalithas, Mulayam Singh Yadavs, Bal Thackerays and Laloo Prasads? The problem is not only their behaviour; it is the impact of their actions that are bringing bad values to public life.

The problem of too many governments in the last decade is a systemic failure. According to my psephologist friend, Dorab Sopariwala, 177 parties contested the 1999 parliamentary election and ninety-four parties got a combined vote of less than 0.005 per cent; 139 parties did not win a single seat, 12 parties won one seat, and 24 won less than five seats. Clearly, we must do something about our marginal parties. Some think that the answer is an American style presidential system. I disagree.

Although the American system will give us a fixed term government for four to five years, we will still need Parliament to make laws and pass budgets. And an unstable Parliament could stop all legislation or even close down the government by not passing the budget. This is what happened in the United States in 1995. The legislative–executive rivalry is a big problem there; we are, if anything, more quarrelsome than the Americans. We are also more feudal and we will turn our president into a monarch. Thus, despite its many attractions, the presidential system is really not suited to our temper.

Another possibility is a multiple vote system of the kind practised in Australia, where a voter ranks candidates according to his preference. The candidate who gets an absolute majority based on the voters' first preference wins. If not, the voters' second preferences are counted. And this goes on till someone gets absolute majority. The virtue of this system is that it will eliminate 175 out of 177 parties, leaving us with a two-party system. Its drawback is that it will eliminate all regional parties and that might be too undemocratic.

A third alternative is the German one, which requires a positive vote of confidence. This means that a sitting government cannot fall unless there is a replacement government ready with a majority. This instrument will give us more stability, and the BJP favours the idea, but this system too suffers from the same defect as the American system. Although there will be a government for five years, Parliament could still remain paralysed, which is as good as having no government. So, we are back to square one.

I favour another German solution, which was avidly debated by Dorab Sopariwala and Ashok Desai in *Business Standard* in 1999. Sopariwala suggested that no party ought to get a seat in Parliament unless it received ten per cent of the vote (in eight of the largest states). This would leave us with only two parties—the BJP and the Congress. Desai offered a simpler criterion—five per cent of the national vote—under which the CPM would also qualify. Sopariwala worried, however, that a coalition of the Yadav cousins might get more than seven per cent (because of their clout in Bihar and Uttar Pradesh) and this may not solve the problem of instability. The ten per cent criterion in eight states would ensure that either national parties would emerge, or regional parties with a national orientation would combine to form a national alternative.

Whatever the solution, the people want urgent electoral reform, and the government in power must give it the highest priority. No single party or grouping can manage the reform on its own. But if the BJP and Congress agree on this—and they should, since a two-party system is in their interest—they should be able to pull it off.

## Indian Paradoxes

India truly is a land of paradoxes. Ever since Independence, political scientists have debated how we became a vibrant democracy despite our poverty, illiteracy and ethnic divisions. A few years ago the political scientist, Adam Przeworski, and his team made an empirical study of 135 countries and published it as a book called *Democracy and Development*. They concluded that given the circumstances of India, it ought to have been a dictatorship. Indeed, the late and gracious Myron Weiner, another political scientist, wrote a charming book called *The Indian Paradox*, in which he wrestled with the contradiction of how democratic politics could endure in our diverse and violent society.

Now, here is another paradox. By most yardsticks, the nineties have been the best decade in our recent economic and social history. Yet, it was also the period of the greatest political instability. How does one begin to explain this contradiction? Conventional wisdom says that prosperity and stability go together and economic growth needs political stability. Does this mean that our economic sphere is slowly becoming autonomous from the political realm? Is this another example of Indian exceptionalism?

As I have already pointed out there are at least five good reasons to believe that the last decade was our best, economically. First, our wealth or GDP grew at an average real rate of 6.3 per cent per year (and crossed 7.5 per cent for three years). No wonder President Bill Clinton kept reminding us during his visit that the world's best-kept secret was that India has been the second fastest growing economy in the world. Second, our population growth has begun to slow down for the first time in decades. Compared to a 2.2 per cent growth rate from 1960 to 1990, it had come down to 1.67 by 1998, giving an average of 1.9 for the decade of the nineties. Third, literacy growth rate doubled in the nineties—from its historic climb of 0.7 per cent a year between 1950 and 1990 to 1.4 per cent between 1991 and 2001. Hence, literacy rose from fifty-two to sixty-five per cent during the decade, with the biggest gainers being women and the backward states. Fourth, at least ninety million Indians rose out of poverty as our poverty ratio declined from thirty-six to twenty-seven per cent between 1993 and 1999. This is almost the same pace as China's in the eighties. We are constantly bickering about our poverty numbers, but most experts are agreed that nine to eleven per cent of Indians crossed the one dollar a day poverty line. Fifth, we may have finally found our global competitive advantage in our booming software and information technology (IT) services—what the economists call the 'lead sector' that can transform the whole economy. This sector rose out of nothing during the nineties and grew at a blistering average compounded growth rate of sixty per cent for the decade to become one of our largest export segments.

When you set these hopeful economic figures beside some political numbers, a dramatic contrast emerges. We had six prime ministers in the nineties. Between 1989 and 1999 we changed our government every two and a half years compared to every four and a half years between 1951 and 1989. No single party has won an overall majority since 1984. Roughly half the incumbent representatives lost their seats in the nineties. And the once mighty Congress Party, which ruled the republic for almost forty years, has been humbled. Today, we have too many weak and silly parties and the ruling coalition has around twenty partners. Compared to India's vibrant economic space, our political stage is somewhat like a comedy, peopled sometimes by clowns who seem to do everything except govern.

Not only is our economic sphere alive, our society is humming. Lower castes have risen and gained confidence primarily through the ballot box and occasionally through caste wars, as a social revolution has taken place in the north. It is the same social revolution that the south experienced decades ago. Cable television and other intrusions have also decolonized millions of young, urban minds. More women are working outside and this is gradually liberating them from the old tyrannies of the family, the caste and the village. We are also losing some of our hypocrisy about money.

How, then, does one begin to explain the paradox of an economic and social revolution happening in the midst of political instability and poor governance? Prof. Devesh Kapur at Harvard has found one answer in our polymorphic institutions, which insulate our political system. While the old formal institutions— the bureaucracy, the parties, public enterprises—have decayed or got clogged by interest groups, new institutions have emerged and old moribund ones have been rejuvenated, such as the Election Commission, the Central Vigilance Commission, the judiciary, NGOs and the new regulatory agencies. This simultaneous cycle of decay and rejuvenation gives our system a certain resilience when political actors keep changing. Weak parties mean unstable coalitions, but they have also brought more federalism, less misuse of the evil Article 356 (which allows Central rule in the states) and a dilution of the BJP's economic nationalism and identity politics. Certainly, this is a believable answer to another Indian paradox!

## E-Governance Will Bring Transparency

We tend to be harsh on our bureaucracy, but I have realized that nowhere do citizens enjoy dealing with their government. They do it because they have to. But that doesn't mean that the experience has to be dismal. Now there is a new wind blowing through government departments around the world, which could take some of this pain away. In the next five years it may well transform not only the way public services are delivered but also the fundamental relationship between governments and citizens. Not surprisingly, it is the Internet that is behind it. After e-commerce and e-business, the next revolution may be e-governance.

Examples abound. *The Economist* reported in early 2000 that the municipality of Phoenix, Arizona, allows its citizens to renew their car registrations, pay traffic fines, replace lost identity cards, etc. online without having to stand in endless queues in a grubby municipal office. The municipality is happy because it saves $5 a transaction—it costs only $1.60 to process an online transaction versus $6.60 to do it across the counter. In Chile, people routinely submit their income tax returns over the Internet, which has increased transparency, drastically reduced the time taken and the number of errors and litigation with the tax department. Both taxpayers and the revenue department are happier.

The furthest ahead, not surprisingly, is the small, rich and entrepreneurial civil service of Singapore, which allows citizens to do more functions online than any other. As in many private companies, the purchasing and buying of Singapore's government departments is now on the Web, and cost benefits come through more competitive bidding, easy access to global suppliers and time saved by online processing of orders. They can post their catalogues, bid for contracts, submit invoices and check their payment status over the Net.

The most useful idea for Indian municipalities is GovWorks, a private sector-run site that collects local taxes, fines and utility bills for 3,600 municipalities across the United States. It is a citizen's site, which also provides information on government jobs, tenders, etc. The most ambitious is the British government, which has targeted to convert 100 per cent of its transactions with its citizens to the Internet by 2005.

Cynics in India will say, 'Oh, e-government will never work in India. We are so poor and we don't have computers.' But they are wrong! There are many experiments afoot in India as well. Citizens in Andhra Pradesh can download government forms and submit applications on the Net without having to bribe clerks. In many districts, land records are online and this has created transparency. Similarly, in Dhar district of Madhya Pradesh, villagers have begun to file applications for land transfers and follow their progress on the Net. In seventy villages in the Kolhapur and Sangli districts in Maharashtra, Internet booths have come up where farmers can daily check the market rates of agricultural commodities in Marathi, along with data on agricultural schemes, information on crop technology, when to spray and plant their crops and bus and railway timetables. They also find vocational guidance on jobs, applications for ration cards, kerosene/gas burners and land record extracts with details of land ownership.

Sam Pitroda's WorldTel, Reliance Industries and the Tamil Nadu government are jointly laying 3,000 km of optic fibre cables to create a Tamil Network which will offer ration cards, school, college and hospital admission forms, land records, and pension records. If successful, WorldTel will expand the network to Gujarat, Karnataka and West Bengal. In Kerala, all the villages are getting linked online to the district headquarters, allowing citizens to compare the development priorities of their village with other villages in the state.

Many are still sceptical of the real impact because so few Indians have computers. The answer lies in interactive cable TV and in Internet kiosks. Although India has only five million computers and thirty-eight million telephones, it has thirty-four million homes with cable TV and these are growing eight per cent a year. By 2005 most cable homes will have access to the Internet from many of the 700,000 local STD/PCO booths. Internet usage may be low today, but it is bound to grow rapidly in the future, and e-governance in India may not be a dream.

# 11

## Making the Nation Competitive

*The men who have changed the universe have never accomplished it
by changing officials but always by inspiring the people.*

—Napoleon I, *Maxims* (1804–15)

$\mathcal{I}$t became fashionable in the nineties to talk of national competitive
advantage. Not just businessmen, but even politicians and
bureaucrats increasingly began to use the phrase. While this is a
useful concept, it is easy to fall into the mercantilist trap of
believing that nations compete in the global market and policy
makers determine market share. The truth is that only companies
compete and they win or lose share based on their capabilities.
When a critical mass of firms in a specific industry from a
particular nation is repeatedly successful in the world market and
helps to generate sizeable export earnings, then that nation is
loosely termed to be competitive *in that particular industry*. There
is no one-on-one competition between nation states.

During the nineties, we were influenced in India by the
American debate on 'strategic trade'. Some Indians enthusiastically
read tracts like Robert Reich's *Work of Nations* and Lester Thurow's
*Head to Head* and we began to view India as a giant corporation
competing with other countries in the global market place. Our
media picked up the phrase 'India Inc' and began to use it widely,
and the Swadeshi Jagran Manch, the rightist protectionist

organization allied to the BJP, tried to persuade the government to target specific industries and lend them support.

Governments can help companies to become competitive by sensible fiscal and monetary policies and investments in social and physical infrastructure. Political stability, law and order and a responsive legal system all make a country a good place to do business and contribute to national competitiveness. But direct intervention by the government in order 'to help industry' is generally counter-productive, inefficient and often insidious. We have learned this lesson painfully in India through all the years of the licence–permit raj. But even richer countries that tried to intervene in the name of industrial policy usually failed. Years ago the Europeans lost millions in an European Economic Community (EEC) attempt to create competitiveness in high definition television. The Japanese lost billions of yen in a government inspired programme to enter into mainframe computers. The lesson is that no industry is more important than another, and even if it were, governments would be the last to find out. Thus, the notion of 'targeting' an industry is fraught with problems and should be avoided. What is important to competitiveness is for governments to create conditions that help raise productivity in every industry.

In Chapter Six, I looked at how our companies could become competitive; this chapter brings together a number of essays on how a government can help create national competitiveness in the post-reform age The first essay introduces the notion of national competitive advantage. The second seeks to learn lessons from China on competitiveness in a number of areas. The third reminds us that military power cannot be sustained unless it is backed by economic strength. Finally, two short pieces: the first is on the Competition Bill; the second is about the trade-off between the environment and jobs.

## The Enemy Is Inside

Once in a while a book comes along that not only influences the minds of policy makers but it creates a new vocabulary for discourse. *The Competitive Advantage of Nations* by Michael Porter was such a book. 'A nation's prosperity does not grow only because of its natural endowments, its labour pool, its interest rates, or its currency's value, as classical economics insists. It grows out of the capacity of its industry to innovate and upgrade,' says Porter. A nation can thus 'create' competitive advantage when its firms insulate themselves from competition through technology or service based on the proprietary skills of their employees. Simply having an educated workforce, as India does, is not enough. The skills of the workforce must be applied to its exporting industries in order to gain national competitive advantage.

Successful exporting nations have always had intensely competitive home markets, and robust competition is the school in which industry learns to succeed, because it creates demanding customers, who continually push companies to improve quality. India failed to understand this, and its greatest mistake was to virtually eliminate competition in its domestic market. Until 1991, our licensing policy restricted domestic competition; FERA and high tariffs inhibited foreign competition. The Monopolies and Restrictive Trade Practices (MRTP) Act, which was meant to foster competition, usually had the opposite effect because it stifled a firm merely on account of size. Porter gives many examples of how intense competition in the domestic market leads to global competitiveness; local rivalry within their country led American software and hardware companies to global leadership. In Japan, fierce competition among 112 machine tool manufacturers, twenty-five makers of music stereos, fifteen camera producers and nine car companies also led to global success. Ten years after the reforms, many Indian markets still do not have the sort of vigorous competition that will teach our companies to become world players.

Porter's second determinant of national advantage is the ability of successful local companies to create a network of top-class suppliers and ancillaries, somewhat in the way that Maruti has done in India. He illustrates this with the example of the Italian footwear industry, where shoe producers interact closely with leather producers on new textures and colours whilst the shoes are still on their drawing boards. Leather producers, in turn, gain early insights into fashion trends because of this early dialogue.

The question is, how do Indian companies expect to compete and gain market share in the global market? Initially, it is bound to be on the primitive basis of factor accumulation—the way all developing countries start, with cheap labour and raw materials—and our present exports of undifferentiated products are based on this advantage. But this also makes them vulnerable to the shifting exchange rates of our competitors and to competition from even lower wage countries.

Gradually, Indian industry will rise to a second stage and become strategic-minded rather than opportunistic. Our companies will focus on excelling in one area of business rather than being a jack of all trades; today the average Indian business house is still engaged in too many business activities. They will seek out more sophisticated customers and higher value-added segments of the market. Rather than make generic products, they will invest in upgrading human, capital and technological resources; establish a formal in-house R&D programme and restructure work practices in order to raise productivity. Although industry will have assimilated modern technology, it will still compete in low price segments with heavy reliance on foreign components, machinery and customers. This is the stage at which South Korea and Taiwan are at the moment.

Eventually, at a third stage, Indian industry will have to be driven by innovation if it has to become world-class. It will have to assume technology and process leadership. Japan and Germany are at this stage. Indian companies will also have to get bigger to be more competitive. Only large companies will be able to make sustained investments in R&D, match the marketing resources and global distribution capabilities of world-scale competitors, and be able to devote huge resources to training and upgrading of their employee skills. Smaller companies will largely play the role of ancillaries or suppliers to the large companies. In Japan, Sony, Panasonic and Toshiba routinely leverage the innovations of their component suppliers into the global market. Microsoft and Intel achieved global leadership on the broad shoulders of IBM. The success of Silicon Valley companies depended on AT&T and Motorola.

The proper role of the government in creating competitive advantage is as a catalyst. The government cannot create competitive industries; only companies can do that. But governments can encourage or even push companies to raise their sights. They can promote sustained investment in human skills and innovation through fiscal policy. They can ensure competition by reducing state and private monopolies, removing price controls and lowering tariff and trade barriers.

Ultimately, it is company leadership that achieves global advantage. A good company chief recognizes the central role of change and innovation—and the uncomfortable truth that innovation grows out of pressure and challenge. This has rich implications for our education policy. How do we get our best talents into export industries like tea, gem-cutting, leather, readymade garments, software? If we value exports then we must attach prestige and rewards to working in them so that young talent will be attracted to them. As Porter says, 'nations tend to be successful in activities and industries that people admire or depend on the activities from which the nation's heroes emerge'. Japan's heroes work for Toyota, Sony and Honda; German heroes work for BMW, Audi and Mercedes. While we did not have national heroes in our traditional exporting businesses, we did begin in the nineties to make our software warriors into national icons. People like Narayana Murthy and Premji increasingly became role models for the young. This is a welcome development.

'Indians are among the brightest people on this earth,' said a German statesman in a candid discussion at Davos in the early nineties, 'and yet India can't seem to take advantage of the global economy. Why can't Indians understand that there is only one game in town? Those who learn to play it well will make it in the twenty-first century; others will be left behind.' That game is, of course, exports, and no nation in modern times has grown rich or economically strong without becoming a successful world trader. India's finest economic years since Independence were between 1993 and 1997. It is not surprising that exports also boomed, increasing twenty per cent a year during the period.

India and China had the same level of exports in 1974—around $13 billion. By 2000, China's exports had crossed $200 billion and India's were languishing below $50 billion. The trade numbers, more than anything else, explain why the world respects China and ignores India. By now most people have realized that East Asia's miraculous success was built on exports. But few realize that to be a top exporter you have to be a top importer. The world's top fifteen exporting nations are also the world's top fifteen importing nations—and virtually in the same order—according to WTO data. This makes sense: the more output you want, the more input you need. Since no country makes everything (or should make everything), they import them.

India has always been bitterly antagonistic to imports. To begin with, we always had very high tariffs. Then, we treated an importer as someone akin to a crook and placed the most terrible hurdles in his or her way. 'But we have always allowed imports for export purposes,' say the bureaucrats. That's true, theoretically. But our systems and procedures are so hostile to imports that they break the back of any honest exporter. One back-broken exporter told me a few years ago, 'Only stupid people will export from India.'

Most Indians cannot begin to fathom how we have suffered from reserving around 800 industries and products for the small-scale industry (SSI) sector. Our policy rewards a small manufacturer for remaining small and prevents him from achieving economies of scale. Ironically, Chinese small industry is sweeping the world because their policy encourages them to mechanize, grow and become large. Foreign buyers give credit and take equity in small Chinese firms and focus them on exports.

What was reserved for the small-scale sector are simple products such as garments, toys, shoes, etc. These are precisely the ones where we have competitive advantage with our cheap labour. The East Asian countries started by exporting these products and built their export miracles on their back. While the global economy needs these products in very large quantities, the Indian exporter was not allowed to make and sell large volumes. Large volumes need large machines, and these exceeded the capital cost limits allowed by law to the small-scale sector. Hence, our exporters became an unprofessional bunch while in our competitor nations, which encouraged economies of scale, exporters are large, professional companies. This explains why we don't find big names such as Tatas, Birlas or Ambanis in the export business.

Our bureaucrats will retort that an exporter is exempted from SSI limits if he gives export guarantees. True, but this is flawed logic. It shows ignorance of the ground reality of how you build a business. The fact is that you must not separate domestic and export businesses in this manner. As Porter has pointed out, companies learn to grow and become strong through robust competition in the domestic market, and only thus do they gain confidence to compete in the savagely competitive world market. If you disbar them from selling in the domestic market, they will never learn to compete.

When I was at Procter and Gamble India, we tried and failed to make India a sourcing base for one of our products for the whole of Asia. The cost of the high technology machine needed exceeded the SSI investment limits and $500 million in potential exports were lost to India. For these and other reasons, the Abid Husain Committee recommended scrapping the small-scale reservations policy. This has finally begun to happen, and a few industries have been de-reserved in recent years, but it is a case of too little too late. Meanwhile, China's exports of toys, garments and small appliances had risen from $3 billion in 1985 to $70 billion in 1997 whereas ours has gone from $2 billion to $14 billion in the same period.

According to the 1996 World Investment Report, as much as one-third of all trade now takes place within transnational firms, and another third between transnationals and other companies. The bulk of world trade is not the export and import of finished goods but a highly complex exchange of components among the subsidiaries of multinational companies based in different countries. Data from the United Nations Council for Trade and Development (UNCTAD) show that American multinationals exported forty per cent of the sales of their subsidiaries in 1993. It was as high as 64.4 per cent from the developing countries of Asia and 84.9 per cent from Malaysia. However, it was only 4.1 per cent from India. Multinationals do not export from India because our systems and procedures for imports are largely antagonistic to the rapid turnaround time that multinationals require to satisfy both internal and external customers. Multinational companies are willing to put up with our inefficiencies when it comes to the domestic market, but they won't risk their global business to the uncertainties of our red tape, corrupt customs officials, congested ports and unionized dock labour. Hewlett Packard (HP) seriously looked at India in the mid-nineties for globally sourcing print heads for its ink jet printers. But it picked Malaysia instead because it was more reliable. HP wanted a turnaround time of twenty-four hours from order to shipment; the best India could do was five days.

Is it surprising that we are a failure as an exporting nation? It is a self-inflicted defeat caused by our policies and procedures. If India wants to win the game and become a successful exporter, it must further reduce duties and non-tariff barriers; it must scrap all SSI reservations; it must improve infrastructure, especially port handling; it must cut red tape and discipline customs officials. Only thus will it become a better place to do business.

Outstanding talent is scarce in any nation. And a nation's success depends on the type of education its talented people choose, where they decide to work and their effort and commitment. If we want to succeed in the world market, it is obvious that we must get some of our best talent into our exporting enterprises.

We export mainly readymade garments and textiles, leather goods, gems and jewellery, low-end engineering products, tea and software. These are products of 'sweat shops' (except software) and our competitive advantage seems to lie in our low wages. As I have pointed out, our policy of reserving simple, labour-intensive manufactures for the small-scale sector ensures that our exports belong generally to small, unorganized and often unprofessional entrepreneurs. It is hard to imagine these enterprises being able to attract real talent (let alone top MBAs), except, perhaps, as 'entrepreneur partners'. Yet every exporter I have spoken to complains about the difficulty of getting good people. So, how do we get our exporters to attract talent?

Every export sector has an industry association. If an industry association and our better institutions of management could come together and if the latter could 'adopt' one export industry, which is local to its area, then we might be able to create a conduit for talent. For example, the Indian Institute of Management (IIM), Ahmedabad might adopt gem-cutting, since it is primarily Gujarat-based; the Indian Institute of Foreign Trade (IIFT) might adopt the readymade garment industry which has a large base around Delhi. IIM, Kolkata might adopt tea which is based in the east while IIM, Bangalore could adopt the software industry. These are merely examples, and institutes other than IIMs might, in fact, be more suited for this purpose.

What do I mean by 'adoption'? I mean the management school would set up, in close collaboration with the adopted industry, training programmes and courses that are relevant to the particular export industry. Industry, in turn, would send its people to teach at the institute as guest faculty and its employees to be trained in the latest skills and in upgrading their knowledge related to the industry. The school would also become a source of fresh, talented young people who would join the industry and make a career in it. It may not be a management graduate. It could even be technicians whom the industry would welcome for the basic skills and the commitment they brought to their jobs.

Industry might argue that they already have their own specialized institutions. This is true, but the majority of these institutes are of indifferent standard and are languishing. In the end, 'adoption' by top schools may not guarantee the highest quality, but I reckon the chances of success will be greater. If it works, then, in course of time, the 'adopted' institutions will create a knowledge base that our rivals will find difficult to imitate and it will provide industry with a sustainable competitive advantage. Obviously, the ability of the industry to attract students and technicians and the track record of the graduates will determine success in the end.

Management institutes will argue that bright young MBAs will not be attracted to our 'hole in the wall' export shops. They may well be right, but if there is commitment to the idea there will be plenty of creative solutions as institutes work in partnership with industry. If MBA graduates are not the answer, it may be more appropriate to work with a different pool of students—perhaps older persons, with experience in exports, and train them to become 'entrepreneur partners' of existing exporters. And you will need a curriculum that prepares managers to become entrepreneurs with special skills related to the specific export industry.

Eventually, with a persistent building up of a knowledge and skill base specific to the industry, our export companies will, one hopes, begin to innovate and upgrade themselves and slowly gain market share. Exporters, I think, should welcome the highly specialized education and a growing pool of talent. The management institution too will benefit by getting a world-class reputation in a specialized area. The country will obviously gain through rising competitiveness and rising exports.

This is the model of the University of California at Davis. Situated in the California wine country, it set up the world's leading centre of winemaking research and talent in cooperation with the local wine industry. This research institution provided the California wine industry a major competitive advantage as it swept the world market in the eighties and early nineties and became one of the best in the world. Porter cites the example of Denmark, which has two hospitals that treat and study diabetes, and it is no wonder that Denmark has been the world's leading exporter of insulin. Similarly, Holland has premier research institutes in cultivating, packing and shipping flowers, a field in which Holland is the world leader.

We have to remember that the competitive advantage of a nation is not general to its entire industry. It is specific to a few industries. Even the most successful nations have only a few industries where they enjoy global market share. The rest of their industries are weak and globally uncompetitive. Therefore, it is important to focus on those industries where we already enjoy a competitive advantage and the challenge is how to increase the advantage over time.

## Ignore Pakistan, Heed China

A few years ago the respected head of a multinational company observed the unreal quality of our public discourse. He said that he had read our newspapers voraciously for two weeks and for every report on China he had counted eight on Pakistan. 'To the world at large only China and India matter in Asia,' he said. 'When people say that the twenty-first century will belong to Asia, they have China in mind, and then India. Japan doesn't count, because its demographics are wrong. Pakistan doesn't even exist in the big picture. Although China is currently ahead, India is the only country that could counter-balance it. I realize Pakistan is your neighbour, but so is China.'

Listening to him I was reminded of one of sage Patanjali's aphorisms: 'What a man thinks, so he becomes.' Patanjali was referring to controlling our thoughts during meditation, but what is true for an individual is also true for a nation. We are obsessed with Pakistan and so we will become like Pakistan—a failed economic and political state. Instead, we should engage with China, the most dynamic economy in the world for two decades. Pakistan is a distraction and pulls us down. China will push us up.

What can China teach us? The first lesson is to have clear national objectives. For twenty years China has had only one objective—to become an economic superpower and lift its people out of poverty—and it is pursuing it single-mindedly. Nations, like individuals, perform best when they are one-pointed. The Chinese have learned that law and order, speedy justice, political stability— all good in themselves—also promote growth by creating a sound climate for investment. Chinese leaders wake up in the morning and they think only one thought—the prosperity of their people. What do *our* leaders think about?

*The New York Times* reported in January 2002 that there were five Chinese delegations in Bangalore in the previous month alone, trying to understand India's success in software. 'They have beaten us in everything, now they also want to defeat us in software,' the CEO of an Indian company, who had refused the Chinese entry into his premises, was quoted as saying. Premier Zhu Rongji visited Bangalore the same month to woo Indian companies to come to China. He went to Delhi not to talk about Aksai Chin or Pakistan but to establish a Beijing–India airlink.

'Foreign investment has been the fuel behind the Chinese miracle,' reported the *Wall Street Journal*. 'Every dollar of foreign investment yields five dollars of additional output to the Chinese economy. That compares with less than two dollars in the state-owned sector.' More than fifty per cent of China's phenomenal exports come from foreign enterprises. Even assuming that seventy per cent of Chinese FDI is from non-resident Chinese, the thirty per cent that is not is four times larger than ours. Yet Indians are the ones who fear foreign investment. Our concerns over swadeshi reflect our inferiority complex and our lack of confidence in our ability to compete in the global market place. How did the notoriously insular Chinese manage to change their attitude to foreign capital? China realizes far more than we do the enormous potential of global capital for creating wealth and eliminating poverty. That is why it is wooing it with much greater vigour and effectiveness. Once investors come to China, they are more hospitably treated by the government. The Chinese government also targets specific multinational companies and goes after them single-mindedly. This is a second lesson China can teach us: how to get more foreign investment.

Why China is growing so fast is the result of a phenomenal rise in labour productivity, according to a study by Zulin Hu and Mohsin Khan of the International Monetary Fund (IMF). They trace this not only to foreign enterprises, but also to Chinese town and village enterprises, 'which have drawn more than 100 million people from low productivity agriculture into higher value-added manufacturing.' Started initially as simple agricultural processing factories, many are now world-class exporters. China's reforms started from below—unlike ours—and the third lesson we can learn is to shift the focus of our reforms on to agriculture and the village.

Another secret of Chinese productivity is flexible labour laws. The Chinese are able to hire and fire workers based on customer demand. Chinese workers in state enterprises are routinely punished for indiscipline. This is not possible in India. Even when a public sector enterprise/company is sick and has stopped production, the workers earn full salary. Hence, a fourth lesson is to reform our labour laws.

There are many more lessons. But first, let's decide as a nation to ignore Pakistan and heed China. Every Indian leader should scrawl 'China' in big letters in his office to remind him every day who is our real competitor. While China is currently ahead (it also has a twelve-year head start in economic reforms) our economy has performed well in the past two decades, and if we accelerate our reforms, especially in agriculture and education, we will gain ground. If we do not, then China is going to push us around and humiliate us in the twenty-first century.

~

What makes a global investor decide to invest in a particular country? When I was member of the operations committee of Procter and Gamble between 1991 and 1994, I had the opportunity to observe the dynamics of investment decisions of a major global investor with operations in more than fifty countries. I learned that what made China and India attractive to multinationals is primarily a growing middle class. China's consuming class is far bigger than India's and it is better off, and this is partially because China has had a head start in reforms, and it has been growing faster. Both societies also have a lively entrepreneurial class, which knows the commercial game. This class is a potential partner of multinationals in distribution, in supplying raw and packaging materials, in wholesaling, retailing and in contract manufacturing.

India's advantages over China are the prevalence of English, and the global economy rewards those who know it. India has also built up a flourishing capital market which is capable of raising ample local funds if needed. India has had open, democratic governments since Independence with a record of orderly succession. Finally, the Indian judicial system is an asset, even though it is extremely slow. These advantages are well known. However, there is one factor that is less well appreciated. In its decision to invest in detergents in India, Procter and Gamble was also strongly motivated because its global competitor, Unilever, was present here and had a strong market position. Being absent from what are potentially the two largest markets in the world, they realized, would put them at a disadvantage in the long term. In short, the hunt for global market share is a strong driving force in investment decisions.

The question is why, despite these assets, has India not been able to attract foreign investment in the nineties when smaller countries in Asia were far more successful? We received less than one per cent of the world's foreign investment. Our biggest disadvantage over China is the attitude of our bureaucracy. I have worked in six countries and nowhere in the world is bureaucratic red tape as big a hurdle as in India. Corruption exists in many countries, but nowhere is it as inefficient. In the words of one foreign investor, the Indian bureaucracy seems to take sadistic pleasure in stopping enterprise.

We can also learn from the Chinese to shed our xenophobic attitude to foreign investors. Our swadeshi activists demand that we be selective about foreign investment and this, on the face of it, appears to be reasonable. But the Chinese have realized that the investment world doesn't work that way. Foreign investors suffer from a herd mentality and act on 'market sentiment'. Before deciding to invest in a distant land they want to know whether their investment will be safe. So, when they view attacks on Pepsi and Kentucky Fried Chicken on their television screens, as it happened in the mid-nineties, everyone becomes concerned.

The Chinese have realized that foreign investors are not lined up outside their doors waiting to come in. The brutal reality of the global market is that the demand for capital is greater than its supply. Global capital goes where opportunities are commensurate with risks and are competitive with alternative options. Indian capital behaves no differently. Why does it flock to Mumbai and Bangalore and ignore Patna? The harsh truth is that India is to global capital what Bihar is to Indian capital. We need foreign capital more than it needs us. We need a massive amount of funds to upgrade our creaky infrastructure and neither our government nor our private industry has these sort of resources. Hence, we have to woo the foreign investor. With our poor image we have to work harder. With the reforms we have signalled to the world that India has opened up, but we are not in a position to say, 'Yes, but.' Thus, we cannot be selective. We cannot be half pregnant.

Even if we could be selective, there are good reasons why we should not be. The point is, who would do the selecting and on what basis? As soon as we give the power of selecting to a politician or a bureaucrat we risk returning to the bad old days of the licence–permit raj. To minimize corruption, it is best to be transparent and not give discretionary powers to anyone. Besides, by being selective we give our industrialists another excuse to demand protection for various products and risk becoming a closed economy again.

I am an admirer of Mahatma Gandhi, but his swadeshi ideology was badly flawed. As a political tactic to galvanize Indians against British rule, swadeshi served its purpose at the time, but as an economic philosophy in today's competitive, borderless economy it is self-destructive. The record of the past fifty years amply shows that countries that were open and encouraged foreign investment have consistently outperformed those which were closed. And none lost its sovereignty. Tiny Singapore built a strong economy based on foreign investment. Today it regularly lectures the United States on moral values and the superiority of the Confucian ethic. So, why is a big country like India afraid?

Lest we forget, we did sincerely try to practise swadeshi for forty years until 1991. And what was the result? We ended up producing high-cost, shoddy goods. And we lost confidence in our ability to export. We became defeatist. Swadeshi bred in us a Third World feeling of inferiority and dependency.

Equally harmful in swadeshi thinking is the presumption that someone should tell me what is good for me. Speaking for myself, I don't eat Kentucky Fried Chicken because I am vegetarian. But I don't deny the freedom to another Indian to eat what he likes. Millions of Americans don't eat junk food, but they don't stop others because they believe it is a small price to pay for one's freedom. I am distrustful of people who tell me what is good for me. For instance, for forty years we were told that telephones were a luxury! Lurking deep in the swadeshi mind is a Chinese style 'command mentality', which ultimately wants to build an authoritarian society. I am more and more convinced that an open economy is our ticket to freedom while swadeshi is the road to slavery.

Although we don't wish to import the command mentality of the Chinese leadership, we ought to learn from the Chinese to be more enthusiastic about the market. I sometimes ask myself why is it that so many Indians, especially intellectuals, hate the market. There may be two reasons, I think. One, there is no one in charge in the market economy and this causes people enormous anxiety. The second reason is that we tend to equate the market with businessmen. Since we think that businessmen are crooked, we tend to transfer this negative image to the market, and feel the need for the heavy hand of government to keep the market in line. Because the market is invisible, nothing anyone can say will convince people that the market is morally blind; that it is merely an arena in which people buy and sell. We forget that the market is, in fact, the best ally of the ordinary citizen, because it forces businessmen to compete. It is like democracy, in this respect, which forces politicians to compete.

This suspicion of markets is magnified when it comes to the global market place, for truly no one is in charge there. And for this reason multinational companies and foreign financial institutions become obvious targets. And to diminish the anxiety, we take comfort in the familiarity of swadeshi objects and protectionism. Although we see today the wondrous spectacle of thousands of young Indians starting new business ventures all around us, the idea that their struggle for personal gain might actually promote the good of the whole society is too bizarre for most people. No wonder Samuel Johnson said, 'There is nothing which requires more to be illustrated by philosophy than trade does.'

Even my mother, who thinks that socialism was the work of the devil, believes in 'fair' prices and 'decent' wages. Although she accepts that people must earn vastly different salaries in order to give incentives for performance, she complains that there is now too much greed in our society. Like most educated Indians, she does not think, as I do, that better results will be achieved if people shamelessly follow their self-interest in the bazaar rather than lofty moral principles.

Critics write much nonsense about the obsolete technology of multinational companies, which they say keeps Indian firms permanently dependent. It is the usual gibberish from the over-active minds of the 'dependency school', which has no basis in the real world and shows a total lack of understanding of how companies operate. A multinational, like any company, invests in order to succeed in the market place, and it will employ whatever technology it takes to win. If it employs old technology against a competitor with the latest technology then it clearly shoots itself in the foot. Multinationals have no interest in neo-colonial constructs.

'Globalization' to us should mean the global expansion of Indian enterprise in areas where India has a comparative advantage. This is what it means to companies like Ranbaxy and Dr Reddy's, who are making it in the global economy. It is the same with our software warriors in Infosys, Wipro and Satyam. Along with generic pharmaceutical and software, another area of potential competitive advantage is agriculture and horticulture. To realize our potential, however, we ought to be more relaxed, like the Chinese, with capitalism and globalization.

The Chinese can also teach us how to harness the power of our diaspora. The Chinese diaspora is fifty-five million, but ours is also substantial, numbering more than twenty million people. The resurgence of China is greatly the work of non-resident Chinese. Almost two-thirds of the annual foreign direct investment of China comes from overseas Chinese. They control an empire from coastal China to hi-tech centres in Silicon Valley, to Manhattan. Their three financial centres of Hong Kong, Singapore and Taiwan together possess foreign reserves twice as large as those of Japan, Germany or the United States. Like the Japanese and the Jews, the success of the Chinese is a result of a passion for education, but unlike the Japanese, the Chinese are less insular and, therefore, better placed to succeed in the global economy.

The wealth of the twenty million Indians abroad is estimated to be equal to the country's GDP, and many have close emotional links with India. They would like to do something for their homeland. We made a good start when PIO, a new three-letter word, entered our vocabulary in the nineties. People of Indian Origin (PIO) began to receive identity cards, along with visa-free entry into India and other benefits available to non-resident Indians. The card was expensive and only a few availed of it, but those who did were able to put their children into school, start a business and make investments in India. This was an unqualifiedly good idea, even though it was not well implemented. We are now moving beyond it to the excellent idea of dual citizenship.

When Chandrababu Naidu visited New York, non-resident Andhrites told him that they would like to help alleviate poverty in Andhra Pradesh, as long as they did not have to deal with the government. Consequently, a foundation has been set up in Hyderabad for this purpose, managed entirely by private citizens. More than the money, the liberated minds of the overseas Indians will make a big difference. Freed from the shackles of India, Indians abroad are hugely successful, and they can teach us management methods, teamwork, the power of technology and a positive attitude.

Harnam Singh Sidhu is the PIO that I know best. He is a prosperous businessman in Columbus, Ohio. His grandfather went to America at the beginning of this century. He worked hard and rose in life. Harnam was bright and got into Harvard. He had no interest in India until he read Sanskrit there. Today, he runs a chain of drugstores in Ohio, is happily married to a white American woman and they have two children. He feels American, but occasionally India tugs at his heart.

Harnam came to Delhi in 1998. As his plane landed, he panicked. He did not know what to expect. He had heard horrendous stories of Indian customs. However, his entry was painless, and he quickly decided that he would stop being American and look at India through Indian eyes. He discarded his elegant

Italian leather jacket and Levis and switched to kurta-pyjama and chappals. He roamed the streets, chatting with ordinary people. He felt in good spirits. However, an aggressive Punjabi woman snapped at him at Lajpat Nagar one day. 'Who are you trying to fool with your American accent?' she said. Harnam felt crushed. He explained that he was an American. She looked him up and down, felt puzzled, and left without saying a word.

A few days later Harnam left for his ancestral village near Ludhiana. He expected to find a bunch of ignorant peasants, living in mud huts like in the old movies. But he was shocked. 'There were no poor in my village,' he said on his return. 'All the houses were pucca, with TV antennae; one even had a dish. The kids were educated. I was the worst dressed around. All the poor are in Delhi!' He left for Ohio with good feelings and great plans for investing in India. A few months later, I got an email from him, saying that he wanted to be among the first to get a PIO card.

The dramatic contrast between the success of Indians abroad and the economic failure of the Indian nation continues to confound people. A book by Joel Kotkin, *Tribes*, in 1992, brought new interest to the debate. In a long chapter titled 'The Greater India', Kotkin argues that overseas Indians are among five global tribes at the hub of the new global economy and are likely to dominate commerce in the twenty-first century. The other four dispersed ethnic groups are the Jews, the Japanese, the overseas Chinese and Anglo-Americans.

Kotkin also says in *Tribes*, 'With the end of the Cold War and the rise of a new global economy, age-old ethnic ties are emerging as the most powerful force in international commerce.' In his study of the evolution of international business, he identifies three characteristics which are shared by these five global diasporas: a strong ethnic identity, with a sense of mutual dependence and emphasis on family structure; a global network based on tribal trust that allows the group to function collectively; and a passion for technology and a belief in scientific progress.

At a time when modern tribalism conjures a vision of a base

clannishness, usually identified with Ayodhya, Afghanistan, Yugoslavia and racial strife in Los Angeles, Kotkin has uncovered a positive and cosmopolitan tribalism among geographically dispersed groups which is feeding the global economy and leading to the diminution of the nation state.

Each of the tribes has something to teach us in India about how to succeed in the world economy. From the oldest tribe, the Jews, we can learn the 'discipline of tradition', in the phrase of Edmond Rothschild, whose family, in the eighteenth century, possessed more influence over the affairs of Europe than most governments. Isolated among hostile strangers, the Jews were forced to develop a powerful tradition of self-help and discipline. The British and their progeny were propelled by the Calvinistic virtues of thrift and hard work as they went abut moulding the pattern of modern technology, commerce and capitalist institutions that define today's global economy. The Japanese diaspora is largely by design as they despatched temporary corporate sojourners to all corners of the globe. Like the Jews, their insularity is combined with openness to new ways to make them conservative yet very innovative.

Overseas Indians 'today represent one of the best educated, affluent groupings in the world, with a strong presence in Britain, North America, Africa and South-east Asia,' says Kotkin. They have 'a long historical memory and a well-developed culture and sense of uniqueness'. Like the Chinese, they followed the British flag to gain a permanent foothold in Africa, Southeast Asia, Fiji and the West Indies. Today they own real estate globally worth $100 billon and boast of 300 multi-millionaires in the United Kingdom alone. Their enormous success has been due to the same reasons as the other ethnic groups. Although their ties to India are not as strong as those of the Chinese to China, they 'keep their *man* (heart) in India even as they place their *dhan* (wealth) in Britain and their *tan* (body) in a third country in Asia or Africa.'

We can also learn from their quiet successes, such as the incredible story of the Gujarati Jains, who have established a commercial empire ranging from their stone-cutting base in Palanpur to Hong Kong, Tel Aviv, Antwerp and New York. Within two decades, they have grown to be second only to Jews in the worldwide diamond trade and by the mid-eighties they accounted for half of the global purchases of rough diamonds. They should be the heroes of modern India; instead they have a feeling of being besieged.

We can also learn from greater India's ethic of self-help. Indians abroad don't blame anyone when they are in trouble; they accept that the world is unfair and pull themselves up by their bootstraps and get on with it. In democratic India we have developed a nasty habit of blaming others. Ever since Mrs Gandhi, our politicians are quick to blame a 'foreign hand'. Businessmen blame the government for over-regulation. Intellectuals blame the West for unequal trade terms, of neo-colonial exploitation by multinational corporations, which appropriates our 'surplus value' and keeps us 'developmentally impaired'.

If we teach these virtues of discipline, hard work, self-help and education to our young, Kotkin's prophecy might well come true: 'Indians boast one of the world's deepest reservoirs of scientific and technical talent. If their homeland can be liberalized and reformed they have the potential to develop into the next powerful global economic force.'

⁓

Another thing we can learn from the Chinese is to regard the WTO as a friend rather than an enemy. It is ironical that throughout the nineties, the Chinese were desperate to get into the WTO while we were trashing it. The Chinese have learned that trade is good, and free trade is even better. This is also one of the first lessons that students of economics learn.

If free trade is good, why do nations put up barriers to it? They do so in the mistaken belief that imports are bad; that they must protect inefficient local companies that cannot compete with cheaper and better products from abroad. In the process, they sacrifice the interests of a majority of their citizens who are denied the world's best and cheapest products. They forget that imports spur local companies to innovate and upgrade their products and force them to lower their costs. In the process, many inefficient companies are driven out of the market, but robust new ones come up, which are able to compete.

We have been debating the wrong question in India. The issue is not whether WTO is fair or unfair. The issue is how do we in India take advantage of the unprecedented opportunity offered by international trade, now that barriers are gradually coming down everywhere. WTO is merely a symbol of this opportunity and it might do more for world prosperity than any institution in the world's history. It frames the rules of trade and is the global umpire in trade disputes. Set up in 1995, it has become the most important international organization; more important, arguably, than the UN Security Council. No nation in it has veto power, and the United States, for example, routinely loses in WTO rulings.

But Indian attitudes have reluctantly begun to change after 1991. Many are finally realizing that in trade there do not have to be losers—everyone who plays the game can win. Since India is not a part of any trading bloc, such as the European Union or the North American Free Trade Association, we have no alternative but to turn to the WTO. The WTO is our friend because it is based on the idea of multilateral trade. Its fundamental principle is that if a nation offers a special concession to another nation—such as lower import duty for a particular product—then it has to offer the same privilege to all the 135 member nations of the WTO. For India, this is an ideal way to gain access to world markets without having to negotiate with each of the 135 countries.

⌒

For two decades now, China has been pursuing a one-child population policy. Is this something that we ought to emulate? Many educated Indians are deeply concerned about our population problem, and let me begin by asking, is there indeed a population problem? In 1798 Thomas Malthus published his famous *Essay on Population*, when the world was nearing a billion people, and he predicted terrible disasters because humans were breeding too rapidly and food would run out. In 1968, Paul Ehrlich predicted that one-fifth of humanity would starve to death by 1985. In 1999, the six billionth child was born on the earth and the one billionth in India, and the Malthusian nightmare has not happened.

The truth is that food supply has consistently outstripped the population, and today people everywhere are eating better than they did in the past. In India, we have consistently produced a food surplus for twenty years, and today we have the largest store of food in the world. Our problem is how to make the poor prosperous so they can get to it. We have thirty-five per cent more food available per head than we did twenty years ago, and it costs less than half of what it did in 1950 in constant rupees. Clearly, food has won the race over population. Our problem is poverty, not food nor population.

If food is not a problem, what about other resources? In 1980, the most celebrated bet in history took place between two professors, Paul Ehrlich, the doomsayer, and Julian Simon, the doom slayer. Ehrlich had forecast that prices of non-renewable commodities would skyrocket because of the exploding population, and they bet $1,000 on the prices of five metals—copper, nickel, tin, tungsten and chrome—over the next ten years. By 1990, the prices of all the resources had declined sharply, although global population had risen by 800 million, the greatest increase in history. Mr Ehrlich sent a cheque to Mr Simon.

Others worry about overcrowded cities and the effects on the environment. This too is an exaggerated fear. Prof. James Tooley calculates that if we packed all the world's six billion people into Uttar Pradesh, each person would still have 500 square feet. In India our density is only 320 persons per square km compared to Holland's 457, South Korea's 460, and Japan's 331, all of whom are richer and whose people seem to manage a reasonable quality of life. I believe that, in time, with more prosperity the poor countries will also improve their air and water, as the rich countries have done.

The world's population growth has also begun to slow down. India's Census 2000 shows a national decline from our 2.2 per cent historic annual growth rate to 1.9 per cent, with the virtuous states declining dramatically. Kerala, Tamil Nadu, Andhra Pradesh, Goa, and the four northeast states have already reached the ideal replacement level of fertility. West Bengal, Orissa, Karnataka, Uttaranchal and Himachal Pradesh will get there by 2010. Maharashtra, Gujarat, Assam and Punjab will reach this point by 2020. These virtuous states are in the midst of what experts call a demographic transition, when population naturally slows in response to economic and social development. The Nobel laureate, Gary Becker, explained this as the natural desire of parents to contain numbers in order to invest more in the quality of each child's life.

But the numbers keep rising relentlessly in the states of the Hindi belt, where neither enough girls go to school, nor do they have access to basic health care and contraceptives. Researcher Mamta Murthi and others have provided statistical evidence from inter-district studies to suggest that population begins to slow when girls go to school and start earning. Hence, there has been a major shift in global thinking on population, away from control and towards the community's health, education and women's empowerment. Evidence shows that women's fertility desires are already at or near the replacement level.

The answer to my rhetorical question then is 'no'. This is not one of the lessons we need to learn from China. Coercive policies such as China's are morally wrong on grounds of human rights. Its one child policy, according to some observers, is also leading to a generation of over-indulged 'super-brats'.

It is a strange irony that humanity's material condition continues to improve in every way, while human beings continue to sit around complaining that things are getting worse. David Hume, the Scottish philosopher, may have a clue about why people worry so much about the population problem. 'The humour of blaming the present and admiring the past is strongly rooted in human nature,' he says, 'and has an influence even on persons endowed with the profoundest judgement.'

## Living in the Post-Bang World

I am not thrilled with owning a nuclear bomb. This puts me, I realize, in a tiny minority of Indians. But I would have been prouder if, instead of Pokhran, our government had announced that India's poverty had come down to twenty per cent, or literacy had risen to eighty per cent, or that we had achieved eight per cent GDP growth. This is because I believe that national security is not only about having bombs and missiles, but its genuine roots lie in economic strength. Raising our ranking on the Human Development Index or on the Per Capita Income Index or on the National Competitiveness Index—we are amongst the lowest in the world on all three—would be a far more satisfying and surer way to achieve national security.

Now that India and Pakistan both have the bomb, I believe, the subcontinent has become a dangerous place to bring up our children. Even if India behaves responsibly in creating safeguards on detonating the bomb, I worry that a mad or angry Pakistani general might decide to pull the trigger and wipe us out. There is stronger logic behind the global nuclear disarmament movement than the logic and rationale behind the doctrine of nuclear deterrence. It goes beyond that. I am not convinced that India, with its overwhelming superiority in conventional weapons over Pakistan, has in fact furthered in its national interest by going nuclear. I fear we might have undermined our flexibility to fight conventional wars with Pakistan by moving towards a situation of nuclear parity.

But now that the deed is done, and the bomb is exploded, we should ask ourselves what benefits can we derive from the pride that has come with it. There is nothing like a good nuclear bang to focus the mind. This is an opportunity, I believe, for the government to take the unpopular actions that the preceding governments have been too cowardly to take. This is the time to tell the people that they have to pay for our nuclear status. This is the time to get rid of the irrational, populist subsidies that burden our economy. Since everyone must tighten their belts, we must tell farmers, for example, that henceforth they must pay for power, water and fertilizers. This action will do wonders to restore the fiscal health of the country. It will also make our SEBs viable, and we can then take a huge leap forward in bringing new power capacity and brighten our twenty-first century.

＊

As we begin to adjust to living in the post-bang world we should ask ourselves what is important to us as a nation. What are our national goals? Where does the bomb fit into our objectives? The BJP wants us to be counted and respected in the community of nations. That obviously cannot be a goal, for respect is the result of something that we achieve. Military power, however, can be a national objective. But history teaches us that unless military power is backed by economic power it cannot be sustained. Russia has many atom bombs; Japan has none. But the world respects Japan.

We, too, have discovered to our chagrin that the atom bomb has not won us the respect of the world. The reason is that it is not backed by economic stature. Even our best friends, who do not condemn our atomic tests, regard us with sad puzzlement. A nation can choose between a number of goals. One national goal could be to achieve a certain quality of life for our people. A second goal could be to raise the status of the lowest castes. A third might be to achieve harmony between different religious communities. If I had to choose and prioritize between them, I would place the economic goal at the top. Now, economics is not everything, but it has to be the most important thing in a country where one-third of the people live degraded lives of unimaginable poverty, and another third live in constant anxiety about making ends meet.

If we agree to define our goal in economic terms, there are many ways to express it—in terms of employment, inflation, productivity, as a poverty index, competitiveness, literacy, exports, and so on. Economists look at all these to capture the proper health of an economy, but they generally hone in on the growth rate as the best indicator. When an economy grows strongly for a sustained period, a lot of good things seem to happen to it. High growth creates jobs, slows down inflationary pressures, raises tax revenues of the government, which can be wisely invested on schools, roads, electricity and on poverty programmes.

If we agree on economic growth as our national goal, then we must be prepared to measure all our actions against this criterion. We must also eschew the temptation to have multiple objectives. Nations, like companies, are most effective when they are one-pointed. We must evaluate every action of every politician and bureaucrat by asking, 'Does it promote economic growth?' For example, law and order, speedy justice, political stability—all good in themselves—also promote growth by creating a sound climate for investment.

Can the bomb promote high growth? It can, conceivably, if it helps reduce the defence budget on the grounds that conventional forces can be cut once there is a nuclear deterrent, and the savings are ploughed into infrastructure. But this is a specious argument. The experience of the last fifty years shows that no nuclear country has been able to cut its conventional arms. Spending on nukes has invariably been an add-on to the existing defence burden of the country. In fact, the bomb will push us into a costly arms race, escalating our defence expenditures and denying funds for economic development.

Does the bomb offer any other benefits? The bomb could possibly have furthered our security if Pakistan did not have it. But how does it help if both sides have the bomb? It only makes the subcontinent a danger zone. To this, the BJP responds with the classic deterrence argument—that the unthinkable horror of a nuclear disaster will deter self-interested, non-suicidal leaders on both sides to even start a conventional war. And thus, it will, paradoxically, promote peace. The empirical evidence in support of this argument is that none of the members of the nuclear club has fought a war. While this argument has some logic, I believe the logic of disarmament is far greater.

But how does this help the Indian child who can't do his homework because of load shedding? In the end, our rulers have to remember that our national goal is not to prove anything to the world or to our enemies. It is to improve the lot of our people.

## The Laws to Compete

The principle of competition, Hesiod pointed out long ago, lies in the very roots of the world. There is something in the nature of things that calls for a real victory and real defeat. The competitive spirit is at the heart of a vibrant economy, and this is precisely what we have been trying to foster through our economic reforms. In the end, competition guarantees individual liberty far better than laws or regulators.

At the end of the decade, a Competition Bill for fostering competition was introduced in Parliament, but it was flawed and ironically, I felt, it might have the opposite effect. With all good intentions, it wanted to ensure that no company becomes dominant in the market and abuses its monopoly power. The bill gave a proposed Competition Commission the power to investigate any acquisition or merger between companies whose combined assets exceeded Rs 1,000 crore or turnover exceeded Rs 3,000 crore. According to economist Omkar Goswami, 144 of our listed companies already exceed that asset limit, and among them were our best companies, the very ones with the potential for building infrastructure and competitiveness. The commission could also investigate an acquisition by an 'industrial group' whose assets exceed Rs 4,000 crore.

The bill did revive foul memories of the MRTP days because

it sought to give 'experts' (read retired bureaucrats and judges) the power once again to decide the fate of our successful companies. They will be able to stop, for example, companies like Reliance or Infosys from acquiring other Indian or foreign companies to become competitive in the global market. Mergers are an essential part of a vibrant economy and they are just beginning to bloom in India. They are already subject to clearances under the Securities and Exchange Board of India's takeover code and the Companies Act. Do we really need a third hurdle of a Competition Commission?

If we are worried that an Indian company may become monopolistic, the simple answer is to protect the consumer by opening our markets to imports and lowering tariffs. We live in a global economy and market dominance can no longer be measured in simplistic terms. We are also a small economy—a little larger than Belgium—that has only recently found its path to growth. Only growth will help us to escape from poverty, and growth will come only if we allow our companies to grow larger and more efficient so that they compete in the world. The new bill will only cut them down.

Fifty years ago, other developing countries envied us because we had robust companies—Tatas, Birlas and others. But the MRTP Commission came and destroyed their drive and ambition. Meanwhile, our competitor countries created giants with global empires. Do we want a repeat performance?

People assume that market concentration inevitably leads to monopoly profits. This assumption has been thoroughly discredited by recent empirical data (including the idea that economies of scale and advertising create barriers to entry for new firms.) Economist William Baumol's theory of 'contestable markets' reaches the same conclusion. Even where there is only one firm left, its behaviour is not necessarily monopolistic. On the other hand, Nobel laureate George J. Stigler has shown that companies inevitably capture government regulatory agencies that regulate them. Thus, a Competition Commission could actually create entry barriers.

Having said that, I must point out that this bill has laudable provisions related to unfair and restrictive trade practices. These are needed, but they can be incorporated in the Consumer Protection Act 1985. We don't need another bureaucracy for that.

The United States, with its giant multinationals, can afford the luxury of chopping down its companies in the name of checking dominance. It has mature policy makers who can be trusted not to destroy the institutions that create wealth. India's bureaucrats, however, have been destroying wealth for fifty years. This bill could seriously undermine investor confidence. The United States does not have the same worry—it is the investment destination of the world. But our investment confidence is fragile. As it is, we do not receive enough foreign investment, and a poor judgement by the Competition Commission could totally undermine our frail edifice.

The only benefit of this law, as far as I can see, is to reassure people who are opposed to liberalization. But a law that could undermine our fragile companies, stifle liberty and slow prosperity is a huge price to pay for this reassurance. I sometimes feel that it is sad that a huge country like India with a potential to grow ten per cent a year is held back because it gets diverted by irrelevancies like competition laws. India needs more competition, but a competition law will not create it. It will come from freer trade and an investor friendly environment.

## Man versus Nature

In the nervous nineties, it was politically correct to be an environmentalist and want to save nature. Who could possibly be against such a sensible pursuit as wanting to make peace with nature and save the green-blue film on which life itself depends? Yet, why do I feel a sense of disquiet because of the actions of our do-gooder environmentalists?

I feel upset when I read that the environmentalists are challenging almost every single power plant in India. Or when I hear an ecologist say that it would be better to live in darkness in the twenty-first century than to degrade our environment. I am distressed to learn that Dabhol had to fight and win more than a dozen environmental cases in the Mumbai High Court before it could get going.

I have heard many entrepreneurs complain that the licence raj has returned in the form of the environmental clearance that is required from the ministry. It appears that bureaucrats and politicians have 'captured' this cause and made it lucrative ground for rent seeking. Nor can the entrepreneur protest too loudly because the bureaucrat owns the high moral ground in this case. Thus, many of our projects suffer endless delays awaiting bureaucratic clearance or court judgements. In the end, some become uncompetitive, while in the case of others that do go ahead, it is the consumer who ultimately pays for the delay. The cost that almost no one calculates is that of young Raju's future in Satara district who will not realize his dreams. When the factory or power plant gets delayed or does not come up for environmental reasons, Raju loses out because his capabilities go wasted.

I used to believe that one could create industry and jobs and still protect the environment. But now I am less sure. Increasingly, it looks as though there is a trade-off, and one has to choose between human beings and nature. The immoderate behaviour of the eco-fundamentalist certainly does not provide the reassurance that both sides can win.

Anna Bramwell, in a fascinating book, *Ecology in the 20th Century: A History*, writes, 'Ecologists believe in the essential harmony of nature. But it is a harmony to which man may have to be sacrificed. Ecologists do not see nature's harmony as especially protective towards or favouring mankind. It looks more and more as though the environment movement is now a secular religion in many parts of the world.' Economist Deepak Lall makes this point in *Unintended Consequences*. He says that although it may appear scientific and modern, the worship of nature is, in fact, closer to religious fundamentalism. It shares with religion a fear of man's instrumental rationality that may undermine humanity's traditional relationship with God or nature and our vanishing, cherished lifestyles.

Although the ecology movement draws on scientists like Malthus and Darwin, it betrays its religious nature because it fails to admit that its earlier predictions were plain wrong. The demographic transition has destroyed, for example, Malthus's prediction about the cataclysmic effects of an exploding population. Modern demography has proved that Third World populations rose primarily as death rates fell with modern medicine, vaccinations and better sanitation. As parents realized, with a time lag, that more children survived, they cut back on the family size. Thus, in country after country population growth rates rose and fell back as fertility rates adjusted. The education of girls and rising incomes, of course, reinforce the demographic transition. This is what is happening in many Indian states as well.

All of us must certainly learn to become sensitive to nature. We should be aware of the consequences of human action on the environment. This is especially true when it comes to the rapid degradation of forest cover in our poorest states (because of limited opportunities in agriculture and industry). But we must also be aware of the religious and 'irrational' nature of the ecology movement, which is willing to sacrifice human opportunities to preserving nature. Obviously, we must protect nature, but when it comes to a choice, human beings, I think, must precede nature. To believe to the contrary is not only elitist but also immoral.

# *Acknowledgements*

My heartfelt thanks to Janaki Kathpalia, Jasbir Singh, Shiv Kumar and David Housego for reading the manuscript and for their valuable suggestions. My gratitude to various kind souls at the *Sunday Times of India*, who have put up with my wayward ways all these years. I also thank Bobby Mathew for his patient help with word processing the text in its different versions. And Krishan Chopra, my editor at Penguin, for his consistent support. Finally, Puru and Kim Das, for being good sounding boards for some of my odder ideas.

# Index